Christopher Isike · Efe Mary Isike
Editors

Conflict and Concord

The Ambivalence of African Migrant/Host
Relations in South Africa

Editors
Christopher Isike
University of Pretoria
Pretoria, South Africa

Efe Mary Isike
University of Pretoria
Pretoria, South Africa

ISBN 978-981-19-1032-6   ISBN 978-981-19-1033-3 (eBook)
https://doi.org/10.1007/978-981-19-1033-3

© The Editor(s) (if applicable) and The Author(s), under exclusive license to Springer Nature Singapore Pte Ltd. 2022
This work is subject to copyright. All rights are solely and exclusively licensed by the Publisher, whether the whole or part of the material is concerned, specifically the rights of translation, reprinting, reuse of illustrations, recitation, broadcasting, reproduction on microfilms or in any other physical way, and transmission or information storage and retrieval, electronic adaptation, computer software, or by similar or dissimilar methodology now known or hereafter developed.
The use of general descriptive names, registered names, trademarks, service marks, etc. in this publication does not imply, even in the absence of a specific statement, that such names are exempt from the relevant protective laws and regulations and therefore free for general use.
The publisher, the authors and the editors are safe to assume that the advice and information in this book are believed to be true and accurate at the date of publication. Neither the publisher nor the authors or the editors give a warranty, expressed or implied, with respect to the material contained herein or for any errors or omissions that may have been made. The publisher remains neutral with regard to jurisdictional claims in published maps and institutional affiliations.

This Palgrave Macmillan imprint is published by the registered company Springer Nature Singapore Pte Ltd.
The registered company address is: 152 Beach Road, #21-01/04 Gateway East, Singapore 189721, Singapore

This book is dedicated to all African migrants and South Africans who have died from xenophobic violence against African migrants in South Africa since 1994. The dedication also goes to all those, African migrants, and South Africans alike, who do their modest best everyday to promote friendship, goodwill and understanding to foster social cohesion between Africans anywhere in the continent. May your efforts lead to a united Africa rooted in the ideals of pan-Africanism and Ubuntu.

Foreword

The subject of migration and integration of migrants into societies they migrate into is not new. Human beings have always been moving from place to place not only in search of greener pastures but also because it is human to be in motion. The idea of firmly fixed boundaries that condition movement and reduce it is new in the long duration of human history. All human civilizations worth the name benefitted from emigration to other civilizations or immigration from others because ideas do not travel themselves, but humans travel with ideas, meaning human contact spreads ideas and these are constantly evolving. For this reason, the Western civilization currently on vogue was once a Greek civilization. The latter too was once an Egyptian civilization, which was once a Nubian civilization. There are many other strands in this miscegenation of human civilizations, growing by giving and taking from others.

Precolonial Africa has a rich history of migration, and historians have long searched for reasons for these migrations and have invariably arrived at several different reasons, none more crucial than human curiosity. This movement of peoples in every direction was misunderstood by racist observers as the absence of population in certain parts, leading to the myth of an empty land, the *terra nubillis* fiction used to justify colonial conquest and imperialist exploitation. For a time and for many people before Western modernization, the border was a mark of respect of coexistence. The border then was understood as a mark of inclusion rather than hardline exclusion. It was a frontier for negotiating interests which could lead to coexistence, intermixing and integration as it happened in so many cases. Although the border could also lead to wars and conquest, it was a conquest that did not establish a class of *conquerors* and the *conquered*, but one by which the conquered came to belong to their new nationality as full members with rights like those of their hosts. We know this about the history of the Afar and Berber in the North, the Fulani and the Akan in the West, the Turkana and the Kalenjin in the Central and Eastern Africa, the Ndebele and the Ngoni in the Southern part of Africa. It is hard to fully identify the immigrant population in Malawi for they have become a nationality that make up the nation-state of Malawi.

This is the kind of conviviality and integration this welcome book on the relations between African migrants and South Africans speaks to. It is the kind of conviviality that did not require the immigrant to completely assimilate but often required them to bring their difference into the mix thus enriching the identity of a host people and nation. There are cases where they lost their unique identity or sometimes fought to rather be an independent and separate nation within a nation to preserve. It is integration that was not necessitated by theories or ideologies but *ubuntu*, a sense of shared humanity that both sides recognized. For example, immigrants that moved from modern Botswana to Zambia did not seek to dominate the people they found in Zambia but sought to contribute to what their Zambian hosts were doing. They displayed their humanity by acting like fellow humans, doing their duties diligently like the people of the areas they got to. Where they did not, they were forced to migrate further or back in search of new locations. But where like the Ngoni they sought to become like the people they settled among, they made integration a little easier.

On the notion of being and belonging, the people of South-East Africa have in their oral tradition a great awe for visitors and foreigners. Found among the Ngunis is a saying, *usisu somhambi asingakanani*, singangenso yenyoni, which means the visitor has such a small hungry stomach that it is the size of a bird's kidney. This means the visitor is not a burden and their needs are not hard to meet. Bearing this notion of belonging in mind, migrants are warmly welcome and when they are hungry, should be fed actually. In East Africa, Swahili speakers say, *mgeni siku bili, siku ya tatu mpe jembe* meaning "a visitor is only a visitor for two days: on the third day you give them also a tool with which to participate in cultivating the land". This means an immigrant is given their responsibility shortly after their arrival so that they do not stay looking like outsiders. The practice of giving them food and of giving them an agricultural implement to work with are powerful metaphors of visitors becoming "like us."

This comes, I suggest, from how the peoples of various parts of Africa understand being. It is from how they understand how to do and be human. Doing and being human is one of the vexing questions revived by the debates on decolonizing *being* alongside *power* and *knowledge* in the decolonial turn. This discussion is reminding us that the encounter with the colonial civilization was accompanied by a civilizing mission whose purpose was to induct Africans into the hierarchical regime of beings with the white Christian, heterosexual, middle-class male as the archetype of the human, as Grosfoguel explains, and others as sub-humans occupying the bottom of the ladder. Thus, ways of *being* came to be conceived in ways that create, in deep and structured terms, insiders and outsiders in the very community of beings. The insider-outsiders are those who are perpetually locked in the struggle to becoming. They are without sovereign power, and they are in a state of exception living a bare life, as Agamben puts it. They are a people struggling with what Aime Cessaire called *nothingness*, a sort of being dead while alive, being the death-bound subject, as Jan-Mohammed puts it. It is these people who are defined by difference made permanent and systematic through socialization and regimes of power. This also defines what Gloria Anzaldua calls the borderlands on which are found people who live on the edges. They are a people with double consciousness like the Black Americans described in WEB Du Bois' Souls of Black Folks, people who are invisible while present, anonymous even when they try to shout their names in pleas and protests, to borrow from Lewis R. Gordon. On this order of being, identity and power people are invented as disposable. At the border, this is accompanied by lots of violence, both structural and physical. Inequality invented becomes normalized as inevitable as Muauz Alemu shows in his work on transborder trajectories of violence in the horn of Africa.

These notions of being formed by competition in the pecking order of beings that produce *non-beings* in Fanonian terms are inimical to ways of being where humans make each other humans, as in Sotho saying that *motho ke motho ka batho* (human beings are human beings by making others human beings too). This reciprocal making of human beings is a virtuous circle displaced by a vicious hierarchy of competitive beings. The view of being as a place of co-creation of human values and intermixing and cross-pollination of everything that makes human beings is one in which migration is an opportunity to expand the human family and its value to life.

Conviviality from contact that enables accommodation, integration and social cohesion is therefore not based on decisions this or that group make about others, but more deeply, it comes from the very construction of *being* over time. In our case, the *being* has long been distorted, used for purpose of dividing us to rule us. Conviviality is formed at the point of decolonization of being that must be accompanied by redefining what the encounters between groups of beings in processes of relocation mean and require. Cessaire has long shown that the colonial civilization was one of decadence because it incubated problems it has no ability of solving. Therefore, something decolonial and anti-colonial is needed as the basis for solving problems the colonial civilization nurtured and normalized, and this is where this welcome book is topical and relevant.

The book is a useful starting point towards understanding what is happening within the context of neocolonialized societies regarding migration and encounters between migrants and prior residents. This helps us characterize how the colonial regime of being continues to shape relations among Africans and what needs fundamental changing. I commend the authors and contributors in this edited volume for their brave discussion of the manifestations of the problem today, and as such they give us what to work with as we think about how to fundamentally solve it. This book is a must-read for all who need insights into the continuing fracas in the encounter between African migrants and South Africans which prevents reciprocal ways of being. Most profoundly, the book also gives insights into how these groups are remaking meaning of being human in the African sense and worldview of Ubuntu.

Siphamandla Zondi
University of Johannesburg
Johannesburg, South Africa

Preface

The impetus for this book came from the findings of the doctoral thesis of one of the editors, Efe Mary Isike, in 2016 which led her to argue that beyond the conflictual aspects of relations between African migrants and their South African hosts, there were also spaces of positive interactions that foster conviviality and concord. Although her study focused on Nigerian migrants in the uMhlathuze municipal area in KwaZulu-Natal, it made Christopher Isike, after reading the thesis, to ponder whether the case would be different for other African migrant groups scattered across South Africa if they were studied in the same way. Thus began the journey to explore this further beginning with proposing and presenting a panel on Reinventing South African/African immigrants' relations for transformation, economic growth and development at the 13th National Conference of the South African Association of Political Studies (SAAPS) in September 2016. Feedback from the panel presentations and methodology meetings during the SAAPS conference allowed for a further exploration of the idea which eventually led to the decision to invite participation from other scholars to be part of an edited book project. The invitation process was concluded in 2018 and the writing began with the title *Conflict and Concord: The Ambivalence of African Migrant/Host Relations in South Africa.*

As articulated in the concept note circulated to contributors, the purpose of the book is to offer some balance in understanding the relations between African migrants in South Africa and their South African hosts by exploring spaces of contact between both groups which produce conviviality and concord. Although much has been written about the conflictual aspects of the relations between both groups in South Africa, there is need for more knowledge on the convivial aspects of the relations which in some instances lead to concord. For example, not much is known about migrants that are well settled in South Africa, are economically well off and sufficiently invested in South Africa to call it home even when they maintain links to their countries of origin. Meanwhile, many African immigrants operate legally in various spaces within both big cities and small towns in South Africa; they occupy the middle and higher economic strata of the country and are much more settled and embedded than has been reported in the literature on conviviality between both groups. In some instances, they are fully integrated into their host communities socially, politically and economically through the use of social capital to bridge diversity. These migrants have children, some with mixed parentage with South African spouses, who bear South African names, speak South African languages and generally see South Africa as their homes, but these relationships are yet brushed together as "friendships of convenience", "transient" and "tactical" for survival purposes only. These are some of the gaps this book was written to fill while acknowledging the conflictual aspects of the relationship between African migrants and South Africans that is well covered in the literature. Divided into two parts that speak to both the conflictual and convivial aspects of intergroup relations between African migrants and South Africans, the book used a social network methodology to explore physical and virtual spaces of conflict and conviviality from contact between both groups in different geographical locations across South Africa. For instance, beyond big cities (Johannesburg, Durban, Cape Town) and urban estuaries which existing studies on conflict and conviviality focus on, other contact spaces explored in this book are small towns (Empangeni, Nelspruit, Bellville, Parow), universities, social media and associations (i.e. the United Nigerian Wives in South Africa) which have not been reported on in the literature. These bring some uniqueness to the book which merits attention from all and sundry that are interested in the subjects of immigration, citizenship, belonging and non-belonging as well as the complexities of intergroup relations between migrant and host communities. More so, the book was written by African migrants who have studied in South Africa, live/lived and/or hold/held an academic appointment with a higher institution or research institute in South Africa. Although this can raise an ethical question around their positionality in the study, it also puts them in good stead to contribute to the book not only from an empirical perspective, but to also write about a subject they know intimately based on their experiences as immigrants in South Africa. This is good for scholarship given the acknowledgement of their positionality and the efforts made to follow established scientific research processes in collecting and analysing data for their various chapters in the book.

We hope this collection of chapters based on empirical research carried out by African migrant scholars with lived experiences in South Africa will help to highlight nuances in the relations between African migrants and their South African hosts. If it sheds some light into a complex issue that is as old as human existence yet ever changing with consequence for future relevance, we shall have achieved our aim as editors and authors in this book. If the light it sheds helps to foster social cohesion between African migrants and South Africans in ways that promote friendship, understanding, goodwill and concord in years to come, we will look back and give ourselves "a Bells" for daring to proceed with this book given the opposition it met from some "intellectual gate-keepers".

Christopher Isike
Efe Mary Isike
University of Pretoria
Pretoria, South Africa

Acknowledgements

So many individuals contributed to making this book from its inception to completion so the list of names will be lengthy if we were to name everyone. However, we want to appreciate the contributors without who there would be no edited book. The project took longer than expected, but it was worth it working with every one of you through the various submissions we all had to make to finalize it. We also want to appreciate the various institutions of the editors and contributors for the varying support they gave to make this project a reality. These include the University of Pretoria, South Africa, University of Johannesburg, South Africa, University of KwaZulu-Natal, South Africa, University of the Western Cape, South Africa, Sol Plaatje University, South Africa, University of South Africa, Cape Peninsula University of Technology, South Africa, Nile University, Nigeria, and Carleton University, Canada.

Contents

1. Contact, Conflict and Concord Between African Migrants and South Africans: An Introduction   1
   Christopher Isike

2. Understanding the Contact, Conflict and Conviviality Discourse   17
   Efe Mary Isike

3. Parities and Disparities in Applying Immigration Legislation/Policies from a World Class National Constitution   37
   Christopher Changwe Nshimbi

4. Xenophobia Against Nigerian Immigrants in South Africa: The *Naijaphobia* Perspective   61
   Hakeem Onapajo

5. Cyberspace Xenophobia in South Africa   85
   Efe Mary Isike, Zainab Olaitan, and Christopher Isike

6. From Paradise Gain to Paradise Loss: Xenophobia and Contradictions of Transformation in South African Universities   109
   Samuel Ojo Oloruntoba

7 Language, Being, Belonging, and Non-belonging
   in South Africa   129
   Ivan Katsere

8 Beyond Xenophobia: Migrants-Locals
   in Socio-Economic Spaces in Cape Town,
   South Africa   145
   Godfrey Maringira and Rosette Sifa Vuninga

9 Foes, Friends or Both? Looking Beyond Hostility
   in Relations Between Congolese Migrants and South
   Africans in Empangeni   157
   Christopher Isike

10 'First Comes Love, then Comes Marriage?': Exploring
   the Narratives and Experiences of South African
   Partners of Nigerian Male Immigrants in South Africa   179
   Dorcas Ettang and Oluwaseun Tella

11 How Can Contact Foster Concord? An Analysis
   of Relations Between Mozambican Migrants
   and South Africans in Mpumalanga Province in South
   Africa   201
   Efe Mary Isike

12 "We Know Each Other": Analyzing Interactions
   Between African International and Local Students
   in South African Universities   219
   Olusola Ogunnubi

13 Conclusion: Contact, Concord and Social Cohesion
   in South Africa   243
   Efe Mary Isike

Index   253

NOTES ON CONTRIBUTORS

Dorcas Ettang is a Senior Lecturer in Political Science at the University of KwaZulu-Natal, South Africa. Her publications have appeared in peer-reviewed journals, including *Africa Development*, *Journal of African Elections*, *Politikon* and *Gender & Behaviour*. Her research covers migration, human security, identity politics and peacebuilding.

Christopher Isike is a Professor of African Politics and International Relations Department of Political Sciences, University of Pretoria, South Africa. He is the current President of the African Association of Political Science (AAPS) haven just completed his term as Vice President of the International Political Science Association (IPSA). He is Editor-in-Chief of Africa's foremost political science journal, *Politikon: South African Journal of Political Studies*, and has been Editor of Ubuntu: Journal of Conflict and Social Transformation since 2017. He also serves on the editorial board of several reputable international journals, such as International Political Science Abstracts. He conducts research from an Africanist lens and teaches international relations theory, strategic and security studies, and security theory at the University of Pretoria. His research interests include African soft power politics, peace and conflict studies, women, and political representation in Africa, rethinking state formation in Africa, human factor development, African immigration to South Africa and politics in a digital era. In 2020, he was appointed by the Minister of Sports, Arts and Culture as a Social Cohesion Advocate of South Africa.

Efe Mary Isike is a Ph.D. (Development Studies) graduate of the School of Development Studies, University of KwaZulu-Natal, South Africa. She is currently a Policy and Development scholar and expert who coordinates the Mastercard Scholarship Program (MCSP) in the Department of Education Innovation at the University of Pretoria, South Africa. Before then, she lectured for 7 years in the Department of Anthropology and Development Studies at the University of Zululand, South Africa. Her research interests include African Migration Studies, Gender and Development Studies and Conflict Transformation and has scores of publications in reputable peer-reviewed journals within and outside South Africa. She is a member of the Canadian Association of African Studies (CASS) and the Ontario International Development Agency (OIDA).

Ivan Katsere is a Research Psychologist with a passion for Social Psychology and a keen interest in how Black bodies perform and are treated in African spaces. His research is embedded in migration, gender studies and impacts of colonialism on relations between Africans. His Master's thesis focused on narratives of language brokers who translate for their parents within South African spaces. This sparked the migration focus and performativity of Blackness holding the roots of his current focus. This research led to his Ph.D. research and work which is focused on gendered journeys—narratives of women who are economic migrants to South Africa.

Godfrey Maringira is an Associate Professor of Anthropology at Sol Plaatje University, Kimberley, Northern Cape, South Africa. He teaches Social Anthropology. He is a Research Associate at the University of Johannesburg, South Africa, Anthropology and Development department. He is a senior Volkswagen Stiftung Foundation Research Fellow and is also a Principal Investigator of the International Development Research Center (IDRC) research on Gang violence in South Africa. His areas of research include armed violence in Africa with a specific focus on the military in post-colonial Africa. His 2017 African Affairs Journal article "Politicisation and resistance in the Zimbabwe national Army", was awarded the best author price in 2018. In 2020, he was awarded the Benedict Vilakazi best author price, *African Studies Journal* (Routledge) for his article titled: "When combatants became peaceful: Azania People Liberation Army ex-combatants in post-apartheid South Africa". He is the author of *Soldiers and the State in Zimbabwe*, Routledge, 2019.

Christopher Changwe Nshimbi is Director of the Institute for Strategic and Political Affairs (ISPA) and Associate Professor in the Department of Political Sciences, University of Pretoria. He researches migration, borders, regional integration, the informal economy and water governance.

Olusola Ogunnubi completed his Ph.D. from the University of KwaZulu-Natal and currently is a Postdoctoral Research Fellow with Cape Peninsula University of Technology. He has published extensively in both local and international journals.

Zainab Olaitan is a Ph.D. candidate at the University of Pretoria where she studied for her master's degree as a 2019 Mastercard foundation scholar. She is presently researching on the impact of gender quotas on the substantive representation of women in Africa. She obtained her first degree in Bachelor of Science (Hons.) in Political Science with First Class from the University of Lagos. She completed her second degree in Philosophy, Politics and Economics Honours at the University of Cape Town as a 2018 Mandela Rhodes Scholars. She was selected as one grantees of Margaret McNamara Education Grant in 2021. She is keenly interested in contributing to research on political thought, gender, conflict and peace studies, African politics and representation.

Samuel Ojo Oloruntoba is an Adjunct Research Professor at the Institute of African Studies, Carleton University, Ottawa, Ontario, Canada, and Honorary Professor at the Thabo Mbeki School of Public and International Affairs, University of South Africa. He is also a Faculty Associate at the African School of Governance and Policy Studies. He obtained Ph.D. in Political Science from the University of Lagos, Nigeria. He was previously a Visiting Scholar at the Program of African Studies, Northwestern University, Evanston, and a Fellow of Brown International Advanced Research Institute, Brown University, Rhode Island, United States. He is the author, editor and co-editor of several books including *Regionalism and Integration in Africa: EU-ACP Economic Partnership Agreements and Euro-Nigeria Relations*, Palgrave Macmillan, New York, United Statess, 2016, and co-editor with Toyin Falola of the *Palgrave Handbook of African Political Economy*, 2020. His research interests are in Political Economy of Development in Africa, Regional Integration, Migration, Democracy and Development, Global Governance of Trade and Finance, Politics of Natural Resources Governance and EU-African Relations.

Hakeem Onapajo is a Senior Lecturer in the Department of Political Science and International Relations, Nile University of Nigeria. He received his Ph.D. in Political Science at the University of KwaZulu-Natal, South Africa. He specializes in conflict, terrorism and elections in Africa. He is a Fellow of the American Council of Learned Societies (ACLS) for his research on child security in North-eastern Nigeria. His research works have appeared in high impact journals and other publishing outlets.

Oluwaseun Tella is Director, the Future of Diplomacy at the University of Johannesburg's Institute for the Future of Knowledge in South Africa. He recently authored a book entitled *Africa's Soft Power* (Routledge, 2021). His research interests include soft power, international relations, migration, peace and conflict studies, African politics and knowledge production in Africa.

Rosette Sifa Vuninga is a Centre for the Humanities and Social Sciences Research Council Doctoral Fellow at the University of the Western Cape's History Department in Cape Town, South Africa. Her Ph.D. project focuses on ways in which ethnic and regional identities are experienced among the Congolese people of Cape Town. Her research is in the field of 'migrating violence' and explores issues related to the politics of identity and belonging.

ABBREVIATIONS

AAD	African Academic Diasporas
ACFTA	African Continental Free Trade Agreement
ANC	African National Congress
BMA	Border Management Authority
CBD	Central Business District
COCOE	Congolese Community of Empangeni
DHA	Department of Home Affairs
DRC	Democratic Republic of Congo
EU	European Union
HEIs	Higher Education Institutions
ICEF	International Consultants for Education and Fairs
IMF	International Monetary Fund
IOM	International Organization for Migration
IPID	The Independent Police Investigative Directorate
LGBTI	Lesbian, Gay, Transgender and Intersex
LHR	Lawyers for Human Rights
NSFAS	National Student Financial Aid Scheme
NUSA	Nigerian Union in South Africa
OECD	Organization for Economic Cooperation and Development
RDP	Reconstruction and Development Programme
RRO	Refugee Reception Office
SADC	Southern Africa Development Community
SALW	Small Arms and Light Weapons
SAPS	South African Police Service
UCT	University of Cape Town
UK	United Kingdom

UKZN	University of KwaZulu-Natal
UNDESA	United Nations Department of Economics and Social Affairs
UNHCR	United Nations High Commissioner for Refugees
UNIZUL	University of Zululand
UNWISA	United Nigerian Wives in South Africa
US	United States
USSR	Union of Soviet Socialist Republics

List of Figures

Fig. 11.1 Age and gender of the migrant sample   206
Fig. 11.2 Income of migrants   207
Fig. 11.3 Duration of stay   208

List of Tables

Table 5.1	Paraphrased xenophobic views expressed on Twitter and Facebook between September 2019 and March 2020	97
Table 12.1	Total number of international registered students in selected South African universities in 2006	225
Table 12.2	International student enrolments in doctoral programs in South Africa	225
Table 12.3	Socio-demographic characteristics of respondents	227
Table 12.4	Responses on the preference of South African higher education system	229
Table 12.5	Responses on integration of international student	230
Table 12.6	Responses on experiences with local students	232
Table 12.7	Responses on assimilation by international African students	233
Table 12.8	Responses of perception of acceptance as international students in South Africa	234

CHAPTER 1

Contact, Conflict and Concord Between African Migrants and South Africans: An Introduction

Christopher Isike

BACKGROUND

Migration enables contact between migrant groups and host communities worldwide, and an enduring theme of this contact in both migration and its study is the relationship between both groups. The arrival of migrants necessarily changes the social, economic, cultural and other aspects of a host community, and one of the main challenges host communities usually face in dealing with migrants is how to respond to the social differences that come with migration (Hugo 2005). Responses range between two extremes of exclusion which breeds hostility/conflict on

[1] Concord as used here can be summarized as the state of agreement, sustainable peace and harmony between different groups in a society which may eventually lead to integration whether intended or not.

C. Isike (✉)
Department of Political Sciences, University of Pretoria, Pretoria, South Africa
e-mail: christopher.isike@up.ac.za

© The Author(s), under exclusive license to Springer Nature Singapore Pte Ltd. 2022
C. Isike and E. M. Isike (eds.), *Conflict and Concord*,
https://doi.org/10.1007/978-981-19-1033-3_1

the one hand, and acceptance/concord (sustainable harmony)[1] which fosters integration on the other hand. However, there are multiple shades or variants of responses in between these two extremes. For example, Efe Isike discusses six categories of responses: exclusion, assimilation, multiculturalism, cosmopolitanism, hybridity, and entanglement and conviviality, which she contends are related but also different from one another in dealing with social differences that come with migration (Isike 2015). According to her, "while exclusion totally abhors the co-existence of differences, assimilation aims to homogenize society by absorbing the different. On the other hand, multiculturalism, cosmopolitanism, hybridity, and entanglement aim to create a space for the existence of differences, but in different ways" (Isike 2015, 36). While multiculturalism boasts of creating a plural society where cultural differences are allowed to exist, cosmopolitanism acknowledges plurality that is rooted in openness and de-territorialization. Hybridity tells us that there is a third space or in-betweenness where homogeneity and heterogeneity meet, and this junction empowers hybrids to renegotiate *othering* and integration. Entanglement and conviviality posit that although differences exist, there is an interdependent relationship, even if for convenience or as a coping mechanism, between diverse groups. The point is that rather than focusing on differences, and how these differences prevent interaction, focus could also be on the spaces of intersection in the varied interactions between migrants and hosts, and how these intersections produce conviviality which is a predictor of concord between migrants and hosts in any given society. This is the aim of this book using the context of African migrants' relations with South Africans. Therefore, its key research question is: besides the conflictual nature of the relations between both groups in South Africa, what convivial spaces of interactions between them exist that could be a predictor of concord?

As James Bennet postulates, two unattainable responses to cultural differences exist on the two extreme poles between exclusion and assimilation/integration. In his words, "on one pole is the ideal of complete non-interaction: we don't engage, and we (and they) don't change. At the other pole is the ideal of complete amalgamation, from which some global homogenization eventually emerges" (Bennet 2011). Along this spectrum, Bennet refers to "models of admixture" wherein he identified three additional overlapping responses: cosmopolitanism, hybridity and entanglement. Similarly, Regout (2011) highlights three responses: exclusion, assimilation and multiculturalism. Clearly then, there are many shades of responses to contact between migrant groups and host communities which extend beyond the two extremes of exclusion, which in worse cases can manifest in conflict or xenophobic violence, and integration, which in the best of cases can be expressed in concord. It is also clear that contact can and does breed both conflict and concord even within the same societies, and studies on the relationships between migrant groups and their host communities actually show this ambivalence (Dominguez and Maya-Jariego 2008). Impliedly, conflict is manifested in xenophobic sentiments and actions against migrants are one side of the contact coin. The other side is concord manifested in convivial relationships developed between migrants and their hosts from contact with each other whether short or long term. In essence then, it is narrow to focus on the one end of the spectrum to describe the complex relationships that often exist between migrant and host communities in any state or society.

In the case of South Africa, in spite of the dominance of the xenophobia discourse in relations between African immigrants and their South African hosts, contact between both groups, which has increased significantly since 1994, has also produced conviviality/concord between them. Unfortunately, this positive aspect of their relationship has not been highlighted enough in research and popular discourses by scholars, policymakers, the media and other civil society stakeholders including the general populace of South Africa. As Isike argues, the literature on relations between South Africans and African immigrants in South Africa largely showcases conflict and hostility (Isike 2015). It paints South Africans as a people that do not tolerate or accommodate foreigners, especially Black Africans and as such mostly xenophobic (Crush 2008), and this is not untrue as xenophobic prejudice particularly targeted at African nationals in South Africa is a real societal and policy problem which remains unresolved. Indeed, as (Crush 2008; Matsinhe 2011; Crush and Ramachandran 2014) found, many South Africans wish for African migrants to "go away" and this is expressed on a daily basis on national radio platforms such as the SAFM[2] and on social media (see Chapter 5). There are numerous examples of xenophobic prejudice and

---

[2] One of the authors records that between August 2019 and February 2020, popular SAFM talk show host, Bongi Gwala made it a point daily to discuss 'the problem' of African migrants in South Africa during his Talking Point segment which flights from 09h00 to 12h00 Monday to Friday.

horrific instances of violence towards African immigrants,[3] and explanations of xenophobia in South Africa are well covered in the literature (see Isike Chapter 2). For example, while there are numerous theories that explain xenophobia globally, some of which apply in varying ways to South Africa, there are also many others that explain the specific drivers and character of xenophobia in South Africa. Several global theories of xenophobia that could also be applicable to explaining xenophobia in South Africa include the relative deprivation theory (Runciman 1972; Aleksynska 2007), realistic group conflict (Tajfel and Turner 1979) and scapegoating (Petersson 2003) which broadly blame economic scarcity and its consequent effect of deprivation as a host community's justification for prejudice against migrants who are perceived as undesirable competitors. Others include social identity theory (Taifel and Turner 1986) and contact hypothesis (Vezzali and Stathi 2017) which broadly use people's sense of self as a group to forge a common identify around common interests which is used to justify the *othering* of people outside the group, especially when there is limited or negative contact between both groups. Amongst others, Isike in Chapter 2 focuses on two theories of xenophobia: false belief and new racism to explain xenophobia targeted at African migrants in South Africa. According to her, government, through its policy actions and inactions, traditional and social media (see Isike, Olaitan and Isike in Chapter 5), all collude consciously and unconsciously to perpetuate false beliefs about African migrants amongst Black South Africans that fuel xenophobia and other forms of intra-racial prejudice against African migrants (see also Matsinhe 2011). Indeed, as Loren Landau noted, "the demons of intolerance and exclusion have not been tamed; it has been given a fancier set of clothes" (Landau 2013), and this persists in 2021 manifesting in ways that are worrying. At the international relations level, the conflictual migrant/host relations in South Africa impede regionalism in the continent with negative implications for the African Continental Free Trade Agreement (ACFTA) which South Africa played a leading role in establishing.

However, there are also spaces of interaction, where contact between these diverse groups has produced conviviality even when they are for convenience or survival on the part of immigrants. For instance, exploring emerging forms of political and normative orders in selected African

---

[3] The May 2008, April 2015 and August 2019 attacks were the worst cases.

cities such as Johannesburg, Loren Landau notes that post-apartheid South Africa is a dual society where "novel modes of accommodation are emerging, double helix-like, with ever-evolving forms of social, economic, political exclusion" (Landau 2014, 360). As Landau (2014) further noted, these challenge "the conceptual foundations typically informing debates over migrant rights, integration, and the boundaries of belonging" as the spatial dynamics in which migration and immigration occur across African cities give cause to reconsider the fundamental distinctions between *guests* and *hosts* as well as rethinking civic, national or municipal belonging as the basis of meaningful membership and rights. Similarly, in exploring the relationships and peculiar friendships that are formed in selected African urban sites or estuaries[4] such as Johannesburg, Landau makes three main arguments with regard to the presence and nature of conviviality or urban friendships, as he calls it. One, that social, political and economic conditions obligate and regulate these friendships resulting in what he calls "communities of convenience" which are often fluid. Second, that "amidst these seemingly anomic, distrustful sites, residents forge shared values and socialities that eschew friendships' potentially confining bonds". And third, these enable friendship fears which "reveal the distinct estuarial spaces shaped by ongoing movements of people into, out of, and through precarious cities of the south" (Landau 2017, 9). This is even when these friendships belie productive or potentially beneficial social relationships. However, Landau's main take on these friendships or emerging solidarities as he calls them is that they are communities of convenience as they are devoid of thick connections, they are not permanent and they are characterized by low levels of trust and regularized engagements. This is because migrants tend to resist deep connections with locals as they see these estuaries as temporary stations in their journey to find better things of life.[5] Thus, for Landau, friendships in estuaries are about how people maintain, by choice or necessity, social connections which allow them to swiftly combine disparate elements of their surroundings according to their current interest and objectives. This allows migrants to enact a broader approach to estuarial life beyond

---

[4] Sites loosely structured by the disciplines of state, formal employment or hegemonic cultural norms.

[5] Friendship in general offers psychological security, respectability and support, but in the case of the urban estuaries as Landau argues, it creates zones of acceptable and respectable behaviour.

national boundaries termed "tactical cosmopolitanism", which enables migrants to partially belong in South Africa without being bound by localized social and political obligations (Landau and Freemantle 2010). Impliedly, they can be neither hosts nor guests or seen to be in South Africa and not of South Africa.

Although most of the convivial sites studied in this book are small communities across South Africa some of which show characteristics of estuaries such as Johannesburg which Landau studied, these friendships (discussed in Chapters 8–12) can and do lead to concord irrespective of whether this was intended or not. Second, some of these friendships such as the intimate ones have permanence as they go beyond relationships of convenience and develop into long-lasting marriages that deepen ties between immigrant and host states. These marriages produce children, many with South African names, that are raised in South Africa, speak local languages and generally tend to see South Africa as their home; to be in South Africa and of South Africa. Third, even when they are transient and tactical, convivial relations between African migrants and their South African hosts leave footprints of positive memories which are useful for broadly improving relations between them in the immediate and long-term future. Studies show that positive contact between in-groups and out-groups improved the in-group's affective reaction towards the out-group even if it may not make the former to support policy changes aimed at making life better for the latter (Everret 2013). Fourth, many of the studies on conviviality in migrant-host relations in South Africa including Landau's have not focused on migrants that are well settled in South Africa, are economically well off and are now sufficiently invested in South Africa to call South Africa home even when they maintain links to their original home countries. As Isike and Isike observe, many African immigrants operate legally in various spaces within South Africa, occupy the middle and higher economic strata of the country and are such more settled and embedded. In some instances, they are fully integrated into their host communities socially, politically and economically through the use of social capital to bridge diversity (Isike and Isike 2012). These are a category of African immigrants whose stories are largely missing in literature as the focus is usually on those who occupy the lower economic strata and live in the fringe areas of society. These stories and accounts need to be examined some more, and the findings reported not only to contribute to and enhance existing knowledge on this subject, but also to promote the effective planning, formulation and implementation of migration and development policies in South Africa. This is the broader purpose this book serves by exploring spaces of contact between African migrants and their South African hosts which produce conviviality and concord.

METHODOLOGY

One of the ways to examine and understand the varied responses of South Africans to contact with African immigrants is to analyse migrants' social networks that foster integration and a sense of belonging through the development of conviviality and entanglement. This is the methodological approach adopted in the second part of the book which explores convivial spaces of interactions between African migrants and their South African hosts. According to Francis Nyamnjoh, migrants "negotiate marginality through relationships (social networks), often romantic, that might make them more accepted, and engage in spaces of popular culture and conviviality" (Nyamnjoh 2015, 11). Although there is a paucity of literature on social networks and the integration of African migrants in the context of South Africa, there are still a few studies that highlight this issue (Kirshner 2012; Brudvig 2013; Adeagbo 2013; Landau 2013; Isike 2015). For example, apart from Landau's detailed treatment of conviviality in urban estuaries in South Africa, Ingrid Brudvig studied the phenomenon in Bellville, a small mining town near Cape Town, and argues that contrary to the exclusion and hostility which many African migrants generally face in South Africa, those in Bellville have experienced conviviality and tolerance (Brudvig 2013). According to her, "Bellville is a place where economic interdependency, social networks and bonding, and bridging social capital prove the resilience of migrants in the face of trends towards exclusion" (Brudvig 2013, 28). She further argues that this tolerance and hospitality is the result of physical space due to the economic interdependency and social capital that exist in Bellville (Brudvig 2013, 29). Economic interdependency is the result of the nature of economic practices in the area which is a well-known migration spot that thrives on the economic benefits provided to host members. Some of these benefits include employment, skills and provision of services, while migrants are allowed to carry on their various businesses unhindered by xenophobic attacks (Brudvig 2013). This space encourages increased contact and interaction with migrants in ways that eliminate hostility and breed conviviality in effect whether intended or not, whether migrants use them as coping strategies or if they are temporal as Landau argues. This supports the contact hypothesis that prejudice and hostility towards a group will eventually decrease when there is increased contact between groups in public spaces (Grim et al. 2005). However, scholars such as Samir Amin argue that spaces of interaction should move beyond public spaces to micro-public spaces where interactions are more frequent, long-lasting and unavoidable, as this would foster convivial interactions and the formation of sustainable ties amongst diverse peoples (Amin 2002). This is reflected in the case of Bellville which is a typical example of a micro-public space that brews convivial relations between migrants and members of the host community. In Brudvig's words, "business operations compel conviviality in Bellville... Groups work together not based on trust but on necessity" (Brudvig 2013). Migrants there thus develop convivial ties with members of their host communities beyond the outsider and insider divide and find a middle space for interaction in order to gain mutual benefits. Although this aligns with Landau's argument of communities of convenience or migrants' tactical cosmopolitanism, there is mutuality based on a shared understanding of norms and economic beneficiation which drives conviviality.

Efe Isike follows up with a similar social network analysis of contact between Nigerian migrants and South Africans in uMhlathuze municipality in the North of KwaZulu-Natal, which found amongst others that dyadic relations between the Nigerian migrants and South Africans in the study area are characterized by mixed responses ranging from exclusion to assimilation, cosmopolitanism and conviviality, that evolve with time, spanning a range of responses from hostile to friendly on both sides (Isike 2015). One of the conclusions of her study is that "the binary question of whether we are friends or foes misses the grey line in between and is therefore too narrow to fully capture everyday realities" (Isike 2015, 198). She thus recommended a network analysis of multiple relationships between African migrants and South Africans to reveal the nuances that shape relations between these groups (Isike 2015, 199). For example, the extracts below from interviews by Efe Isike with two of her respondents: Shola,[6] a male Nigerian migrant, and Ntuli, his South African friend, offer some insight into the core argument this book makes; that xenophobia does not fully describe the varied everyday relationships that exist between

[6] This is a pseudonym to maintain the anonymity of the respondent. This is the case with other respondents who took part in the various studies conducted by contributors towards this book unless otherwise stated.

South Africans and African immigrants in the country. Shola is 50 years old and hails from Western Nigeria. He is a medical practitioner based in Empangeni and classified as middle class on account of his income bracket. Shola moved to Empangeni 15 years ago (in 2015), is married to a South African woman and has been friends with Ntuli since he has been living in South Africa:

Interview with Shola:

> *Efe*: How would you describe your relationship with your South African neighbors?
> *Shola*: Because of my busy schedule at work, I usually don't have time to socialize with neighbors but whenever I meet them unexpectedly, we interact pleasantly... But there are some neighbors that are not so friendly, and I don't interact with them.... otherwise, my neighborhood is generally friendly... There is one incident that I would never forget that happened in 2008. During the xenophobic mayhem, two of my neighbours came to my house to check up on me... One in particular apologised for what his fellow countrymen were doing. He reassured me it is not all South Africans that have such predatory attitude towards foreigners... One thing that struck me is that he offered me accommodation in his home if there was any problem.
> *Efe*: Do cultural differences affect your relationship with your South African friends and colleagues?
> *Shola*: ....I enlighten them about my culture and they do the same. I am partly South African not by location but by blood. My children are of South African heritage and I have come to accept the culture as mine. I practice some of the Zulu cultures that do not go against my beliefs.

Interview with Ntuli:

> *Efe*: You were named by Shola as his most important South African tie. How would you describe your relationship with him?
> *Ntuli*: ... my relationship with him is more than friendship... At first I was apprehensive. I had heard a lot about Nigerians... We began to talk and I think he invited me for his party and the relationship grew thereafter.
> *Efe*: Did cultural differences affect your relationship with Shola?
> *Ntuli*: Maybe initially, but as we became friends, that disappeared as I came to know more about Nigerians. ... From close contact, I can see we are almost the same... He changed my mind-set not just about Nigerians but about Africans and our common humanity.

As these interviews show, South Africans have responded in varying ways beyond xenophobia (a form of exclusion) to the challenges of their contact with other Africans, in this case, Nigerian immigrants. Similarly, Nigerians have not simply reacted to xenophobia with self-exclusion but have built various kinds of relationships with South Africans which have fostered their integration into their host society. In this particular case, Shola and his South African wife have two children who straddle Nigerian and South African cultures, showing that, in practice, identities are hybrid and fluid. Overall, Shola's daily contact with South Africans varies from unfriendly to convivial or hospitable, and he has also responded in a variety of ways. For example, he adopted some aspects of Zulu culture from his friend Ntuli, and this indicates a form of hybridity. Therefore, in this case, as Efe Isike argues, "cultural differences did not hinder the development of convivial relations but led to cultural exchange which enhanced the cosmopolitanism of both Shola and Ntuli" (Isike 2015, 1). This is just one of many examples of everyday relationships and realities of African migrants' interactions with South Africans in micro-public spaces such as small towns and university environments, which are not told as much as the conflictual responses of exclusion and xenophobia are told, hence the attempt in this book to offer some balance in the discourse.

Organization and Structure

The book is set out in three parts: Part I which introduces and lays out the theoretical and policy frameworks for the book, Part II which focuses on conflict and exclusion as the South African response to contact with African immigrants in the country and Part III which focusses on the convivial and integration aspects of this contact. In Chapter 2, Efe Isike lays out the theoretical framework for the book by explaining contact and its ambivalence as both a facilitator of conflict and concord depending on factors that foster the fluidity of social identity. In Chapter 3, Christopher Nshimbi provides a policy framework to underscore how the migration policy environment in South Africa sets the stage for conflict between South Africans and African immigrants. He argues that legislation and policies that govern immigration, immigrants' lives and co-existence with hosts in the country should be consistent with these instruments. Besides a thorough examination of South Africa's migration and related legislation and policies and the literature on migration, the chapter also purposively analyses selected immigrants' accounts of living in South

Africa and concludes that some of the national constitution's best intentions fall off as the supreme law of the land distils into idiosyncratic legislation, policies, practices and lived experiences on the ground. The law is, however, perfected in instruments and lives that adhere to it to the letter. Hakeem Onapajo's Chapter 4 sets the tone for the second part of the book: conflict and exclusion. It contextualizes the conflictual nature of the relationship between African immigrants and South Africans by using the case of Nigerians in South Africa. It introduces the concept of Naijaphobia and analyses the patterns and causes of its rise in South Africa in different facets of society. Zainab Olaitan and Efe Isike further underscore the conflictual nature of the relations between African migrants and their South African hosts in Chapter 5 where they analyse the social media comments of South Africans on Twitter and Facebook and argue that cyberspace xenophobia is a third space of contestation between South Africans and African migrants where hostile and xenophobic sentiments are expressed daily by the former against the latter group. In their view, these sentiments are important drivers of the relationship between African migrants and South Africans on the ground because social media is used as a platform to mobilize for xenophobic attacks against African migrants. In Chapter 6, Samuel Oloruntoba examined the challenges with transformation in South African universities, underscoring how transformation has been used as politics of nationalism and xenophobia to reinforce the exclusion of foreign African academics in the country's universities. He argued that although transformation is necessary on issues such as decolonization of curricula and diversification of faculty members, the ways it is being implemented could have a long-term sub-optimal outcomes or what he calls "paradise loss" which erode the immense benefits ("paradise gains") South African universities got from attracting top African academics in the early years after the end of apartheid. Ivan Katsere ends Part II of the book with his Chapter 7 that focuses on the experiences and narratives of African migrant families whose children serve as language brokers in various families. He delves into the behavioural expectations of Black bodies in South African spaces including the implications of failing to behave in these expected ways. According to Katsere, as English is the *lingua franca* in South Africa, brokering and translating in general are not necessary in any South African spaces. However, the South African context is a unique one to highlight how discrimination, Black on Black racism through "othering" of blackness and Black bodies by local South Africans highlight the daily realities of Afrophobia.

The last segment of the book, Part III, which focusses on the convivial and integrative aspects of the contact between African migrants and South Africans, starts with Chapter 8 where Godfrey Maringa and Rosette Sifa Vuninga use ethnographic and social network analysis of Zimbabweans and Congolese migrants in Cape Town to argue that migrants are not only victims of xenophobia, but they are also actors within these socio-economic spaces which they themselves re-create and re-produce overtime. The chapter focuses on spaces such as barber shops, saloons, street and train station vending amongst others in Black settlements and found that migrants and locals co-exist as a community, with migrants emerging as *abangani* meaning friends in IsiXhosa, which is a dominant local language. In Chapter 9, Christopher Isike examines the nature of dyadic (two-way) relations that exist between Congolese migrants and South Africans in the small town of Empangeni in KwaZulu-Natal. It x-rays the nature of the linkages/ties between both groups and contends that beyond the hostility/xenophobia discourse, there is a conviviality/integration reality which should also be presented in the literature with a view to giving a much more balanced discourse on the relations between African migrants and South Africans in general. The chapter concludes that the binary question of friends or foes misses the grey line in between and is therefore too narrow to fully capture everyday realities in the relationship between Congolese migrants and South Africans in the study area as their relationships are characterized by mixed responses ranging from exclusion to assimilation, cosmopolitanism and conviviality. In Chapter 10, Dorcas Ettang and Oluwaseun Tella use semi-structured key informant interviews and focus group discussions with members of the United Nigerian Wives in South Africa (UNWISA)[7] to examine the processes of integration that Nigerian men have experienced in South Africa while highlighting positive and negative experiences and narratives on integration. They also examine the challenges South African spouses of the Nigerian men have faced and share their recommendations on how integration can be better attained in these contexts. Efe Isike, like the previous two chapters before, uses Chapter 11 to examine the existence of positive relations between Mozambicans migrants and South Africans in Mpumalanga, a province known to host a high number of Mozambican

---

[7] UNISWA is a Johannesburg-based non-governmental organization of women married to Nigerians living in South Africa. The organisation's main objective is to fight the different forms of discrimination and victimization that they and their families face.

migrants. She employed the contact hypothesis as a theoretical framework to answer whether contact between South Africans and Mozambicans only exacerbated conflict or also reduced discord and fostered concord between them. The chapter found that the relationship between both groups illuminates friendships and ties beyond the prevalent discourse of xenophobia thus confirming the thesis of contact theory that interaction between diverse groups reduces discord and promotes concord, thereby creating conviviality between them. Olusola Ogunnubi in Chapter 12 reports a survey of African international students across two universities in KwaZulu-Natal with a view to determine levels of acceptance within their university communities and the South African society in general. The chapter uses the students' perception to argue for a deeper appreciation of South Africa's contribution to internationalization and regional integration in Africa not only for building a stronger global reputation for the Republic but also in providing a recipe for socio-economic transformation of Africa in the face of challenging political-economic realities. The concluding chapter by Efe Isike brings the chapters together to advance the central argument made in the book that notwithstanding the reality of the xenophobia discourse, there are many positive spaces of interactions between both South Africans and African immigrants in South Africa which need to be studied. Acknowledging that contact does not always reduce prejudice, tension and conflict, the argument is made that the presence of the predisposing conditions and mediators of the contact-prejudice effect mentioned above do yield conviviality and concord that foster integration with consequence for regionalism. Therefore, given the inevitability of African migration to South Africa and the resulting challenges from group contact, the chapter also offers some policy suggestions for enabling social cohesion in the light of South Africa's stake and leading role in fostering regional integration in Africa.

REFERENCES

Adeagbo, Oluwafemi. 2013. We Are Not Criminals; We Are Just Victims of Circumstances: An Exploration of Experiences of Nigerian Immigrants' Men That Married South African Women in Johannesburg. *National Identities* 15 (3): 277–296.

Aleksynska, Mariya. 2007. Attitudes Towards Immigrants and Relative Deprivation: The Case of a Middle-Income Country, MPRA Paper No. 4595, Munich Personal RePEc Archive. http://mpra.ub.uni-muenchen.de/4595/.

Amin, Ash. 2002. Ethnicity and the Multicultural City: Living with Diversity. *Environment and Planning* 34 (6): 959–980.
Bennet, C. James. 2011. Assimilation and the Persistence of Culture. *The New Criterion* 33 (4): 29–34.
Brudvig, Ingrid. 2013. Conviviality in Bellville: An Ethnography of Space, Place, Mobility and Being. Master's Dissertation, University of Cape Town.
Crush, Jonathan. 2008. The Perfect Storm: The Realities of Xenophobia in Contemporary South Africa. Southern African Migration Project. http://www.genocidewatch.org/images/South_Africa_09_03_30_the_perfect_s torm.pdf.
Crush, Jonathan, and Sujata Ramachandran. 2014. Migrant Entrepreneurship Collective Violence and Xenophobia in South Africa. Migration Policy Series No. 67. Southern African Migration Programme.
Dominguez, Silvia, and Isidro Maya-Jariego. 2008. Acculturation of Host Individuals: Immigrants and Personal Networks. *American Journal of Community Psychology* 42: 309–327.
Everret, Jim. 2013. Intergroup Contact Theory: Past, Present, and Future. https://www.in-mind.org/article/intergroup-contact-theory-past-present-and-future.
Grim, Patrick, Evan Selinger, William Braynen, Robert Rosenberger, Randy Au, Nancy Louie, and John Connolly. 2005. Modelling Prejudice Reduction: Specialized Game Theory and Contact Hypothesis. *Public Affairs Quarterly* 19: 95–126.
Hugo, Graeme. 2005. Migrants in Society: Diversity and Cohesion. A paper prepared for the Policy Analysis and Research Programme of the Global Commission on International Migration. http://iom.ch/jahia/webdav/site/myjahiasite/shared/shared/mainsite/policy_and_research/gcim/tp/TP6.pdf.
Isike, Efe. 2015. Ties That Bind: A Network Analysis of Relationships Between Nigerian Migrants and South Africans in Umhlathuze. PhD Dissertation, University of KwaZulu-Natal.
Isike, Christopher, and Efe Isike. 2012. A Socio-Cultural Analysis of African Immigration to South Africa. *Alternation, Interdisciplinary Journal for the Study of the Arts and Humanities in Southern Africa* 19 (1): 93–116.
Kirshner, D. Joshua. 2012. We Are Gauteng People: Challenging the Politics of Xenophobia in Khutsong, South Africa. *Antipode: A Radical Journal of Geography* 44 (4): 1307–1328.
Landau, Loren. 2013. Xenophobic Demons Linger in SA. *Mail & Guardian*, May 17. https://mg.co.za/article/2013-05-17-00-xenophobic-demons-linger-in-sa/.
Landau, Loren. 2014. Conviviality, Rights, and Conflict in Africa's Urban Estuaries. *Politics and Society* 42 (3): 359–380.

Landau, Loren. 2017. Friendship Fears and Communities of Convenience in Africa's Urban Estuaries: Connection as Measure of Urban Condition. *Urban Studies*, Special Issue.
Landau, Loren, and Iriann Freemantle. 2010. Tactical Cosmopolitanism and Idioms of Belonging: Insertion and Self-Exclusion in Johannesburg. *Journal of Ethnic and Migration Studies* 36 (3): 375–390.
Matsinhe, D. Mario. 2011. Africa's Fear of Itself: The Ideology of Makwerekwere in South Africa. *Third World Quarterly* 32 (2): 295–313.
Nyamnjoh, B. Francis. 2015. Incompleteness: Frontier Africa and the Currency of Conviviality. *Journal of Asian and African Studies* 52 (3): 253–270.
Petersson, Bo. 2003. Combating Uncertainty, Combating the Global: Scapegoating, Xenophobia, and the National-Local Nexus. *International Journal of Peace Studies*, Spring/Summer 8 (1): 85–102.
Regout, Sybille. 2011. The Integration of Immigrant Communities in France, the United Kingdom, and the Netherlands: National Models in a European Context. In Migration Studies Unit Working Papers, London: London School of Economics and Political Science.
Runciman, G. Walter. 1972. *Relative Deprivation and Social Justice: A Study of Attitudes to Social Inequality in Twentieth-Century England*. London: Penguin Books.
Tajfel, Henri, and John Turner. 1979. An Integrative Theory of Intergroup Conflict. In *The Social Psychology of Intergroup Relations*, ed. W.G. Austin and S. Worchel. Monterey: Brooks/Cole.
Tajfel, Henri, and Turner John. 1986. The Social Identity Theory of Intergroup Behaviour. In *Psychology of Intergroup Relations*, ed. S. Worchel and G.W. Austin, 7–24. Chicago: Hall Publishers.
Vezzali, Loris, and Sofia Stathi. 2017. *Intergroup Contact Theory: Recent Developments and Future Directions*. London: Routledge.

CHAPTER 2

Understanding the Contact, Conflict and Conviviality Discourse

Efe Mary Isike

INTRODUCTION

Migration from one state or society to another leads to contact between individuals and groups within both states and societies which can produce either of two extreme outcomes: conflict and conviviality. Conviviality, irrespective of the motive driving it, is a predictor of concord which has been operationalized in this book as sustainable peace and harmony between migrant and host communities which may eventually lead to the full integration of the former whether intended or not. However, there are other categories of outcomes in this spectrum which contact can produce, and often both extreme outcomes (conflict and conviviality) are present and discernable in the relationships between migrants and their hosts. Taking them one after the other, conflict in the relations between migrant and host communities manifests in a variety of ways including

E. M. Isike (✉)
Department of Education Innovation,
University of Pretoria, Pretoria, South Africa
e-mail: efe.isike@up.ac.za

structural and physical violence against migrants which are often motivated by xenophobic sentiments. Scholars have defined xenophobia as the fear, distrust and dislike of others that are foreign, and within the South African context, the response to this fear is usually through violence, exclusion and hostility (Harris 2002; Nyamnjoh 2006; Bordeau 2010). It has been argued that although xenophobia and racism are similar in terms of *othering* of the other, they differ in terms of the socio-biological markers. Bordeau (2010) states that the *othering* in xenophobia is because of the foreignness of the other while that of racism is based on the different race of the other. This is broadly true in the global context. However, in South Africa, the difference between these two is blurry as xenophobia is a new form of racism that has evolved from the apartheid era within the same racial group where one sub-group has been profiled and dehumanized as a different kind of blackness from the one indigenous to South Africa (Matsinhe 2011). Impliedly, xenophobia goes beyond hostility or open violence against foreigners as it is a consciousness of being that prejudices the other based on real or imagined difference. Tafira terms this as new racism "practised by black people on other blacks, who belong to the community but are seen as socially and culturally inferior... not necessarily based on skin colour... but on differences in culture, nationality, language, dress, habits and ethnicity" (Tafira 2011). It could be inferred from Tafira's (2011) analogy of xenophobia in South Africa that belonging to the community does not produce conviviality from the host towards the other group if their blackness is defined and characterized by socio-cultural differences. Given the centrality of xenophobia to the discourse of contact, conflict and conviviality between migrants and their hosts in any country, in this case South Africa, this chapter undertakes a brief engagement with theories that seek to explain xenophobia and zero in on two that align with the focus of the chapter, which is a theoretical discussion of the mutually reinforcing nexus between identity, contact, conflict and conviviality which play out in intergroup relations.

Explaining Xenophobia in South Africa

There is a plethora of theories that seek to explain xenophobia globally and nationally in South Africa. Some of the theories within the former category include relative deprivation, social identity theory, realistic group conflict, scapegoating, contact hypothesis and anomy (Runciman 1972; Tajfel and Turner 1979; Taifel and Turner 1986; Petersson 2003; Aleksynska, 2007). In South Africa, some perspectives espoused to explain xenophobia include the post-apartheid nation-building arguments; the isolation hypothesis; xenophobia as a by-product of apartheid racism which led to a fear of the other; and lack of trust between South Africans and African immigrants (Morris 1998; Harris 2002; Landau 2004; Steenkamp 2009; Mazars et al. 2013). A more recent and compelling comprehensive review of the theories of xenophobia was by Peterie and Neil (2019) which surveyed the theories of false belief, new racism, socio-biological explanations and effects of capitalist globalization as explanatory factors for xenophobia in South Africa (Peterie and Neil 2019). The false belief theory and new racism discourse are pertinent here to explain xenophobia in South Africa as they fit better with the focus of this chapter.

False Belief Theory

False belief paradigm sees xenophobia as an effect of fake news and information generated through government and media platforms. Government policies do not just address needs but communicate government's positions which inherently shape citizens' views and perceptions on diverse issues. Peterie and Neil (2019) describe this as "communicative function that influences community attitudes". In South Africa, research shows that government's immigration policies from post-apartheid to democratic era have fostered exclusion and segregation (Hamill 2014). Also, government officials are known to make xenophobic statements that propagate conflict and hostility towards African migrants in South Africa (Savo 2019). Media houses also propagate false information that encourages the stereotyping of African migrants as criminals that does not fit the new South African dream (McDonald and Jacobs 2005; Crush 2008). These views have trickled down from the top to the bottom and stirred xenophobic sentiments at the grass-roots level towards African migrants in South Africa.

New Racism

In simple terms, New Racism theory argues that the migrant group is labelled foreign to the national character of the host nation and is as such perceived as a threat to the presumed homogeneous character of the host nation. Presumed identity being the operational term because most societies lack an internal homogeneous identity (Brubaker 2000, 2002). The perceived threat posed by the migrant becomes a contest between a presumed homogeneity and heterogeneity. In this case, anyone—mostly asylum seekers—perceived to be different in terms of skin colour, cultural and national background is labelled as the *other* who is a threat to the national self of the host nation (Peterie and Neil 2019). This breeds xenophobic tendencies against these heterogeneous group. It differs from traditional racism as it does not use the physical marker, race, as a rationale for exclusion, even though it is targeted towards groups with similar race. Rather, it focuses on the socio-cultural and national differences (Peterie and Neil 2019). Simply put, the culture of the immigrants is seen as alien and different from the presumed homogeneous culture of the host country. This can be related to the xenophobic attitudes and actions in South Africa against African migrants who happen to be seen as the only "foreigners" in South Africa. This explains why Misago contends that the xenophobic attacks against African migrants in South Africa are racialized (Misago 2011). The democratic nation that emerged post-1994 sought to create a rainbow nation, a novel type of nationalism aimed at uniting the diverse races within the country, but this gave birth to a new kind of racism against those perceived as outside the new rainbow nation of many colours. Neocosmos iterates that this nationalism was based on the notion of exceptionalism that produces a twin effect of difference and superiority in relations to other Africans within the continent (Neocosmos 2008). African migrants were thus perceived as a threat to the new nationalism that was evolving and treated as such (Landau and Freemantle 2010). This did not exist in a bubble, as it was a fallout from past apartheid practice of racism. The old racism produced an "inferiority syndrome" among black South Africans which not only led to self-hate, but the hatred of anyone who shares similar identities (Matsinhe 2011). In this case, the African migrants that shared same racial characteristics became the victims of this self-hate. This is an ingrained consciousness of self vs the *African other* which drives the xenophobic sentiments daily expressed by South Africans of all hues in public and private forums, in institutions and in traditional and social media spaces, which in many instances has culminated in open violence on the streets against African migrants and their businesses.

However, conflictual relations brought on by xenophobia between South Africans and African migrants are one of the many types of relations that exist between the two groups. However, the former has dominated studies on migration in South Africa. At the other end of this spectrum is conviviality which though has been written about, needs to be researched and reported more. The next section seeks to show the nexus between identity formation and intergroup relations and how both conflict and conviviality play out in this equation.

SOCIAL IDENTITY THEORY AND INTERGROUP RELATIONS

Intergroup relations is an important social science field due to the complexities of diversities and the impact it has on how group members perceive themselves. The arguments put forward by the social identity theory capture this complex web of intergroup relations. The theory emphasizes differentiation and categorization. One of such arguments of the theory is that individuals possess various identities; these identities are grouped into personal identity and social identity. An individual's personal identity is drawn from his social identity. Haslam (2001) explains that social identities speak in a fundamental way to who individuals are in the world. Simply put, how people see themselves is usually socially constructed or developed in social groupings. Padilla and Perez (2003) add that individuals' behaviour and values are often times a reflection of the views of the group they identify with. Therefore, the theory posits that individual identities are drawn from their social identities. The latter shapes the former and the two identities do not exist in isolation.

In addition, the theory argues that members of social groups tend to be fused together based on a sense of a shared common identity. In fact, Stets and Burke (2000) explain that social identity implies "being at one with a certain group, being like others in the group, and seeing things from the group's perspective". Hogg (1993) adds that people's sense of self and how they perceive themselves are largely influenced by the social group they belong to. Simply put, individuals' identity is drawn from that of the group. It is, therefore, the sense of homogeneity or common shared identity that binds members within a social group together. However, the paradox of this is that it propagates both unification and differentiation.

Oldmeadow and Fiske (2010) state that "social identity theory argues that discrimination is driven by a fundamental motivation to maintain a positive and distinctive social identity". In other words, the social identity that unifies one group invariably excludes a diverse group. As Briesacher (2014, 12) explains,

> similarities between the actor and other individuals in the social situation define the in-group, while differences between the actor and other individuals are defined as the out-groups. Meanings that are applied to the out-groups (whether accurate or not) are stereotypes.

Simply put, the theory argues that group classification propagates the *we* and *them* divide.

This chapter does not oppose the ideas of the social identity theory. However, it further argues that in some cases between the *we* and *them* divide there is an *us*, where diverse identities intersect. It is important at this point to take into cognizance the fluidity of identity. Identities are not rigid but flexible and can be described as a continuum of being renegotiated and reconstructed. This idea corresponds with that of the non-essentialist school of identity. To this school,

> cultural identity is a matter of 'becoming' as well as 'being'. It belongs to the future as much as to the past. It is not something which already exists, transcending place, time, history and culture. Cultural identities come from somewhere, have histories. But, like everything which is historical, they undergo constant transformation. Far from being eternally fixed in some essentialised past, they are subject to the continuous 'play' of history, culture and power. (Halls 1990, 225)

Therefore, identity is an ever-changing plane. It rejects the notion that culture is "holistic, bounded, static and deterministic", and describes it as a process which is characterized by "shifting multiple intersecting identities…" (Nathan 2015, 101–124). Individuals do not possess a single but multiple identities. Over-generalizing individuals' identity to a singular as portrayed by essentialist thinkers does not provide a vivid picture of the complexities of identity (Nathan 2015). It is possible that a single identity may dominate an individual's sense of self in relation to the world, but this does not remove other recessive identities that individual possesses. For instance, a middle-class female may see herself as an African or Black person, but she could also be a Catholic, a woman, rich, Zulu, among others. She therefore possesses multiple intersecting identities, and they are expressed based on the context she finds herself at a particular point.

Flowing from these arguments, identity is not always rigid and bounded; rather, it is dynamic and fluid—characterized by intermingling and intersecting, which is founded on social border transgression. It is therefore plausible for spaces of interaction to evolve, where diversities intermingle and evanescence to produce conviviality across diverse social groups. In some studies, such as that of Landau and Freemantle (2010), it is evident that migrants develop networks as a strategy to cope with xenophobia and exclusion in South Africa. The networks in this context produce conviviality between them although more for convenience and survival than concord or integration. Conviviality is a concept employed in the study of relations between diverse groups. Gilroy (2004) defines it as

> a social pattern in which different metropolitan groups dwell in close proximity but where their racial, linguistic, and religious particularities do not—as the logic of ethnic absolutism suggests they must—add up to discontinuities of experience or insuperable problems of communication.

His definition of conviviality does not remove the existence of differences but explains how they do not preclude the interaction of these diverse groups. In fact, Nyamnjoh (2015) captures conviviality as a state of "incompleteness". His description recognizes that identity is unbounded. He further adds that conviviality makes us more receptive to different identities. Clearly, it is the void or incompleteness—to borrow Nyamnjoh's term—in one that makes one open and susceptible to develop positive interaction, with an aim to fill in this void. Therefore, incompleteness or conviviality is not necessarily a weakness but a means to an end. According to him:

> conviviality encourages us to reach out, encounter and explore ways of enhancing or complementing ourselves with the added possibilities of potency brought our way by the incompleteness of others (human, natural, superhuman and supernatural alike), never as a ploy to becoming complete (an extravagant illusion ultimately), but to make us more efficacious in our relationships and sociality. (Nyamnjoh 2015, 14)

Brudvig (2013) provides another piece of the puzzle when she explains that the development of convivial relationship is brought on by mutual interdependence of the diverse groups. Mutual interdependence in this context speaks to the notion of entanglement and the intersection of diverse relationships, resulting in the inclusion of various groups irrespective of their similarities and differences. This is what Nuttall (2009, 1 and 11) calls an entanglement of relationships that is

> complicated, ensnaring, in a tangle, but which also implies a human foldedness. It works with difference and sameness but also with their limits, their predicaments, their moments of complication… It is an idea which signals largely unexplored terrains of mutuality, wrought from a common, though often coercive, and confrontational, experience.

This kind of entanglement based on mutual interdependence is clear in some of the relationships between African migrants and South Africans. According to Landau and Freemantle (2010), African migrants in South Africa developed a strategy termed tactical cosmopolitanism aimed at coping with xenophobia and exclusion. In this process, the migrants "shallowly" create networks and enter spaces of positive relations as a strategy to cope with exclusion (Landau and Freemantle 2010, 380). The depth of the network may be shallow, and the density of the entanglement may be loose; however, this does not remove the presence of mutual interdependence, which may also be one purpose for formatting the network in the first place even if short-lived or temporary. In this regard, this chapter argues that in coping with exclusion and xenophobia, the networks and strategies African migrants form help to foster conviviality, whether intended or not, given the long-term positive effects of group contact which can come from imagined group contact and positive presentation of intergroup friendships in the media (Everett 2013). Therefore, without claiming that all migrants' relations with South Africans develop to convivial relations, conviviality can be one of the long-term outcomes of these relationships between the two diverse groups even if not intended. Conviviality does not eradicate hostility towards differences, but it creates an enabling space for "different groups and individuals to focus on commonalities that intercut the dimensions of fixed difference which may cause fear and anxiety about the other" (Rzepnikowska 2013). The long-term effects of this conviviality are positive predictors of concord.

In summary, conviviality involves a process where diverse groups find a common ground or space for interaction without doing away with their differences but rather making them inconsequential to attain mutual interests or benefits. The "finding process" of a common ground is not always a smooth sailing journey that is devoid of conflict and hostility. Bearing in mind that the goal is not to produce a sense of homogeneity, which is impossible and idealistic, but to attain a compromise, where interactions or relationships are not defined by differences that still exist, but the need each group has for each other. This is what scholars such as Loren Landau have described in their works as friendships and communities of convenience, utilitarian extraction and tactical cosmopolitanism (Landau 2018) which can be approximated either as coping mechanisms, strategies of survival or modalities for negotiating through difference. As Brudvig (2013) asserts, "conviviality may emerge from a resolution of frictions …" In effect, intersecting the "we" and "them" divide to produce an "us" may entail renegotiating and shifting boundaries. The effect which is an "us" cannot be produced in isolation, but through contact between the "we" and "them". This notion is connected to the contact theory which presupposes that contact between majority and minority groups is an effective way to reduce prejudice and conflict between them, provided certain predisposing conditions are present. Impliedly, the absence of these predisposing conditions will result in conflict between the groups.

Contact Theory, Conflict and Conviviality

Contact theory can be traced to the mid-twentieth century when Allport (1954) developed the intergroup contact hypothesis which suggested that an effective way to reduce prejudice and hostility between diverse groups is through contact between them. Studies indeed show, in terms of immigration, that contact between diverse groups fosters conviviality and removes hostility (Isike 2015, 2017). The premise of contact theory in this context is that the in-group (hosts) can develop positive relations and attitude towards the out-group (migrants) when there is contact between these different groups (Vezzali and Stathi 2017). In this way, contact implies conducive spaces of interaction as opposed to isolation, which acts as a breeding ground for relationships to develop. Brameld (1946, 245) argued that when diverse groups "are isolated from one another, prejudice and conflict grow like disease". This argument supports the isolation hypothesis put forward by migration scholars such as Morris (1998) to explain xenophobia in South Africa. According to him, South Africans are hostile to migrants from the African continent because they are not accustomed to interacting or integrating with members of these groups because of the stringent apartheid laws prevented them from relating with the rest of Africa. At that time, these laws did not only create geographical but also social boundaries that hindered contact. Where contact exists, perceived threat and hostility among diverse groups are replaced with empathy and cultural understanding (Pettigrew and Tropp 2008) which removes the "us" and "them" divide and creates a sense of a "we" between them. This is somewhat related to Landau's discussion of conviviality, rights and conflict in Africa's urban spaces (in Maputo, Johannesburg, and Nairobi) that are largely unregulated by the state. Although he sought to understand the solidarities and communities people form to meet their daily needs, find rights and recognition in these spaces or estuaries, Landau argued that the spatial dynamics in which migration and immigration occur across African cities give cause to reconsider the fundamental distinctions between guests and hosts as these are blurred from convivial relationships enabled through contact (Landau 2014). Similarly, showing how diverse, peri-urban residents negotiate modalities of accommodating difference, Landau and Freemantle (2016) use the cases of residents of Rongai on Nairobi's urban edge and Katlehong on Johannesburg's periphery, to argue that conviviality is rooted in utilitarian extraction, not a desire for shared identity or enduring bonds. In this sense, coexistence within communities of disconnection and distance means that in place of territorial ownership or strict social boundaries, people (co)operate through a largely instrumental ethics: oriented towards accessing and extracting the "fruits" of urban space while simultaneously imagining or enacting life elsewhere (Landau and Freemantle 2016).

However, there is a flip side to the argument, and it is that contact is not always an elixir that removes hostility and in turn produces conviviality between diverse groups. Landau and Freemantle (2016) challenge the emphasis on cohesion as the basis of conviviality; that the ultimate goal of policy-makers and residents is to turn every-day interactions into "positive" and transformative encounters that produce a society based on respect, common goals and mutual recognition. Other studies have also shown that contact between diverse groups does not always produce the ideal result of conviviality espoused by contact theory (Vezzali and Stathi 2017). They argue that to ensure conviviality, certain favourable conditions need to be put in place. Simply put, when these conditions are absent, then the space of interaction becomes unconducive for conviviality to exist between the diverse groups irrespective of contact, instead of producing a counter-effect of hostility and conflict. This is the case of South Africans where contact with other Africans in the country enabled by post-apartheid democratization, which opened the country to African migration, has produced hostility and conflict reflected in the widespread incidences of xenophobic violence across South Africa. Indeed, there are cases where contact fuels up hostility and prejudice against the *other* rather than reducing such tensions as espoused by contact theory (Dixon and Durrheim 2003). This is the paradoxical effect of contact. However, this does not totally reject the postulations of contact theory but argue that the theory overgeneralizes and exaggerates the influence of contact. In their view, the "problem with research on the contact hypothesis is that it tends to detach intergroup dynamics from their societal contexts, focusing on factors within the immediate environment of interaction that are easily manipulated and measured" (Dixon and Durrheim 2003, 2). To address the over simplicity of this theory, other scholars have argued that the paradoxical effect of contact does not necessarily imply that contact theory is not valid. In fact, Pettigrew and Tropp (2006), in interrogating the paradoxical effect of contact, acknowledge that the argument that contact produces conviviality is valid; however, it is not a given. Furthermore, Forbes (2004) states that there is a "right kind of contact" that reduces prejudice and stereotypes across diverse groups. It could be inferred that prejudice and hostility will prevail in contact across diverse groups because of the absence of the right kind of contact. The question is what is the right kind of contact?

Scholars of this school argue that the right kind of contact is the one that exists under favourable conditions. The favourable conditions include four determinants that must be present to stimulate the desirable effect of contact, which is the production of conviviality across diverse groups. These determinants include the equality of status of the diverse groups; cooperation among members of diverse groups; the pursuit of shared or interdependent goals; and the presence of social norms (Everett and Onu 2013; Hodson and Hewstone 2013). Equality of status refers to hierarchies within social relationships. By implication, there must not be unequal power relations between and within members of the diverse groups. Maoz (2005) reiterates that the relations between the diverse groups must be symmetrical. Where the reverse is the case, that is, a contact that is asymmetrical in nature, it is most likely to buttress prejudice. He further adds that equality of status also implies mutuality in intergroup relations. In his words:

> ...an intervention that is responsive primarily to the needs of only one group will often be marked by the less dominant's group's interest... In more extreme cases, a dramatic lack of symmetry can lead to resistance and hostility toward the encounter by the group that is underrepresented. (Maoz 2005, 136)

Therefore, equality of status does imply equal perceptions not only of identity but also of interests among members of the diverse groups. The second condition involves cooperation of members across groups and across multiple planes. Dixon and Durrheim (2003) explain that cooperation between members of two diverse groups entails both groups working together as a team and this would help bridge their differences. The wrong type of contact in this regard emphasizes competition as opposed to cooperation, and rivalry as opposed to teamwork. Dovidio et al. (2010, 9) expound that "positive interdependence (cooperation) produces more favourable attitudes toward out-group members, whereas negative interdependence (competition) generates more unfavourable attitudes". When a group perceives the other as a competitor for space of any kind, then contact produces hostility. This is because it becomes a game of win or lose or a zero–sum relationship (Dovidio et al. 2010). Cooperation is therefore intrinsic in producing conviviality through contact across diverse groups. The third prerequisite for the development of the right kind of contact is pursuit of a shared goal. This factor is closely linked to cooperation. It has to do with members having an interdependent relationship. In this situation, the out-group's goal and that of the in-group are essentially connected. No one's goal is mutually exclusive of the other or takes priority over another. Freeman (2012) explicates that in such pursuit "of common goals and activities, animosities wane and tolerance grows". Members of the diverse group would cooperate and set differences aside if only they share a common interest. This corresponds with the arguments of conviviality that diverse group develop interdependent relationship when they have a common interest. Therefore, pursuit of a shared goal is a stimulus for bridging diversity across groups, through contact. The fourth factor here, which speaks to the presence of institutional and social norm, has to do with the implementation of policies that favour contact and discourage prejudice and hostility. Kinloch (1991) posits that societal norms influence the effect contact has on intergroup relations. This implies that contact at lower levels across diverse groups will not be futile; they materialize in conviviality if the external arena creates an environment that propagates prejudice. In this regard, Everett and Onu (2013) contend that "there should not be social or institutional authorities that explicitly or implicitly sanction contact, and there should be authorities that support contact". This stipulates that at a larger scale contact should not be discouraged but also encouraged. Clearly then, with these conditions in place, contact can change the attitude of the in-group towards the out-group within the context and extend to the wider out-group (Pettigrew 2009). Meaning that, the in-group's attitude may not only change towards those who they have contact with, but to a large extent, towards those outside the immediate parameters of their contact and interaction.

Finally, having established that contact can reduce hostility and foster conviviality, it is imperative to also examine how this happens. Pettigrew and Tropp (2008) provide three mediators of the contact-prejudice effect. First, they state that the knowledge about the out-group diminishes the prejudice from the in-group. Hutchison et al. (2006) argue that the in-group usually perceives the out-group members as a homogeneous group characterized as sharing a common identity. Various studies like that of Isike (2015) show that this is not always the case, as out-group members have multiple identities, which make them diverse within their own group. Through contact, the in-group becomes aware of the social identities which form the characteristics of the out-group. During the course of this new discovery, they learn more not just about the differences but also the similarities they both share (Pettigrew and Tropp 2008). This knowledge gain about their similarities forms a bridge between the two diverse groups, thereby fostering conviviality and reducing hostility. The second mediator is intergroup anxiety. This has been defined as "the anxiety individuals (in-group members) experience when anticipating a future encounter with one or more outgroup members and is likely to occur in contexts characterized by intergroup conflict or minimal previous intergroup contact" (Swart et al. 2010, 311). In this case, the in-group has a preconceived notion about the out-group, who they envisage as a threat even before having any contact with the out-group. This negative anxiety stems from limited or no intergroup relations, previous hostilities between these groups, class differentials, prejudicial stereotyping of the out-group or higher population of out-group than the in-group (Brown and Hewstone 2005; Tredoux and Finchilescu 2010). As a result of this, contact and intergroup relations are discouraged. Anxiety, therefore, can be a breeding ground for intergroup hostility. It is a well-known fact that anxiety is a critical mediator of the effects of intergroup contact; that is, it mediates the relationship between contact and prejudice (Harwood and Kocovsk 2017); therefore, encouraging positive contact will create a space for the development of convivial relations, which would ultimately reduce anxiety. Lastly, empathy is an affective positive response towards another and the ability to accept their perspective irrespective of the disparity that exists between them (Swart et al. 2010). These two aspects of empathy produce tolerance and magnanimity towards the *other*. Contact between members of the in-group and out-group can foster empathy, which could lead to the development of convivial relations. Pettigrew and Tropp (2008) explain that empathy has to do with a self-expansion process, where members of the in-group "extend their sense of self to include the out-group". It is at this point that the *we* and *them* divide vanishes and the two merge, not into a single entity but a third part, which forms the *us*. Therefore, knowledge, intergroup anxiety and empathy form the three mediators of the contact-prejudice effect. Knowledge and empathy are positive mediators that need to be increased, while intergroup anxiety is the negative mediator that must be reduced if contact is to result in conviviality in intergroup relations.

The discourse of conviviality and contact theory is useful in explaining relations between diverse migrant groups and host communities. Convivial relations can exist where there are spaces of interaction brought on by frequent contact, which does not necessarily make differences evanesce but tolerate and accommodate them as a result of mutual interdependence. This is bearing in mind that contact is a two-edged sword that can produce conflict or conviviality. The pendulum swings towards the latter (conviviality) when certain favourable conditions are put in place. These include the fostering equality of status of the diverse groups; cooperation among members of diverse groups; the pursuit of shared or interdependent goals; and the presence of social norms. The presence of these alongside other mediators of the prejudicial effects of contact such as mutual knowledge of each other which can reduce anxiety that breed conflict can also mitigate conflict that comes from contact. This shows that conviviality within migrant and host relationships is not cast in stone but is an ever evolving plane, characterized by negotiations, mutuality and compromises. As Ashby and Diener (2014, 5) contend, this is a result of the intersection and entanglement of identities which are a "complex social construct encompassing various constantly (re) negotiated aspects... the meanings attached to these are inevitably subject to shifts and changes through migration". In reference to the case of African migrants and South Africans, the question is what knowledge do the latter have of the former, and how the lack of knowledge or false beliefs from fake news fuel anxiety against African migrants for example? Certainly, given the apartheid shielding of Black South Africa from the rest of the continent, many continue to have limited knowledge of Africa including of African migrants in South Africa. This has opened the space for falsehoods and fake news to gain ground in ways that perpetuate anxiety and the resulting lack of empathy many South Africans feel towards African migrants in the country. This knowledge gap and false beliefs also play a role in perpetuating the ingrained consciousness of self vs the *African other* that drives xenophobia targeted only at African migrants in South Africa. However, these are also bridged on a daily basis by conviviality in other spaces where contact enables common ground of understanding which fosters intergroup cooperation and the pursuit of shared goals that are markers or social predictors of concord. This is irrespective of whether or not concord and integration were the motives behind such convivial interactions since in many cases, as Loren Landau has variously argued, they are coping or survival mechanisms which are often fluid.

Conclusion

Intergroup relations is either conflictual or convivial and this is a function of the nature of interaction among them. Simply put, contact can lead to either conflict or conviviality and this depends on the predisposing conditions which include equality of status of the diverse groups, cooperation among its members, the pursuit of shared or interdependent goals and the presence of social norms. When these predisposing conditions are absent, contact produces conflict rather than conviviality. Relatedly, there are three mediators of the contact-prejudice effect and these include: the knowledge of the out-group, which enables the formation of bridges across diversity, the anxiety of members within the groups and the attitude of empathy present within intergroup relations. The first and last are positive mediators that create an enabling space for contact to produce conviviality, while the second (anxiety) produces the opposite effect. Therefore, intergroup contact does not necessarily produce only conviviality, but can also produce a paradoxical effect of conflict in the absence of the predisposing and mediating conditions discussed above. What one gets in terms of either conflict or conviviality would depend largely not only on the presence or absence of these conditions, but also on the degree to which they are present or absent in the relations between African migrants and South Africans.

References

Aleksynska, M. 2007. Attitudes Towards Immigrants and Relative Deprivation: The Case of a Middle-Income Country, MPRA Paper No. 4595, Munich Personal RePEc Archive. http://mpra.ub.uni-muenchen.de/4595/.
Allport, G.W. 1954. *The Nature of Prejudice*. Cambridge and Reading, MA: Addison-Wesley.
Ashby, D.J., and W. Diener. 2014. You Are a Foreigner, You Are a Foreigner, as If You Are an Outcast; Exploring the Dynamics Between Discrimination and Identification Amongst Nigerian Immigrants in Durban, South Africa. Dissertation, Aalborg University, Denmark.
Bordeau, J. 2010. *Xenophobia: The Violence of Fear and Hate*. New York: Rohen Publishing Group.
Brameld, T. 1946. *Minority Problems in the Public Schools*. New York: Harper.
Briesacher, A.B. 2014. Integrating Stereotype Threat into Identity Theory and Social Identity Theory. PhD Dissertation, Kent State University.
Brown, R., and M. Hewstone. 2005. An Integrative Theory of Intergroup Contact. In *Advances in Experimental Social Psychology*, vol. 37, ed. M. Zanna, 255–343. San Diego, CA: Academic Press.
Brubaker, R. 2000. Beyond Identity. *Theory and Society* 29 (1): 1–47.
Brubaker, R. 2002. Ethnicity Without Groups. *Archives européènes de sociologie* XLIII (2): 163–189.
Brudvig, I. 2013. Conviviality in Bellville: An Ethnography of Space, Place, Mobility and Being. Master's Dissertation, University of Cape Town.
Crush, J. 2008. The Perfect Storm: The Realities of Xenophobia in Contemporary South Africa. Southern African Migration Project. http://www.genoci dewatch.org/images/South_Africa_09_03_30_the_perfect_storm.pdf.
Dixon, J.A., and K. Durrheim. 2003. Contact and the Ecology of Racial Division: Some Varieties of Informal Segregation. *British Journal of Social Psychology* 42: 1–23.

Dovidio, J.F., J.D. Johnson, S.L. Gaertner, A.R. Pearson, T. Saguy, and L. Ashburn-Nardo. 2010. Empathy and Intergroup Relations. In *Prosocial Motives, Emotions, and Behavior: The Better Angels of our Nature*, ed. M. Mikulincer and P.R. Shaver, 393–408. Washington, DC, US: American Psychological Association.
Everett, J. 2013. Intergroup Contact Theory: Past, Present, and Future. https://www.in-mind.org/article/intergroup-contact-theory-past-present-and-future.
Everett, J.A.C., and D. Onu. 2013. Intergroup Contact Theory: Past, Present, and Future. *The Inquisitive Mind* 13 (2). http://www.in-mind.org/article/intergroup-contact-theory-past-present-and-future.
Forbes, H.D. 2004. Ethnic Conflict and the Contact Hypothesis. In *Psychological Dimensions to War and Peace: The Psychology of Ethnic and Cultural Conflict*, ed. Y.T. Lee, C. McCauley, F. Moghaddam, and S. Worchel, 69–88. Westport, CT: Praeger Publishers and Greenwood Publishing Group.
Freeman, C.M.L. 2012. The Psychosocial Need for Intergroup Contact: Practical Suggestions for Reconciliation Initiatives in Bosnia and Herzegovina and Beyond. *Intervention* 10 (1): 17–29.
Gilroy, P. 2004. *After Empire: Melancholia or Convivial Culture?* London: Routledge.
Hall, S. 1990. Cultural Identity and Diaspora: Identity. In *Identity: Community, Culture, Difference*, ed. J. Rutherford, 222–237. London: Lawrence and Wishart.
Hamill, J. 2014. Africa: Closing the Door—South Africa's Draconian Immigration Reforms. *World Politics Review*. http://imcosa.co.za/news/458-sa-s-new-immigration.html
Harris, B. 2002. Xenophobia: A New Pathology for a New South Africa? In *Psychopathology and Social Prejudice*, ed. D. Hook and G. Eagle. Cape Town: University of Cape Town Press.
Harwood, E.M. and N.L. Kocovsk. 2017. Self-Compassion Induction Reduces Anticipatory Anxiety Among Socially Anxious Students. *Mindfulness*. https://self-compassion.org/wp-content/uploads/2018/05/Harwood2017.pdf.
Haslam, S.A. 2001. *Psychology in Organizations*. London: Sage.
Hodson, G., and M. Hewstone. 2013. *Advances in Intergroup Contact*. London: Psychology Press.
Hogg, M.A. 1993. Group Cohesiveness: A Critical Review and Some New Directions. *European Review of Social Psychology* 4: 85–111.
Hutchison, P., T. Jetten, J. Christian, and E. Haycraft. 2006. Protecting Threatened Identity: Sticking with the Group by Emphasizing In-Group Heterogeneity. *Personality and Social Psychology Bulletin* 32: 1620–1633.
Isike, E. 2015. Ties That Bind: A Network Analysis of Relationships Between Nigerian Migrants and South Africans in Umhlathuze. PhD Dissertation, University of KwaZulu-Natal.

Isike, E. 2017. A Contact Theory Analysis of South Africans' Perceptions of Nigerian Immigration. *African Population Studies* 31 (1): 3225–3233.
Isike, C., and E. Isike. 2012. A Socio-Cultural Analysis of African Immigration to South Africa. *Alternation* 19 (1): 93–116.
Kinloch, G.C. 1991. Inequality, Repression, Discrimination and Violence: A Comparative Study. *International Journal of Contemporary Sociology* 28: 85–98.
Landau, L.B. 2004. The Laws of (In)Hospitality: Black Africans in South Africa. Forced Migration Working Paper Series, 7. University of the Witwatersrand, Johannesburg. http://www.repository.forcedmigration.org/pdf/?pid=fmo:5808.
Landau, L. 2014. Conviviality, Rights, and Conflict in Africa's Urban Estuaries. *Politics and Society* 42 (3): 359–380.
Landau, L.B. 2018. Friendship Fears and Communities of Convenience in Africa's Urban Estuaries: Connection as Measure of Urban Condition. *Urban Studies* 55 (3): 505–521.
Landau, L., and I. Freemantle. 2010. Tactical Cosmopolitanism and Idioms of Belonging: Insertion and Self-Exclusion in Johannesburg. *Journal of Ethnic and Migration Studies* 36 (3): 375–390.
Landau, L., and I. Freemantle. 2016. Beggaring Belonging in Africa's No-Man's Lands: Diversity, Usufruct and the Ethics of Accommodation. *Journal of Ethnic and Migration Studies* 42 (6): 933–951.
Maoz, I. 2005. Evaluating the Communication Between Groups in Dispute: Equality in Contact Interventions Between Jews and Arabs in Israel. *Negotiation Journal* 21 (1): 131–146.
Matsinhe, D.M. 2011. Africa's Fear of Itself: The Ideology of Makwerekwere in South Africa. *Third World Quarterly* 32 (2): 295–313.
Mazars, C., R. Matsuyama, J. Rispoli, and J. Vearey. 2013. The Well-Being of Economic Migrants in South Africa: Health, Gender and Development. Working Paper for the World Migration Report. http://www.iom.int/files/live/sites/iom/files/What-We-Do/wmr2013/en/Working-Paper_SouthAfrica.pdf.
McDonald, D., and S. Jacobs. 2005. (Re)Writing Xenophobia: Understanding Press Coverage of Cross-Border Migration in Southern Africa. *Journal of Contemporary African Studies* 23 (3): 295–325.
Misago, J.P. 2011. Disorder in a Changing Society: Authority and the Micro-Politics of Violence. In *Exorcising the Demons Within*, ed. L.B. Landau. Johannesburg: Wits University Press.
Morris, A. 1998. Our Fellow Africans Make Our Lives Hell: The Lives of Congolese and Nigerians Living in Johannesburg. *Ethnic and Racial Studies* 21 (6): 1116–1136.

Nathan, G. 2015. A Non-Essentialist Model of Culture: Implications of Identity, Agency and Structure Within Multinational/Multicultural Organizations. *International Journal of Cross Cultural Management* 15 (1): 101–124.

Neocosmos, M. 2008. The Politics of Fear and the Fear of Politics. *Journal of Asian and African Studies* 43 (6): 586–594.

Nuttall, S. 2009. *Entanglement: Literary and Cultural Reflection on Post-apartheid*. Johannesburg: Wits University Press.

Nyamnjoh, F.B. 2006. *Insiders and Outsiders: Citizenship and Xenophobia in Contemporary South Africa*. Dakar and London: CODESRIA and Zed Books.

Nyamnjoh, F.B. 2015. Incompleteness: Frontier Africa and the Currency of Conviviality. *Journal of Asian and African Studies* 52: 1–18.

Oldmeadow, J.A., and S.T. Fiske. 2010. Social Status and the Pursuit of Positive Social Identity: Systematic Domains of Intergroup Differentiation and Discrimination for High and Low Status Groups. *Group Processes and Intergroup Relations* 13: 425–444.

Padilla, A.M., and W. Perez. 2003. Acculturation, Social Identity, and Social Cognition: A New Perspective. *Hispanic Journal of Behavioral Sciences* 25 (1): 35–55.

Peterie, M., and D. Neil. 2019. Xenophobia Towards Asylum Seekers: A Survey of Social Theories. *Journal of Sociology* 56 (1): 23–35.

Petersson, B. 2003. Combating Uncertainty, Combating the Global: Scapegoating, Xenophobia and the National-Local Nexus. *International Journal of Peace Studies, Spring/Summer* 8 (1): 85–102.

Pettigrew, T.F. 2009. Secondary Transfer Effect of Contact: Do Intergroup Contact Effects Spread to Non-Contacted Outgroups? *Social Psychology* 40: 55–65.

Pettigrew, T.F., and L.R. Tropp. 2006. A Meta-Analytic Test of Intergroup Contact Theory. *Journal of Personality and Social Psychology* 90: 751–783.

Pettigrew, T.F., and L.R. Tropp. 2008. How Does Intergroup Contact Reduce Prejudice? Meta-Analytic Tests of Three Mediators. *European Journal of Social Psychology* 38: 922–934.

Runciman, W.G. 1972. *Relative Deprivation and Social Justice: A Study of Attitudes to Social Inequality in Twentieth-Century England*. Harmondsworth, Middlesex: Penguin Books.

Rzepnikowska, A. 2013. Convivial Cultures in Multicultural Manchester and Barcelona: Narratives of Polish Migrant Women. Paper from Euroemigranci Conference, Kraków. http://www.euroemigranci.pl/dokumenty/pokonferencyjna/Rzepnikowska.pdf.

Savo, H. 2019. Politics: Xenophobia and Party Politics in South Africa. *Mail and Guardian*, September 3.

Steenkamp, C. 2009. Xenophobia in South Africa: What Does It Say About Trust? The Round Table. *Commonwealth Journal of International Affairs* 9: 439–447.

Stets, J.E., and P.J. Burke. 2000. Identity Theory and Social Identity Theory. *Social Psychology Quarterly* 63: 224–237.

Swart, H., M. Hewstone, O. Christ, and A. Voci. 2010. The Impact of Cross-Group Friendships in South Africa: Affective Mediators and Multi-Group Comparisons. *Journal of Social Issues* 66 (2): 309–333.

Tafira, K. 2011. Is Xenophobia Racism? *Anthropology Southern Africa* 34 (3 & 4): 114–121.

Taifel, H., and J.C. Turner. 1986. The Social Identity Theory of Intergroup Behaviour. In *Psychology of Intergroup Relations*, ed. M. Hewstore and R. Brown, 7–24. Chicago: Nelson-Hall.

Tajfel, H., and J.C. Turner. 1979. An Integrative Theory of Intergroup Conflict. In *The Social Psychology of Intergroup Relations*, ed. W.G. Austin and S. Worchel. Monterey, CA: Brooks/Cole.

Tredoux, C., and G. Finchilescu. 2010. Mediators of the Contact-Prejudice Relation Among South African Students on Four University Campuses. *Journal of Social Issues* 66: 289–308.

Vezzali, L., and S. Stathi. 2017. *Intergroup Contact Theory: Recent Developments and Future Directions*. Abingdon, UK: Routledge.

CHAPTER 3

Parities and Disparities in Applying Immigration Legislation/Policies from a World Class National Constitution

Christopher Changwe Nshimbi

INTRODUCTION

South Africa is touted as a country with one of the best constitutions in the world. A nation's constitution essentially lays out a framework that establishes, defines, regulates and sets out the powers and authority of a government (Allott 1979). For a democratically and constitutionally governed country such as South Africa, this means that the government is limited in its ability to act (Sajó 1999). This is because, through its provisions, the constitution frames the state's power. And in doing so, it limits that power in a couple of ways.

Firstly, the constitution lays out the composition and specific powers of government. Secondly, it draws up a Bill of Rights. In the former, a national constitution establishes and stipulates the responsibilities of

C. C. Nshimbi (✉)
Department of Political Sciences, University of Pretoria, Pretoria, South Africa
e-mail: christopher.nshimbi@up.ac.za

© The Author(s), under exclusive license to Springer Nature Singapore Pte Ltd. 2022
C. Isike and E. M. Isike (eds.), *Conflict and Concord*,
https://doi.org/10.1007/978-981-19-1033-3_3

Parliament (Calland and Taylor 1997; Lakin 2008) as that part of government which carries out legislative activities, and the Executive (Hassan 2015) as the branch of government that implements legislation. The latter grants human rights to the people in the country under the guidance of the constitution in question and cements the protection of those rights (Sakala 2010). The Courts, or better still the Judiciary, as a third wing of government (in addition to the Executive and Parliament) are not only guided by, but also inhere power from the constitution to interpret the constitution and legislation as well as declare legislation and the behaviour of government constitutional or unconstitutional (Akiba 2004; Ellett 2013). The Courts may, for instance, declare unconstitutional, any conduct or legislation that exceeds that for which the constitution technically and procedurally provides.

Accordingly, the Constitutional Court of South Africa (2017) in the June 2017 case, *Lawyers for Human Rights v Minister of Home Affairs and Others* declared that sections 34(1)(b) and (d) of South Africa's Immigration Act, 2002 (Act No. 13 of 2002) were inconsistent with sections 12(1) and 35(2)(d) of the Constitution of the Republic of South Africa, 1996. The inconsistency, according to the Court, lay in two facts for which the sections of the principal Act did not allow: automatic judicial intervention when an "illegal" foreigner was detained in order to be deported; and for a detained "illegal" foreigner to challenge the lawfulness of their detention in person, in court.

This case and judgement underscore a technical provision which constitutions in democratically and constitutionally governed countries produce, namely the separation of powers. Through this doctrine, the constitution decentralises power in government vis-à-vis legislation or law making, implementing, and adjudicating on matters concerning the law. In the cited example, the South African courts as a separate entity from, but equal in power with, the Executive (which implements laws) checked the Executive by interpreting and applying the law. Consequently, the Executive drafted the Immigration Amendment Bill 2018 to address the judgement of the Constitutional Court and to amend sections of the principal Act that the Court had declared inconsistent with the Constitution of the Republic of South Africa. The doctrine of separation of powers in this way decentralises the location of power between the three arms of and in government.

Besides making laws, Parliament also represents the people in/of a country. It, further, exercises oversight over the Executive, whose other function is to keep the peace and order in the country. This action constitutes the doctrine of checks and balances. The Courts participate in that too, in addition to settling disputes between the government and people as well as between people in the country. The three arms of government check and balance each other's power.

Democratically and constitutionally governed countries that endeavour to adhere to their national constitutions through these and other technical or procedural provisions that constitutions make, further claim to observe the Rule of Law. They claim that they do not engage in arbitrary actions towards or against the people or any other entities in the country. Instead, they argue, they act on the basis of predictable and objective law that is accessible to all. So, if an individual, group of individuals or any other entity in the country sought the services, assistance of or engaged with government or its officials, those actors would be treated in a predictable way based on criteria established by or in the law.

This chapter is not about constitutionalism. It rather discusses South Africa's policy and legislative framework in relation to immigration. Specifically, it discusses the life experiences and interactions of selected immigrants with officials in the Executive branch of government as well as with some ordinary South African people on the ground under the country's law. In doing so, the chapter also parenthetically tests the validity of claims that South Africa's is one of the best constitutions in the world. Ultimately, the aim is to peek into the lived experiences of ordinary South Africans and immigrants under the law in the country and within the communities in which they dwell, together.

The rationale behind this objective is sensible in that, national constitutions in and of themselves constitute the core of the premise that government is limited. That, government cannot engage in conduct that falls outside of the provisions of the constitution. Further to the theoretical postulations laid out so far concerning the ways that constitutions limit the power of government, the constitution through the Bill of Rights restricts the extent to which government can use its authority, relative to people's consciences, expressions and association. It also declares that Parliament may not formulate any legislation that restricts such freedoms. People in a country such as South Africa should be free to voluntarily associate with others in the pursuit of common purposes (Republic of South Africa [RSA] 1996). The Bill of Rights also specifies procedures meant to prevent the government from engaging in arbitrary or capricious or unfair conduct that might include subjecting the people living in the country to having their homes and property searched or their property seized (Republic of South Africa [RSA] 1996, Chapter 2, section 14: Bill of Rights) without any due process of the law. Not only so, the Bill of Rights in the Constitution of the Republic of South Africa (section 21) bestows on everyone in the country the freedom of movement and residence and to leave the Republic.

From the foregoing, this chapter asks, how consistent is the conduct of the Executive branch of the Government of the Republic of South Africa with the stipulations of the constitution when dealing with immigrants? Are the engagements of the Executive with immigrants really limited by the provisions of the Constitution of the Republic of South Africa? What about the local people or South Africans and immigrants who co-exist as hosts and visitors on the ground? Do their actions and interactions fall within the ambit of the law? The conduct in question is viewed through policies, designated agencies and officials of/in the Executive.

Many studies examine immigration and the state and people's respective responses in post-apartheid South Africa. Peberdy (2001), for example, documents the evolution of state and exclusionary discourses in immigration policies and argues that because South Africa has shifted towards inclusivity and citizenship as markers of belonging, its immigration policy has increasingly become exclusive and restrictionist. Vigneswara argues that non-immigration policymakers can potentially play an equally important role in enforcing immigration laws and demonstrates how the capacity of South Africa to deport foreign nationals is impacted by decisions to develop new methods of policing and to ban segregation (Vigneswaran 2020). The politics of migration and belonging, among other things, play out at the community level too. For example, foreign nationals in South Africa live alongside and interact with South African nationals in cosmopolitan urban settings where tense "deficit of belonging" conditions occur and precipitate xenophobia (Gordon 2011, 2020; Landau 2005; Landau and Freemantle 2010).

To the best of my knowledge, however, no studies incorporate policy, the activities of actors in and the Executive and tie these up with the life stories of immigrants as well as their lived experiences with actors in the communities they live. The discussion in this chapter therefore aligns with the theme of this book in that, it does not so much dwell on the discriminatory nature and tightening of South Africa's immigration policy and the xenophobic attitudes of South African locals towards foreign nationals. It rather attempts to meander the spirit and letter of the law to determine how officials in the Executive—as implementor of policy and legislation—follow through with the provisions thereof and the actualisation of policy in the lived realities of people on the ground. Moreover, the chapter uniquely compares and contrasts as well as attempts to distil the provisions of South Africa's constitution in the lived experiences of officials in the Executive branch of government, ordinary people as well as the asylum seekers and immigrants.

The chapter is informed by a qualitative research design and thematic content analysis of the Executive or Department of Home Affairs and immigration realities as well as of/and a couple of anecdotal evidences from the lived experiences of a Kenyan asylum seeker and a Mozambican immigrant and their interactions with the law, officials of the Executive and people in South African communities. Besides a thorough examination of South Africa's migration and related policies and legislation, the literature on migration and newspaper articles, the chapter also analyses two purposively selected immigrants' accounts of life experiences in South Africa. The qualitative research approach helps gain insight into how South Africa's immigration legalisation, regulations and policy are lived out in the country. The anecdotal evidence then attests to this. The aim being to shine a spotlight at the interface between policy and reality or life on the ground. It is also to highlight conviviality and/or frostiness between hosts and immigrants under the same supreme and rule of law that consider both parties equal (Republic of South Africa [RSA] 1996). The policies and legislation and migration-related literature are observed and analysed for content, to draw meaning and make sense of assumptions that hosts and immigrants in South Africa convivially and/or frostily live together. This is the basis upon which the chapter gathers data from which it draws inferences, interprets and explains reality insofar as concerns immigrants and their hosts in South Africa.

After this introductory section, the next section briefly conceptualises immigration. This is done in the general context of a couple of the policy and legislative instruments under which issues concerning human mobility occur. The focus is on mobility that occurs across nation-state borders. The section also outlines some of South African's key pieces of policy and legislation on and that relate to immigration, and which impact on immigrants and immigrants' lives in the country as well as the lives of ordinary South Africans and their co-existence with immigrants. The section also highlights some of the implications of those instruments for immigrants, South Africans and government. The next section examines immigration realities in South Africa, in the shadow of the country's immigration policies and legislation. Besides examining government's interaction with and conduct towards immigrants, the section mainly provides anecdotal evidence of hospitality and/or hostility between hosts and immigrants under the law. The last section concludes by touching on the validity of claims that South Africa's constitution is one of the best in the world.

OF HONEY AND HONEYCOMBS: THE CONSTITUTION AND IMMIGRATION LEGISLATION/POLICIES OF SOUTH AFRICA

Human Mobility and the Crossing of Nation-State Borders

Difficulties exist in defining and interpreting migration and related concepts. The notion migration is itself complex. The same applies to determining who qualifies as a migrant. A reason for the difficulty and complexity is that the ways that migration and migrants are defined differ from one country to another. This is besides differences in definition drawn up by and across intellectual disciplines or subject areas of study that conduct inquiries into migration and migrant-related issues.

For its purposes, this chapter simplifies the challenging and daunting task of getting around establishing an operational definition of migration and migrants, in two ways. Firstly, it focuses on human mobility that, though still difficult to define, occurs when a person crosses a nation-state border into a country in which relations between such a person and their host government and communities live—in this case South Africa. This chapter considers such movement to be immigration and the person thus entering the country, an immigrant. Secondly, the chapter takes time into consideration and focuses on only those persons who move into and remain in the country for a period of one year and more. Thus, the chapter considers a person to be an immigrant if they cross the nation-state borders of the Republic of South Africa and remain in the country for periods extending beyond one year.

Thus conceptualised, the understanding of immigrant deployed in this chapter is consistent with the way that the United Nations Department of Economic and Social Affairs (UNDESA 1998, para. 36) defines an international migrant: as, "a person who moves to a country other than that of his or her usual residence for a period of at least a year (12 months), so that the country of destination effectively becomes his or her new country of usual residence". This conceptualisation is more specific and suits the purposes of this chapter better than the broader way that the International Organisation for Migration (IOM) (2003, 8) defines international migration: as, "the movement of a person or group of persons from one geographical unit to another across an administrative or political border, wishing to settle definitely or temporarily in a place other than their place of origin".

The Constitution and Immigration Legislation/Policies of South Africa

Migration is a historical, international and global reality. This can be deduced from the fact that many international conventions define or touch on issues that concern the subject and migrants. South Africa acknowledges and is a signatory to some of these instruments. According to the 1948 Universal Declaration of Human Rights, for example, every person has the right to freedom of movement and residence within the borders of each state and the freedom to leave any country, including their own, and to return to their country (Art. 13). South Africa has also signed in on to the 1966 International Covenant on Civil and Political Rights, which confers on everyone lawfully within the territory of a state the right, within that territory, to liberty of movement, freedom to choose their residence and also the freedom to leave any country, including their own (Arts. 12.1 and 12.2). Another is the 1951 Convention Relating to the Status of Refugees. As far as African conventions are concerned, South Africa is a signatory to the African Charter, among other continental and regional instruments. The African Charter (Art. 12) states that every individual shall have the right to freedom of movement and residence within the borders of a state, to leave any country, including their own, and to return to that country.

The extent to which international conventions and legislation, such as the ones cited in this chapter, have effect on/in a country only goes so far as that country ratifies, complies with and incorporates them into its own national legislation and implements them (Nshimbi and Fioramonti 2013, 20). And, as the theoretical introduction of this chapter has demonstrated, South Africa has to some extent adopted most of the cited international conventions in its republican constitution. The question, however, is whether the Executive branch of the government and South African citizens and locals in communities respect and observe these provisions when engaging and interacting with immigrants? That, really is the point at which the goodness and clout of the country's constitution as a world class instrument gets tested.

Ideally, policies and legislation that govern immigration, immigrants' lives and immigrant co-existence with hosts in the country should be consistent with the country's national constitution. This is because those instruments are formulated in the shadow of the constitution, given that it is the supreme law of the land. For instance, among the policies and legislation whose content this chapter examined for provisions that potentially promote or inhibit cordiality and immigrant integration at community level in South Africa include the White Paper on International Migration for South Africa of 1999 and 2017, respectively; the White Paper on Local Government, 1998; the 1998 Municipal Structures Act No. 17; and the Municipal Systems Act No. 32 of 2000. These pieces of policy and legislation when read together with section 152 of the Constitution of the Republic of South Africa [RSA] (1996) promote the participation of grassroots people in local governance. Therefore, the question insofar as this chapter is concerned is whether immigrants participate in such activities too, in the communities in which they live.

As of May 2020, the 2017 White Paper on International Migration for South Africa and the Immigration Amendment Bill 2018 represented some of government's latest efforts to update South Africa's immigration and related policy and law.

The latter sought

> To amend the Immigration Act, 2002, so as to insert a definition; to revise and align the provisions relating to the detention of illegal foreigners for purposes of deportation with constitutional principles; to provide for further extensions of detention of an illegal foreigner in certain circumstances; to provide guidance to an immigration officer as to when he or she may arrest and detain an illegal foreigner for purposes of deportation; and to provide for matters connected therewith. (Department of Home Affairs [DHA] 2018, 6)

According to then Minister of Home Affairs, Honourable Prof Hlengiwe Mkhize, MP, efforts to update were driven by the need to comprehensively review the immigration policy framework to inform the systematic reform of the country's immigration and related legislation (DHA 2017b, iii). At the time, the 1999 White Paper on International Migration defined the country's policy on international migration, which is implemented and achieved through Immigration Act, 2002 (Act No. 13 of 2002), as amended, and, partly, the Refugees Act, 1998 (Act No. 130 of 1998), as amended (Department of Home Affairs [DHA] 2017b, iii). But the 1999 policy, the Minister argued, had significant policy gaps in areas such as the management of integration for international migrants, emigration, and asylum seekers and refuges. According to the Minister, the new White Paper on International Migration for South Africa would, therefore, approach international migration holistically given the interconnected nature of many aspects of migration that were evident in concrete processes and people's lives.

The 2017 White Paper on International Migration for South Africa itself argues that the migration paradigm established by the 1999 White Paper on International Migration for South Africa exposed the country to various risks in a world that was volatile, and that the 1999 policy strengthened colonial patterns of production, trade and labour (Department of Home Affairs [DHA] 2017b, v). This was besides perpetuating irregular migration and, consequently, corruption, the abuse of human rights and posing risks to national security. Because of this, the 2017 White Paper on International Migration for South Africa argues, the previous policy inhibited South Africa from adequately embracing global opportunities and safeguarding national sovereignty as well as the safety of the South African public.

The 2017 White Paper on International Migration for South Africa outlines eight areas in which it recommends strategic and policy interventions on international migration including, management of admissions and departures; residency and naturalisation; international migrants with skills and capital; ties with South African expatriates; international migration within the African context; asylum seekers and refugees; the integration process for migrants; and enforcement (Department of Home Affairs [DHA] 2017b, iii).

Two distinctive aspects of the new policy include, some immediately implementable administrative elements and those elements that the government will have to significantly change and, therefore, involve legislative amendment. The Border Management Authority Bill, 2016 (BMA) (DHA 2016), for example, is borne out of and speaks to the immigration or the first of the eight policy and strategic interventions of the 2017 White Paper on International Migration for South Africa. It is plausible to argue that the Bill is clearly one of those measures Minister

Prof Mkhize said would need legislative intervention in the policy and is, therefore, part of the institutional capacity the DHA will set up in order in order to control immigration. As of May 2020, the BMA had been passed by both Houses of the National Assembly and sent to the republican President for assent.

When the Bill becomes law, the BMA will consolidate South Africa's fragmented border management in order to address threats to its territorial integrity (Department of Home Affairs [DHA] 2016). With the power to set up and control a new agency to administer South Africa's borders vested in the DHA that comes with this legislation, the DHA will take the lead in on all matters concerning the country's borders including, for instance, policing, movement of people and customs administration.

Another piece of immigration-related legislation government amended between 2015 and 2020 is the Refugees Amendment Act, 2017 (Act No. 11 of 2017). The amendment was necessitated by the need to deal with challenges in the system of asylum management (DHA 2017a). The amended Act grants the DHA authority to designate or close a refugee reception office (RRO); it provides conditions for exclusion and cessation from refugee status; and restricts asylum seekers' rights to study, work or be self-employed (Department of Home Affairs [DHA] 2017a).

Although the Minister acknowledged that the 1999 policy was outdated and imposed serious limitations on the country's ability to exploit global opportunities, the 2017 White paper on International Migration for South Africa, nonetheless, "incorporates much of the content of the 1999 White Paper" (Department of Home Affairs [DHA] 2017b, iii). This, therefore, suggests that although the new policy seeks to respond to realities and developments in the global political economy, it still builds on past policies and legislation.

IMMIGRATION REALITIES UNDER SOUTH AFRICA'S CONSTITUTION AND IMMIGRATION LEGISLATION/POLICIES

Immigration under one of the world's best constitutions presents contrasting realities. In the broader context of migration, some foreign nationals find protection and safety from the factors that drove them into seeking asylum and refuge in South Africa. The promise of a better life and incomes, however, turns sour when others face the grim reality of borders and life inside the country (Moyo and Nshimbi 2017; Nshimbi et al. 2018). Two anecdotal cases presented in this section illustrate this disparity in the practice and outworking of immigration policy and legislation, on the one hand, and the impact on the lives and living of immigrants and host government and communities, on the other hand, in South Africa.

The Executive and Immigration Realities

The Department of Home Affairs (DHA) is the primary custodian of immigration policy and legislation in the Executive branch of the Government of the Republic of South Africa. In the 2017 White Paper on International Migration for South Africa, the DHA introduced interventions to increase the international competitiveness of South Africa by prioritising the retention and attraction of "high-valued migrants" (Department of Home Affairs [DHA] 2017b).

The department is, however, greatly concerned that "the majority of international migrants [in the country] are either low-skilled, asylum seekers or those who are granted residence on the basis of relationships (relative's visas)" (Department of Home Affairs [DHA] 2017b, 30). Most of these are from neighbouring and other countries in Africa. The concern, especially with asylum seekers and low-skilled immigrants, is that they burden and threaten the security of the country as opposed to positively contributing to its development (Department of Home Affairs [DHA] 2017b). DHA argues that some unskilled and low-skilled migrants abuse the asylum seeker management system and use it as an avenue to enter the country and legitimise their stay. In essence, it argues, the abusers do not qualify for asylum but largely comprise people who come to the country in search of economic opportunities even when they lack the skills that the country desires. But because those migrants do not qualify for visas that are open to and seek to attract skilled human resources, they resort to abusing the asylum seeker management system. Consequently, the system is overwhelmed. And this, the DHA argues, further, creates opportunities for as well as an environment that fuels corruption.

In response, the state through the DHA has followed this up by, among other things, deporting (those said to be violating immigration rules), tightening asylum seeker legislation and regulations, and creating asylum processing centres.

The 2017 White Paper on International Migration for South Africa acknowledges that the larger proportion of the people the DHA annually deports include low-skilled migrants from neighbouring countries and that, between 2012 and 2016, South Africa deported 369,726 irregular migrants in total (Department of Home Affairs [DHA] 2017b, 29–30). Mozambican, Sotho and Zimbabwean nationals comprised 88% of the total deported during that period (Department of Home Affairs [DHA] 2017b, 29, 30). The total number deported would have been higher had the country not issued amnesties and special permits to nationals of those countries (Nshimbi and Fioramonti 2013). Still, Nshimbi and Fioramonti (2013) argue that the deportation scheme of post-apartheid South Africa is probably one of the largest in the world—having systematically (Segatti 2011) detained and deported approximately 2.5 million undocumented (and mostly Zimbabwean and Mozambican) immigrants between 1988 and 2010.

The DHA amended the Refugees Act 1998 (Act No. 130 of 1998) in order to tighten asylum seeker legislation and regulations. The amendment was effectively a policy response, on the part of government, to the perceived high levels of inflows of irregular migrants. It also represented government's effort to stop and provide a solution to the abuse of the asylum seeker management system and, thus, seems cognisant of Nshimbi and Fioramonti's (2013) argument that migrants attempt to circumvent measures that are restrictive to their movement by seeking amnesty or asylum. However, the authors are quick to point out that challenges plague policies that restrict the movement and entry of migrants. The abuse of the asylum seeker management system that the DHA seeks to cap is, indeed, itself a consequence of restrictions on the movement of unskilled and semi-skilled migrants from South Africa's neighbours. And such is not unique to South Africa but evident elsewhere in Africa and the rest of the world, wherever strict measures against free movement exist.

The amended Refugees Act 1998 introduces a couple of new measures meant to resolve some of DHA's concerns just highlighted. This chapter points to only two among the many including, the opening up and closure of RROs and the repeal of asylum seekers' right to work and study.

In effecting the former, the DHA argues that it aims to decongest or free up the overwhelmed asylum seeker management system. The Amendment Act thus empowers the Director-General of DHA to establish RROs at land borders and disestablish them (DHA 2017a). The DHA argues that the centres will not only help reduce irregular inflows of migrants but costs related to managing many asylum seekers too as well as provide for a transparent and responsive system (Department of Home Affairs [DHA] 2017a).

Rights organisations and critics, however, are concerned that the act paves way for RROs to serve as detention centres for asylum seekers. This is because the methods deployed for operating the centres, for example, are typical of detention. And with this, the probability is high that officials will engage in inhumane actions that will translate into the violation and abuse of migrants' rights as well as corrupt practices and abuse of authority. And such concerns are not unfounded. The South African Human Rights Commission (SAHRC) (2012, 2017), Amnesty International (2018) and Lawyers for Human Rights (LHR) (2017) as well as researchers (see, e.g., Amit 2015b; Nethery and Silverman 2015) have over the years released reports that detail and examine the ways in which migrants (including children) are exposed to and have their rights infringed upon and abused by police and officials of the DHA at RROs such as the Lindela Repatriation Centre. The organisations and researchers examine and tell of unlawful detentions, procedural violations and unsafe and inhuman conditions. They reveal lacunas in immigration legislation/policy and its implementation by the state and/or its agencies.

Considering that immigration legislation is made under the gaze of the Constitution of the Republic of South Africa, another way of saying this is that a clear disparity seems to exist between a world class legal instrument and reality. Or, better still, there seems to exist disparity between the intents of the law and policy and its implementation. And this is manifested in the (mis)application and official (ab)use of that law in certain sections or by certain actors in the state's agencies.

Besides attributing corruption to irregular migration, the 2017 White Paper on International Migration for South Africa justifies the creation of RROs as a measure to combat it (Department of Home Affairs [DHA] 2017b). It could, however, also be posited that DHA actually adopted the measure in reaction to allegations of widespread corruption in the asylum seeker management system in the first place. Rights organisations and studies of migration in South Africa paint a picture contrary to DHA assertions that corruption in the system is due to irregular migration. The contrary posits and provides evidence that DHA officials and police extort bribes from immigrants and asylum seekers and that this occurs at various stages in the process of obtaining asylum seeker/refugee documents (Alfaro-Velcamp et al. 2017; Amit 2015a, b; Grant and Thompson 2015; Jinnah 2010; Landau 2006; Mbelle 2005; Vigneswaran 2011).

Besides opening up and closing down RROs, the Refugees Amendment Act 2017 repeals asylum seekers' automatic right to study and work in South Africa. An asylum seeker would only access the right to work upon DHA satisfactorily determining (on the basis of support from the United Nations High Commissioner for Refugees (UNHCR) and through a process that assesses) that the person applying for asylum can support themselves. The DHA would then "endorse" the right on the applicant's visa. Otherwise, the applicant would have the right endorsed on their visa but then need to prove that they were employed within two weeks. Failure to do that risked their employer paying a hefty fine. Asylum seekers engaged in study too would have to prove that they were studying, although at the time of writing this chapter the matter was not yet very clear. The Draft Regulations of the Refugees Amendment Act 2017 should probably clarify this issue when they are published.

Relevant to the discussion in this chapter regarding the revision of the Refugees Act is the undoing of a previous Court ruling that sought to promote the dignity of asylum seekers. This was in the case, *Minister of Home Affairs and Others v Watchenuka and Others* (The Supreme Court of Appeal of South Africa 2003). In the case, the Courts had ruled that asylum seekers had the right to work in South Africa. It had argued that, that right was interwoven with the constitutional right of an individual's dignity. What the Refugees Amendment Act, 2017 does, therefore, is effectively reverse a past court decision that protected asylum seekers.

The DHA's amending of legislation to "overrule" the Supreme Court's earlier ruling could be considered a sign of a healthy and functioning democracy. That is, in the sense that one branch of government (in this case, the Executive) checks and balances another (the Judiciary). But considering the fact that the Courts had initially checked the Executive in the 2003 ruling, tweaking and altering existing legislation on issues adjudicated over in a previous ruling concerning asylum seekers' dignity suggests otherwise. It indicates regression and action that targets the subject of the ruling, and not to check or balance the actions of the entity that made the ruling. This is the sense in which Crush et al. (2017) as well as Odunayo et al. (2017), for instance, argue that the Refugees Amendment Act 2017 along with the 2017 White Paper on International Migration for South Africa represent growing restrictionism and exclusion in a previously generous rights-based approach to asylum.

Social Life and Immigration Realities

South Africa is a preferred destination for migrants from the Southern African Development Community (SADC) region and beyond (Nshimbi and Fioramonti 2013). Besides the promise of better incomes and refuge from civil wars and conflicts, it promises protection, safety, freedom and happiness to victims of less visible threats and violence against them. This is based on the impression that the country's constitution and law is progressive.

Gay Kenyan Asylum Seeker in South Africa

Media, rights organisations and the academe report on and examine cases of immigrants with different sexual orientations in Africa (Beetar 2016; Bornman and Frame 2020; PASSOP 2020). As of 2018, homosexuality was illegal in 33 African countries, and attracted the death penalty in another four (Amnesty International UK 2018). Besides these damning legal provisions, many families, communities and societies in Africa are homophobic. Their sociocultural attitudes and actions towards this group of people make the latter outcasts. Among the 21 African countries in which homosexuality was legal in 2018, South Africa was leader in terms of constitutional rights, marriage equality and legal protection against discrimination for Lesbian, Gay, Bisexual, Transgender and Intersex (LGBTI) people (Amnesty International UK 2018; The author wishes to remain anonymous 2019). Hence, many people from other African countries that consider or treat them as outcasts flee to South Africa, for the promise it offers of individual freedom, safety, protection and security.

Upon arrival, however, LGBT asylum seekers and refugees encounter new challenges including, discrimination in places of work, robbery, corrective rape, stigma, homophobia, harassment and even murder (Beetar 2016; PASSOP 2012; The author wishes to remain anonymous 2019). This does not uniquely happen to asylum seekers and refugees, however. South Africa generally records high rates of homophobic crime and corrective rape, which suggests that robust or progressive legislation and laws do not necessarily mean societal acceptance (The author wishes to remain anonymous 2019). Still, this huge gap between legislation and reality also manifests itself in the treatment of asylum seekers by state authorities. Many LGBT asylum seekers do not even cross the country's borders, as they are turned away when their sexual orientation is revealed (Beetar 2016; The author wishes to remain anonymous 2019). Many more remain undocumented in the country.

Bornman (2019) tells the story of Kenyan musician George Barasa that provides a limited anecdotal illustration of the gap between legislation and practice in South Africa. Barasa fled Kenya (where homosexuality is illegal) for refuge in South Africa, when the Kenyan authorities issued a warrant of arrest for him, after he came out as gay in 2017 (Bornman 2019; The author wishes to remain anonymous 2019). Bornman says Barasa's application for asylum in South Africa was, however, rejected upon arrival. According to Bornman, the refugee officers that attended to Barasa were homophobic, questioned his sexuality and dismissed the claim that he was afraid for his life.

Mozambican Immigrant Cuffed and Dragged Behind a Police Van in South Africa

Emidio Josias Macia from Mozambique had lived in South Africa for over a decade and worked as a taxi driver when he died in police custody in 2013. Two points regarding the immigrant's death are relevant in the discussion here: the brutal and violent way in which the arresting police officers treated Macia and the final consequence on the officers. The officers pulled Macia over and claimed he had caused a traffic jam by illegally parking his taxi in Daveyton, Johannesburg (BBC News 2013). According to them, he then resisted arrest. They, thus, overpowered and cuffed him to the rear of a police van and then dragged him along a street to a holding cell (Clayton 2013). A witness in a crowed filmed the incident on their mobile phone. The Independent Police Investigative Directorate (IPID) later released a post-mortem report that indicated that Macia, who was found dead in a pool of blood in the holding cell, had died from internal bleeding and head injuries (BBC News 2015; Siddique 2013). The North Gauteng High Court convicted all eight accused policemen for killing the immigrant (Independent Police Investigative Directorate [IPID] 2015; Jacaranda FM 2018).

IPID and the Courts' responses in this matter suggest that the rule of law was observed. Then head of the Executive branch of government himself, President Jacob Zuma, was shocked by the police action, calling it horrific and unacceptable (BBC News 2013). In his judgement, Judge Bert Bam called the killing of Macia barbaric, an assessment echoed by Jose Nasciment, Macia's family lawyer (BBC News 2015; Jacaranda FM 2018). In his statement, Nasciment further said most foreign nationals in

South Africa felt they were victims of xenophobia (Jacaranda FM 2018). His was not a lone voice on the matter. Human Rights Watch South Africa Director, Cameron Jacobs, is reported to have expressed deep concern that the incident affected a foreign national (Clayton 2013). The way Macia was treated might have been partly because he was a foreign national, according to Jacobs, because (as something that had been seen before in the country) if one were "different", the police were more likely to stop them.

Immigration Realities in South African Communities
Further arguments hold anti-migrant violence in South African communities to have continued, since the large-scale violence against foreign nationals in 2008 (Beetar 2019; Crush and Ramachandran 2014). Crush and Ramachandran, for instance, argue that most violent incidences against foreign nationals occur sporadically in marginal areas of the country including, informal settlements, inner-city suburbs and townships (Crush and Ramachandran 2014). They explain the anti-migrant violence in three broad categories—"xenophobia denialism", "xenophobia minimalism" and "xenophobia realism".

The first category according to Crush and Ramachandran, obviously, rejects suggestions that xenophobia has anything to do with the violence against immigrants in South Africa. The second posits that the violence is symptomatic of people's discontent arising from structural economic inequalities and the capture of the ruling party, the African National Congress (ANC), by neo-liberalism. Because the state has not transformed the country, the argument goes, poverty, inequality and competition for resources in marginalised areas leads to the victimisation of immigrants. The third category, xenophobia realism, according to Crush and Ramachandran, is pervasive throughout South African society, where a significant number of South Africans are predisposed to violence. This view is informed by the perceptions and attitudes that South Africans hold towards refugees and migrants and is drawn from a systematic representative sampling of the whole South African population (Crush and Ramachandran 2014, 14–20; Crush et al. 2013). According to Crush and Ramachandran, the periodic surveys of the population clearly show that hostility and animosity towards immigrants in South Africa is deep-rooted and pervasive.

Beetar seems to agree with Crush and Ramachandran's third category, xenophobia realism, as he considers xenophobia to be an unavoidable and inevitable pointer to South Africa's nation-building project (Beetar 2019). Beetar points to South Africa's environment of hostility and intolerance, which he attributes to socially and politically embedded characteristics that he traces over a decade, from the 2008 incident to 2018. He, further, adds on to xenophobia denialism by considering narratives of South African exceptionalism and denialism to be necropolitical because they "render certain bodies as worthy of life in the country, and relegate migrant bodies to zones of figurative and literal death" (Beetar 2019, 122).

A couple of issues come out of the three cases—the DHA; the Kenyan immigrant; and the Mozambican immigrant—described in this section. A disparity exists between the national constitution, immigration law and policies in South Africa and their application to real life and the lived experiences of officials in the Executive branch of government, asylum seekers, immigrants and South African people in communities. The DHA has concerns that immigrants are unskilled, pose a security threat and are a burden rather than benefit South Africa. Because of this, the department resorts to deporting them. The department's determination to restrict migration is also evident in the observation made in this section that, it even "undoes" rulings of the Courts about the need to consider asylum seekers' dignity. Additionally, the department reforms legislation to prevent abuse of and corruption in the asylum seeker management system. However, the challenges which the system faces seem to be a consequence of restrictive measures against the mobility of unskilled and semi-skilled migrants. Civil society in South Africa expresses concern that measures designed to reform policy and legislation lead to inhuman actions and the abuse of the human rights of asylum seekers, refugees and immigrants. Some actors in certain sections of the Executive branch of government do misapply and abuse the law, which in and of itself has good intention. Thus, despite being a preferred destination on the basis of perceptions of progressive legal environment and promise of freedom, protection and safety, asylum seekers, refugees and migrants who manage to enter South Africa soon discover that a huge discrepancy exists between legislation and the ways in which they are treated by state authorities and ordinary people on the ground.

Concluding Remarks

This chapter discussed South Africa's legislative and policy framework in relation to immigration. It told of the life experiences and interactions of a couple of purposively selected immigrants with actors in the Executive branch of government and with some South African locals under the country's law. The chapter also, in a related manner, tested the validity of claims that South Africa has one of the best constitutions in the world. Ultimately, it sought to peek into the lived experiences of people and, especially, immigrants, actors in the Executive branch of government and South African nationals under that law. Upon examining the immigration law and policies, the actions of implementors of the law and policies in the Executive and their engagements with asylum seekers and immigrants, the chapter revealed a gap between written law and the reality of life in the Executive as well as in the lived experiences of immigrants and asylum seekers and the communities in which they dwell.

Some of the best intentions of the 1996 Constitution of the Republic of South Africa fall off as the supreme law of the land distils into idiosyncratic policies, legislation, practices and lived experiences on the ground. The law is, however, perfected in instruments and people's lives that adhere to it to the letter. The intentions of the supreme law are good.

Challenges and frivolities arise, however, when the issues and people it seeks to protect and on which it provides guidance manifest themselves in the way the Executive interprets some of its provisions, in interpersonal relationships both in government and at local level, in communities. At those levels, interests come into play and seem to rule supreme. This chapter has shown how the Executive branch of the Government of the Republic of South Africa, for instance, faced legal challenges and suits from organisations that represent immigrant, asylum and refugee interests.

And in some instances, the Courts, in their interpretation of the law, ruled the state out of order and in favour of immigrants and/or asylum seekers and refugees. Thus, immigrants sometimes find refuge in South Africa, under the protection of the law. That protection is also, sometimes, from threats originating from outside of the country. In this regard, the chapter has discussed some immigrants that seek refuge in the Republic of South Africa and how they are shielded from threats that are external to the country. The threats vary and range from social to political. But the chapter restricted itself to the case of a refugee fleeing sociocultural threats in their country of origin and one that sought economic wellbeing. However, the reality of life in the land of refuge or that promises greener pastures is not always rosy. The chapter has demonstrated that whereas the law provides for immigrants to co-exist and dwell in harmony with the hosts (including government), life does not quite pan out that way for many. In the most extreme of cases some immigrants have been murdered. And this has even happened at the hands of state agencies.

That the South African constitution is progressive or alive to issues that need attention in the twenty-first century is undeniable. But, to cite Prof Hlengiwe Mkhize, "glaring gaps in legislation…and…serious policy gaps" (Department of Home Affairs [DHA] 2017b, iii), hiccups in implementation thereof, and negative perceptions of immigrants in some communities persist. As no condition is permanent, improvements in each of these areas would be commendable.

References

Akiba, Okon (ed.). 2004. *Constitutionalism and Society in Africa*. London: Routledge.
Alfaro-Velcamp, Theresa, et al. 2017. 'Getting Angry with Honest People': The Illicit Market for Immigrant 'Papers' in Cape Town, South Africa. *Migration Studies* 5 (2): 216–236.
Allott, Philip. 1979. The Courts and Parliament: Who Whom? *The Cambridge Law Journal* 38 (1): 79–117.
Amit, Roni. 2015a. *Queue Here for Corruption: Measuring Irregularities in South Africa's Asylum System*. Johannesburg: Lawyers for Human Rights and ACMS.
Amit, Roni. 2015b. The Expansion of Illegality: Immigration Detention in South Africa. In *Immigration Detention: The Migration of a Policy and Its Human Impact*, 145–153. London: Routledge.
Amnesty International. 2018. South Africa 2017/2018. https://www.amnesty.org/en/countries/africa/south-africa/report-south-africa/ (May 15, 2020).
Amnesty International UK. 2018. Mapping Anti-Gay Laws in Africa | Amnesty International UK. https://www.amnesty.org.uk/lgbti-lgbt-gay-human-rights-law-africa-uganda-kenya-nigeria-cameroon (May 20, 2020).
BBC News. 2013. President Zuma of South Africa Shocked Over 'Police Dragging.' https://www.bbc.com/news/world-africa-21625395 (May 19, 2020).
BBC News. 2015. South African Police Jailed for Murder of Taxi Driver Mido Macia. https://www.bbc.com/news/world-africa-34786559 (May 19, 2020).

Beetar, Matthew. 2016. Intersectional (Un)Belongings: Lived Experiences of Xenophobia and Homophobia. *Agenda* 30 (1): 96–103.
Beetar, Matthew. 2019. A Contextualisation of the 2008 and 2015 Xenophobic Attacks: Tracing South African Necropolitics. *Current Sociology* 67 (1): 122–140. http://journals.sagepub.com/doi/10.1177/0011392118807528 (May 19, 2020).
Bornman, J. 2019. A Gay Kenyan's Asylum Struggle in South Africa. *New Frame*. https://www.newframe.com/a-gay-kenyans-asylum-struggle-in-south-africa/ (May 20, 2020).
Bornman, J., and N. Frame. 2020. Violence Follows Gay Asylum Seeker in SA. *Times Live*. https://www.timeslive.co.za/news/south-africa/2020-01-06-violence-follows-gay-asylum-seeker-in-sa/ (May 20, 2020).
Calland, Richard, and Mandy Taylor. 1997. Parliament and the Socio-Economic Imperative—What Is the Role of the National Legislature. *Law, Democracy and Development* 1: 193. https://heinonline.org/HOL/Page?handle=hein.journals/laacydev1&id=196&div=&collection= (May 8, 2020).
Clayton, Jonathan. 2013. Eight South African Police Arrested Over Death of Man Dragged Behind Van | World News | *The Guardian*. https://www.theguardian.com/world/2013/mar/01/eight-south-african-police-arrested (May 19, 2020).
Constitutional Court of South Africa. 2017. Lawyers for Human Rights v Minister of Home Affairs and Others (CCT38/16) [2017] ZACC 22; 2017 (10) BCLR 1242 (CC); 2017 (5) SA 480 (CC) (29 June 2017). http://www.saflii.org/za/cases/ZACC/2017/22.html (May 21, 2020).
Crush, Jonathan, S. Ramachandran, and W. Pendleton. 2013. *Soft Targets: Xenophobia, Public Violence and Changing Attitudes to Migrants in South Africa After May 2008*. SAMP Migra. Waterloo, ON: Southern African Migration Programme (SAMP).
Crush, Jonathan, C. Skinner, and M. Stulgaitis. 2017. Benign Neglect or Active Destruction? A Critical Analysis of Refugee and Informal Sector Policy and Practice in South Africa. *African Human Mobility Review* 3: 751–782.
Crush, Jonathan, and Sujata Ramachandran. 2014. *Xenophobic Violence in South Africa: Denialism, Minimalism, Realism*. Southern African Migration Programme (SAMP).
Department of Home Affairs (DHA). 2016. *Border Management Authority Bill, 2016*. Pretoria, South Africa: Government Printing Works.
Department of Home Affairs (DHA). 2017a. *Refugees Amendment Act, 2017a*. Pretoria, South Africa: Government Printing Works.
Department of Home Affairs (DHA). 2017b. *White Paper on International Migration for South Africa, 2017b*. Republic of South Africa: Government Printing Works.

Department of Home Affairs (DHA). 2018. *Immigration Amendment Bill, 2018*. Republic of South Africa: Government Gazette.

Ellett, Rachel L. 2013. *Pathways to Judicial Power in Transitional States: Perspectives from African Courts*. Abingdon and New York: Routledge.

Gordon, Steven Lawrence. 2011. Migrants in a State of Exception: Xenophobia and the Role of the Post-Apartheid State. In *Contemporary Social Issues in Africa: Cases in Gaborone, Kampala and Durban*, ed. M.S. Mapadimeng and S. Khan, 45–64. Pretoria: Africa Institute of South Africa.

Gordon, Steven Lawrence. 2020. Understanding the Attitude–Behaviour Relationship: A Quantitative Analysis of Public Participation in Anti-Immigrant Violence in South Africa. *South African Journal of Psychology* 50 (1): 103–114. http://journals.sagepub.com/doi/10.1177/0081246319831626 (September 21, 2020).

Grant, Richard, and Daniel Thompson. 2015. City on Edge: Immigrant Businesses and the Right to Urban Space in Inner-City Johannesburg. *Urban Geography* 36 (2): 181–200.

Hassan, Mai. 2015. Continuity Despite Change: Kenya's New Constitution and Executive Power. *Democratization* 22 (4): 587–609.

Independent Police Investigative Directorate (IPID). 2015. Independent Police Investigative Directorate Secures Conviction for Mido Macia Murder Case | South African Government. https://www.gov.za/speeches/ipid-secured-conviction-mido-macia-murder-case-25-aug-2015-0000 (May 19, 2020).

International Organisation for Migration (IOM). 2003. *World Migration Report 2003*. Geneva: International Organisation for Migration.

Jacaranda FM. 2018. Court Grants Damages in Mido Macia Case. https://www.jacarandafm.com/news/news/court-grants-damages-in-mido-macia-case-/ (May 19, 2020).

Jinnah, Zaheera. 2010. Making Home in a Hostile Land: Understanding Somali Identity, Integration, Livelihood and Risks in Johannesburg. *Journal of Sociology and Social Anthropology* 1 (1–2): 91–99.

Lakin, Stuart. 2008. Debunking the Idea of Parliamentary Sovereignty: The Controlling Factor of Legality in the British Constitution. *Oxford Journal of Legal Studies* 28 (4): 709–734.

Landau, L.B. 2005. Migration, Urbanisation and Sustainable Livelihoods in South Africa.

Landau, L.B., and I. Freemantle. 2010. Tactical Cosmopolitanism and Idioms of Belonging: Insertion and Self-Exclusion in Johannesburg. *Journal of Ethnic and Migration Studies* 36 (3): 375–390. http://www.tandfonline.com/doi/abs/10.1080/13691830903494901.

Landau, Loren B. 2006. Protection and Dignity in Johannesburg: Shortcomings of South Africa's Urban Refugee Policy. *Journal of Refugee Studies* 21 (4): 308–327.

Lawyers for Human Rights. 2017. *Violence and Violations at Lindela Repatriation Centre*.
Mbelle, Nobuntu. 2005. *Living on the Margins: Inadequate Protection for Refugees and Asylum Seekers in Johannesburg | HRW*. Johannesburg. https://www.hrw.org/report/2005/11/16/living-margins/inadeq uate-protection-refugees-and-asylum-seekers-johannesburg (May 17, 2020).
Moyo, I., and C.C. Nshimbi. 2017. Of Borders and Fortresses: Attitudes Towards Immigrants from the SADC Region in South Africa as a Critical Factor in the Integration of Southern Africa. *Journal of Borderlands Studies* 35 (1): 131–146.
Nethery, Amy, and Stephanie J. Silverman. 2015. Immigration Detention: The Migration of a Policy and Its Human Impact. In *Immigration Detention: The Migration of a Policy and Its Human Impact*, ed. Amy Nethery and Stephanie J. Silverman. London: Taylor and Francis.
Nshimbi, Christopher C., and Lorenzo Fioramonti. 2013. *A Region Without Borders? Policy Frameworks for Regional Labour Migration Towards South Africa*. Johannesburg: African Centre for Migration and Society, University of the Witwatersrand. http://www.miworc.org.za/docs/MiWORC-Report-1.pdf.
Nshimbi, Christopher C., Inocent Moyo, and Trynos Gumbo. 2018. Between Neoliberal Orthodoxy and Securitisation: Prospects and Challenges for a Borderless Southern African Community. In *Crisis, Identity and Migration in Post-Colonial Southern Africa*, ed. H. Magidimisha et al., 167–186. Cham: Springer.
Odunayo, Moyosore A., Lucky E. Asuelime, and Andrew E. Okem. 2017. South African Policy on Migration and Its Alignment with the UNO Charter on Refugee and Asylum-Seekers. *Journal of African Union Studies* 6 (1): 81–96. https://journals.co.za/content/journal/10520/EJC-791fcab35 (May 17, 2020).
PASSOP. 2012. *A Dream Deferred: Is the Equality Clause in the South African Constitution's Bill of Rights (1996) Just a Far-Off Hope for LGBTI Asylum Seekers and Refugees?* Johannesburg.
PASSOP. 2020. People Against Suffering Oppression and Poverty. https://www.passop.co.za/ (May 20, 2020).
Peberdy, S. 2001. Imagining Immigration: Inclusive Identities and Exclusive Policies in Post 1994 South Africa. *Africa Today* 48 (3): 15–32.
Republic of South Africa (RSA). 1996. *Constitution of the Republic of South Africa*. Pretoria, South Africa: Government Printing Works.
Sajó, András. 1999. *Limiting Government: An Introduction to Constitutionalism*. New York: Central European University Press.
Sakala, J.B. 2010. *The Role of the Judiciary in the Enforcement of Human Rights in Zambia*. Lusaka: Image Publishers Limited.

Segatti, Aurelia. 2011. Reforming South African Immigration Policy in Post-Apartheid Period (1990–2006): What It Means and What It Takes. In *Migration in Post-Apartheid South Africa: Challenges and Questions to Policy Makers*, ed. Aurelia Wa Kabwe-Segatti and Loren Landau, 33–79. Paris: FASOPO.

Siddique, Haroon. 2013. South African Police Suspended Over Death of Man 'Dragged Behind Van' | World News | *The Guardian*. https://www.theguardian.com/world/2013/feb/28/man-dies-south-africa-police-van (May 19, 2020).

South African Human Rights Commission. 2012. *Investigative Reports*. Johannesburg. https://www.sahrc.org.za/home/21/files/4%20SAHRC%20Investigative%20Reports%20VOLUME%20FOUR%2025062015%20to%20print.pdf.

South African Human Rights Commission. 2017. Children Illegally Detained Under Bosasa's Watch at Lindela as Healthcare Crumbles. https://www.sahrc.org.za/index.php/sahrc-media/news/item/1075-children-illegally-detained-under-bosasa-s-watch-at-lindela-as-healthcare-crumbles (May 15, 2020).

The author wishes to remain anonymous. 2019. Small Victories Add Up in Southern Africa. In *State-Sponsored Homophobia 2019*, ed. Lucas Ramón International Lesbian, Gay, Bisexual, Trans and Intersex Association: Mendos, 93–97. Geneva: ILGA.

The Supreme Court of Appeal of South Africa. 2003. *Minister of Home Affairs and Others v Watchenuka and Others (010/2003) [2003] ZASCA 142; [2004] 1 All SA 21 (SCA)* (28 November 2003).

United Nations Department of Economic and Social Affairs (UNDESA). 1998. Recommendations on Statistics of International Migration. Statistical Papers, Serie M, No. 58, Revision 1. New York: United Nations

Vigneswaran, Darshan. 2020. The Complex Sources of Immigration Control. *International Migration Review* 54 (1): 262–288. http://journals.sagepub.com/doi/10.1177/0197918318823191 (September 20, 2020).

Vigneswaran, Darshan Vijay. 2011. Incident Reporting: A Technique for Studying Police Corruption. *Policing and Society* 21 (2): 190–213.

CHAPTER 4

Xenophobia Against Nigerian Immigrants in South Africa: The *Naijaphobia* Perspective

Hakeem Onapajo

INTRODUCTION

Notwithstanding consistent denials by the government, it is incontrovertible that xenophobia has become a reality and common phenomenon in South Africa. Since 2008 when the first major attacks on foreigners were experienced, the country has been in the news for xenophobic violence, which is responsible for gruesome deaths and large-scale destruction of property. Indeed, the shocking part of the increasing anti-foreigners' attacks is that black Africans, who were in the forefront of the anti-apartheid struggles in support of their fellow Africans under the apartheid regime, have been the major targets. This surprising action informed the popularisation of concepts such as 'Afrophobia' and 'Negrophobia' in the public space, which captures the idea that the unfolding event being experienced in the 'Rainbow Nation' is more of abhorrence for, and deliberate

---

H. Onapajo (✉)
Department of Political Science and International Relations,
Nile University of Nigeria, Abuja, Nigeria
e-mail: hakeem.onapajo@nileuniversity.edu.ng

attack on, fellow blacks (Tafira 2011). Although several Asian immigrants, especially the Pakistani and Bangladeshi shop owners, have also been victims of the xenophobic attacks, their closeness in physical appearance to the Indian South Africans often saves them in the vicious attacks when they occur.

While African immigrants have been the major victims of the growing anti-foreigners' sentiments and attacks in South Africa, the Nigerian immigrants are specifically identified as a central problem in the category of unwanted immigrants. This is why a Nigerian remarked at a national association meeting that, 'I can say it boldly that if there are no Nigerians in this country (South Africa), there will be nothing like xenophobia.'[1] In his claims, he insisted that South Africa's xenophobia incidents represent a violent expression of the indigenes' hostility towards the presence of Nigerians in their communities. Truly, Nigerians, notwithstanding their statuses, do not attract a positive perception in their host community. To many South Africans, an average Nigerian is a drug dealer and human trafficker and should not be accommodated in their country. This negative perception and criminalisation of this group of immigrants has led to occasional mob actions against them in different cities. For example, in February 2017, violence was unleashed on Nigerians in Pretoria and other areas in South Africa by irate youth claiming to get rid of the 'Nigerian' drug dealers and human traffickers allegedly exploiting young girls for prostitution.

While the focus of the book is on areas of cooperation and friendship between South Africans and Nigerians, this chapter takes a critical approach by offering analysis of the patterns and causes of rising 'Naijaphobia' in South Africa. Naijaphobia is used as a term to capture the phenomenon of growing prejudices, fear and stereotyping of Nigerians. 'Naija' as a shorter version of Nigeria has become a term increasingly used by the Nigerian youth to portray the unique characteristics of their country and its peoples (Labaran 2010). Furthermore, the term has gained increased acceptance in the literature to identify the Nigerian version of broken English language—Pidgin English—used by most Nigerians across different ethnic groups for easy communication, which is also gaining currency in the West African sub-region (see Onyeche 2004). Even though it is officially rejected by the Nigerian government

---

[1] The researcher attended the meeting of the Nigerian Union in South Africa (NUSA) in Pietermaritzburg, KwaZulu-Natal, in February 2017.

given the thinking that it may replace the original name of the country, formal organisations are beginning to show preference for 'Naija' as a marketing strategy to appeal to Nigerians. For example, a popular reality television show 'Big Brother Africa' produced by Multichoice Company, watched by millions of Africans, suddenly changed its Nigerian version from 'Big Brother Nigeria' to 'Big Brother Naija,' which has recorded unprecedented record of viewership across the continent since it started in 2003.

I contextualise the phenomenon of Naijaphobia in South Africa within the general theoretical frameworks on racism and xenophobia in the contemporary world. The paper is a product of personal observations and content analysis of secondary materials including published articles and media reports containing experiences of Nigerian migrants in South Africa. The principal aim of this chapter is to demonstrate the patterns and causes of xenophobia against Nigerians in South Africa, using the terminology of Naijaphobia.

RACISM, XENOPHOBIA AND THE SOUTH AFRICAN CONTEXT: A LITERATURE REVIEW

More relevant to this study is the literature concerning racism and xenophobia as both terms relate to the issue under discussion. As I argue in this paper, 'Nigerians' represent a group of people who are subject of prejudices specifically as a group of nationals from a state in the West African sub-region, and on the other hand, as a group of African immigrants in South Africa. This preamble underscores the conceptual clarification scholars have made about the two inter-related concepts: 'racism' and 'xenophobia.' To some, both concepts are completely different and with distinct meanings. In their analyses, racism relates to negative attitudes and discrimination towards a particular social group based on their different social membership, while xenophobia concerns negative attitudes and behaviours towards foreigners (Tafira 2011; Misago et al. 2015).

Despite the differentiation, some scholars have gone ahead to prove that xenophobia cannot be totally dissociated from racism; it is indeed an aspect of racism. According to Tafira (2011), the reason why xenophobia is a form of racism can be well understood if it is agreed that the concept of racism is dependent on 'social and epistemological conditions,' to such extent that the concept assumes different meanings at different times. As such, it is argued that xenophobia represents some sort of 'New Racism' going by the idea that racism has changed overtime from being conceptualised in biological terms to cultural terms (Rydgren 2003; Tafira 2011). In the analysis of Rydgren (2003, 48), it is noted that:

> [t]his type of 'new' or 'cultural' racism comes close to the conception of "xenophobia", that is, fear of individuals who are different or 'strange.' Like the new cultural racism, xenophobia also is characterised by a belief that it is 'natural' for people to live amongst other of 'their own kind', and a corresponding hostility towards the presence of people of a 'different' kind.

In this study, the approach emphasising a close connection between racism and xenophobia is favoured. It speaks more to the condition of the Nigerian migrants in South Africa given that the intersection of nationality and immigration forms the basis for prejudices, stereotyping and discrimination against them in the country. Furthermore, this conceptualisation reflects the working definition of the United Nations High Commissioner for Refugees (UNHCR) in its report on xenophobic violence in South Africa, which is defined as 'any form of violence that mobilises and exploits differences based on spatial, linguistic, or ethnic origins as xenophobic' (Misago et al. 2015, 17). To be sure, this definition also captures the problem of growing Islamophobia in the Western countries. A combination of religion and nationality of a group of people has become a basis for hate, fear and prejudices against them in those countries.

With emphasis on the South African situation, many studies have advanced useful explanations on the causes and triggering factors of xenophobia (Nieftagodien 2008; Charman and Piper 2012). In her study, Dodson (2010) usefully organised the explanations around three general arguments: the economic, political and social factors. The economic explanations, which are popular in the literature, are hinged on arguments suggesting that anti-foreigners' sentiments and attacks are driven by perceptions from the local population that the presence of migrants presents a threat to economic opportunities in their country. In South Africa, the black population—who are mostly involved in the attacks and the supposedly economically disadvantaged group—find the foreign nationals competing with them for jobs and other economic benefits in their country (Dodson 2010, 5). In a study by Charman and Piper (2012), it was argued that recurrent violence against Somali shopkeepers in South Africa represents an extreme form of economic competition, which they capture as 'violent entrepreneurship'. This is because the Somali entrepreneurs are seen to be smarter and making more sales than their local competitors; hence the attacks against them. To substantiate this, those who hold the economic perspective often present the evidence that most of the cases of xenophobic violence occur in the poor communities in South Africa (Tevera 2013).

The political argument focuses on poor leadership and the increased use of anti-foreigners' rhetoric by the political leaders to distract the people from their failures, especially the vexed issue of poor service delivery (Steinberg 2008; Mosselson 2010). The use of anti-foreigners' rhetoric by the leaders has been seen as a useful instrument to project some form of South African nationalism. Important political personalities have used it to advance their political agenda. Jacob Zuma, for example, in the wake of attacks against Nigerians in 2017 stated that: 'We cannot close our eyes to the concerns of the communities that most of the crimes, such as drug dealing, prostitution, and human trafficking are allegedly perpetuated by foreign nationals' (de Villiers 2017). This statement was made at the time of his many troubles over mounting corruption scandals. Clearly, these statements—advertently or inadvertently—provide an official criminalisation of the African immigrants in South Africa. Also, it underlines the seemingly weak political will of the leadership to wholeheartedly address the problem of xenophobia in the country.

In addition, the political argument captures the deliberate and consistent denials of the government on the problem and extent of xenophobia. For example, Thabo Mbeki stated in 2008, after the first major xenophobic attacks, that 'I heard it said insistently that my people have turned or become xenophobic…. I wondered what the accusers knew about my people which I did not know' (cited in Dodson 2010, 7). During the 2015 xenophobic violence, President Zuma also said 'I think we love using phrases in South Africa that at the time cause unnecessary perceptions about us. I think we are not [xenophobic], it's not the first time we are with foreigners here' (Sekhotho 2015). The denials may be important for the leaders in respect of their projection of South Africa as a regional leader and a major promoter of human freedom and peace in the international environment. However, choosing to use another language because of political correctness and ignoring the enormity of the problem has allowed xenophobia to linger than expected.

Arguments around cultural stereotyping and social differentiation constitute the social dimension to the problem. According to Crush and Dodson (2007), post-apartheid South Africa has seen a sudden rise in the number of African migrants who saw new opportunities in the newly democratised and free state. Increased contacts with other Africans and the poor knowledge of happenings in other African countries by South Africans give room for 'mutual stereotyping' to the extent that cultural differences are exaggerated, leading to 'prejudice and antagonisms' (Dodson 2010). In this regard, the media has played a significant role in promoting stereotype against the foreigners as proven in many studies (Danso and McDonald 2001; McDonald and Jacobs 2005). It is also important to note that South African's history of apartheid, especially the way the indigenes were treated by the settlers, should provide a reason for animosity towards foreigners.

Journey to the South: History of Nigerians' migration to South Africa

Although Nigerians have been migrating to other countries before the independence of the country in 1960, emigration became more popular amongst the people following the economic hardship and political instability experienced in the military era, particularly under the regimes of Ibrahim Babangida (1985–1993) and Sani Abacha (1993–1998) (Bangura 1994; Adepoju 2003). In response to the economic contraction occasioned by falling oil prices in the international market, the Babangida regime introduced the International Monetary Fund (IMF) prescribed Structural Adjustment Programme (SAP), which was poorly implemented, and compounded the socio-economic crisis (Adejumobi 1996). In a bid to escape the worsening economic situation and find greener pastures, many Nigerians left the country for countries in Europe and America. The situation was later aggravated by the harsh political climate that characterised Abacha's military government. That government unleashed violence on its opposition, which necessitated another wave of migration consisting of Nigerians largely seeking asylum outside the country. At the initial stage, South Africa was not a popular destination for the Nigerian migrants because of the apartheid government's closed immigration policy and the horrendous treatment of blacks. It was after the end of apartheid and the beginning of a new South Africa in the 1990s that Nigerians started seeing the country as a good option for new opportunities. This is because South Africa was increasingly demonstrating good economic prospects, largely because of the expansive physical and economic infrastructure inherited from the white-dominated government. However, it was only in the 2000s that the presence of Nigerians in major cities of South Africa, especially Johannesburg, Durban and Cape Town, started becoming substantial.

A useful research carried out by the African Center for Migration and Society of the University of the Witwatersrand (2012) reported that by 2004 monthly entries of Nigerians rose to 2000. By 2008 and 2010, the number had grown to about 3000–4000 monthly. At inception, Nigerians were found mainly in Gauteng, KwaZulu-Natal and the Western Cape provinces. The Nigerian migrants include entrepreneurs, highly and medium-skilled workers, students, dependents and asylum seekers. It was reported that although many Nigerians apply for refugee status in South Africa, but the government had been refusing the applications. This is founded on the fact that Nigerians, since their country experienced democratic transition in 1999, do not qualify for a political asylum, although reports suggest that a number of the rejected applicants do not return to their home country (African Center for Migration and Society 2012).

Due to poor records, the exact number of Nigerians in South Africa cannot be ascertained. However, some figures in the public domain can be useful. The Nigerian Union in South Africa (NUSA) claims that 800,000 Nigerians are residing in the country. However, upon enquiry, the spokesperson of NUSA, Emeka Ezinteje clarified that the figure is only 'an approximated figure based on projections from current data' (Oshin 2017). A more reliable data is derived from Statistics South Africa's (StatsSA) 2016 Community Survey which estimated that 30,314 foreign-born people living in South Africa are Nigerians (https://africa check.org). In addition, StatsSA shows that Nigeria is one of the top ten sending countries in South Africa. Obviously, this represents the data of documented Nigerian migrants in the country. There is no sufficient information on the number of undocumented Nigerians, as well as those that are carrying identities of other countries. In another useful report sponsored by the European Union (EU) and International Organization for Migration (IOM) (Muhwava and Chiroro 2014), it was stated that 'there are Nigerian professionals in almost all sectors of the economy in South Africa.' This especially includes the academic and the health sectors. Furthermore, it is useful to note that rising numbers of visa applicants from Nigeria has necessitated the South African government to open a third visa application centre in Port Harcourt (Rivers State) in 2015, in addition to the ones in Lagos and Abuja. Clearly, this points to the growing community of Nigerians in South Africa.

XENOPHOBIC ATTACKS ON NIGERIANS: FACTS, NOT FICTION

As a background to the xenophobic attacks on Nigerians, it is useful to start by illustrating the extent of the problem of xenophobia in South Africa. A UNHCR report (Misago et al. 2015) noted that 'at least one attack on groups of foreign nationals' is being recorded on a monthly basis since mid-2008. In mid-2009 and late 2010, it was reported that 'there were at least 20 deaths, over 40 serious injuries, at least 200 foreign-run shops looted and more than 4000 persons displaced due to violence targeting foreign nationals' (Misago 2016, 448). The report further stated that 'in 2011, at least 120 foreign nationals were killed, five of them burnt alive, 100 were seriously injured, at least 1000 displaced, and 120 shops and businesses permanently or temporarily closed through violence or selective enforcement of bylaws.' For the year 2012, the incidents increased with the following statistics: 250 incidents that led to 140 deaths and 250 serious injuries. 'In 2013, an average of three major violence incidents was recorded per week with attacks regularly reported in many areas across the country during 2014' (Misago et al. 2015, 21). By March 2014, 'an estimated 300 incidents of violence against asylum seekers and refugees had been reported, an estimated 200 shops had been looted and 900 persons had been displaced' (Misago et al. 2015, 21). The escalated xenophobic riots in 2015, after the Zulu King Goodwill Zwelithini's infamous statement against foreign nationals in KwaZulu-Natal, were followed with eight deaths and displacement of many foreign nationals (Essa 2015).

In the wake of increasing attacks on her fellow nationals, Nigeria's Senior Special Adviser to the President on Foreign Affairs and Diaspora, Abike Dabiri, stated that 'in the last two years, 116 Nigerians have been killed in South Africa and according to statistics, 63% of them were killed by the police' (Salau 2017). The statistics was not substantiated with any evidence, which makes it weak. However, it is true that Nigerians have increasingly been subjects of xenophobic attacks in South Africa, which is under-reported in the South African media. There may be lack of adequate data to demonstrate the extent of attacks on the Nigerian immigrants, but there are some press statements by NUSA which have proven useful in documenting the rising cases of Naijaphobia. A summary of the organisation's report between 2016 and 2018 is presented below:

- 14 September 2016, A Nigerian trader, Monday Okorie, was killed in Potchefstroom, North West. Twenty Nigerians were later arrested for protesting the murder (Ajasa 2016).
- 24 December 2016, Austin Agunwa was abducted by unknown persons in Rustenburg, North West. The car was later found but without the victim (Vanguard 2017).
- 30 August 2017, Kingsely Ikeri, a businessman was killed in Vryheid town in KwaZulu-Natal (The Nation 2017a, b).
- September 2017, Victor Nnadi was suffocated to death in Cape Town by the South African police (Premium Times 2017a, b).
- October 2017, a 25-year-old Nigerian was killed at his residence at Deforest Street in, Vereeniging (Premium Times 2017a, b).
- 13 November 2017, two Nigerians were confirmed killed on different occasions by the local gangs. It was reported that one of the victims 'pleaded with the police to take him to the hospital for treatment but they refused. After searching his house without finding anything, he died as a result of severe beating' (PM News 2017).
- 18 January 2018, Nigerians' shops and property were attacked in Krugersdorp in Johannesburg which led to the death of two Nigerians and the displacement of many of them (The Nation 2018). This attack occurred as a result of allegations that Nigerians were responsible for the abduction and rape of a South African girl, which was later discovered to be false after the said girl was found.
- 18 January 2018, a 27-year-old Nigerian was killed by the police in Durban (The News 2018).
- 14 February 2018, knife attack on a Nigerian in Rustenburg in North West who sustained multiple injuries. According to the report, 'he was rescued when he was about to be set ablaze after being wet with petrol' (*Daily Post* 2018, n.p).
- 17 February 2018, report of abduction, extortion and murder over refusal to pay requested money. According to NUSA, 'Nigerians and their families told us the situation is very dangerous and that their lives are not safe. They also alleged that some group of people were abducting Nigerians and requesting money to bail themselves.

A Nigerian who couldn't pay was murdered last month' (Vanguard 2018, n.p).
- 9 April 2018, an unnamed Nigerian was shot by the police in Roodeport (van Zyl 2018).
- 9 April 2018, ThankGod Okoro (aged 30) was killed by the South African police in West Rand, Johannesburg (*Sahara Reporters* 2018).
- 22 April 2018, Clement Nwaogu was burnt to death in a mob attack in Rustenburg, North West (Premium Times 2018).

Most of the incidents above are usually classified and treated as regular criminal cases by the government, while the circumstances around them, as shown in subsequent sections, have clear trappings of xenophobia. Clearly, these cases cannot be likened to some other killings and attacks on Nigerians in other countries. For example, in the United Kingdom, where there has been a sudden increase in the killing of Nigerian youths, it can be observed that the actors and circumstances around the incidents make them criminal cases. The victims are caught up in the menace of gang violence increasingly spreading amongst youths in the black communities in the United Kingdom. Indeed, some of the perpetrators of violence in the community are African migrants including Nigerians. However, in the South African situation, the opposite is the case. Even despite persistent denials, the South African government in April 2017 had to reach an agreement with their Nigerian counterpart to establish an early warning system to prevent xenophobic attacks targeting Nigerians. Evidently, this is an admission that there are issues of Naijaphobia in the country, which required urgent attention by the authorities. The early warning system was designed as a framework that will provide a platform for engagement of the officials of both countries by the Nigerian migrants' association (NUSA) on a regular basis. However, the system has not been effective because the attacks and killings against Nigerians rose considerably after the agreement.

Patterns of Naijaphobia

In this section, an analysis of the ways in which Nigerians are subject of prejudices and discrimination is undertaken. Because this comes in various ways, I categorise them into four patterns: criminalisation; professional Naijaphobia; institutional Naijaphobia; and societal Naijaphobia. While they may be seen to be interconnected, I believe a better understanding of Naijaphobia in South Africa will be enhanced if each of the categories is treated and analysed separately.

Criminalisation

This is the most popular pattern of Naijaphobia in South Africa. Apparently, Nigerians are before anything seen as criminals who indulge in a wide range of crimes, especially drug trafficking, human trafficking, fraud and robbery, before considering any other important qualities in them. This stereotype is mostly promoted by the South African media and affects the way Nigerians are perceived and treated across the country. The security agencies including the police and immigration officers are also important agents responsible for the conveyance of this negative perception of Nigerians. There are several examples to support this argument. For example, in a social media post on an incident concerning the killing of a Nigerian, the comments by South Africans illustrate clearly this criminalisation narrative. One commentator said, 'Nigerians are thieving conniving bastards and should not even be allowed to enter South Africa. All they know is sell drugs, rape, kidnap and rob us while our policemen are not helping matters at all. Most of the idiots should be killed to send a message to them that they are welcome here.' Another one stated that, 'in my own opinion, very few South Africans love Nigerians and they know this very well. They come into our country, steal our money, sell drugs to our people, corrupt our young men and treat our women as prostitutes' (Pulseng 2017).

Indeed, media representation of Nigerians in South Africa has proven as a major promoter of this perception. As noted in other studies, the South African media play a significant role in the negative portrayal of other Africans, which contribute to growing xenophobia (Danso and McDonald 2001; McDonald and Jacobs 2005). In the case of Nigerians, most media outfits characteristically associate them with crime incidents, even in the absence of substantial evidence. For example, the headline of a Johannesburg-based newspaper went thus 'Nigerians arrested in drug raid on city hotel,' while in the article it was only revealed that '[w]hile no drug related arrests were made ... two Nigerian nationals were arrested for being in the country illegally' (quoted in Valji 2003).

In this regard, public officials and analysts also use formal platforms to advance Naijaphobic narratives. For example, at a meeting, a security expert who was the guest speaker at the programme consistently made use of 'Nigerians' in describing the problem of drug and prostitution in major cities in South Africa. According to him, 'Nigerians and the like' are the major culprits (Vahed 2013, 205). While discussing the issue of prostitution, he argued that:

> … these women have a drug dependency or alcohol dependency problem, so they attract the Nigerians, and all of a sudden you have got everybody attracted here just because of the prostitutes. If you get rid of the prostitutes I guarantee you, you will get rid of the rest of the bulk of the petty crime, because it all follows. (Vahed 2013, 205–206)

The stereotyping of Nigerians also extends to academic research, thereby promoting the negative narrative about the social group in scholarly discourses. A researcher affiliated with the University of Cape Town chose to research the phenomenon of crime in South Africa but with a focus on what she termed 'the Nigerian Mafia.' According to the researcher, Nigerians have become the largest distributor of drugs in South Africa, while 'Johannesburg remains the headquarters for Nigerian illicit activities in South Africa' (Bernardo 2017). While trying to avoid being seen as subjective and promoting xenophobia, the researcher rationalised an invalid argument that 'Nigeria is the most populous country in Africa so it has a greater chance of having a higher number of people involved in criminal activities' (Bernardo 2017). However, the researcher failed to acknowledge that high population is not a very significant factor in explaining crime rate because there are countries with lower population which are still notorious for record-high crime rates. For instance, a recent report on countries with the highest murder rates—based on the number of homicides per 100,000 inhabitants per year—includes countries with relatively smaller population sizes such as Panama, Botswana, Equatorial Guinea, Dominica, Saint Lucia, Dominican Republic, Rwanda, Democratic Republic of Congo, South Africa, Trinidad and Tobago, The Bahamas and Columbia (https://list25.com/25-countries-with-the-highest-murder-rates-in-the-world/3/).

Surprisingly, despite increasing claims that Nigerians are the chief perpetrators of crime in South Africa, there are official reports showing that this category of migrants should really be seen as the victims of crimes. According to Valji (2003), African migrants in South Africa, 'regardless of their legal status, by approaching police officials…risk being arrested themselves, leaving them without state protection and vulnerable to criminal victimisation.' With emphasis on Nigerians, the author noted, while citing (Leggett 2003) that 'If one looked specifically at the Nigerian nationals (for whom the stereotypes of wealth and drugs are particularly entrenched in mainstream consciousness) the discrepancy between those who were victims of robbery, assault, or murder was between two and three times that of nationals' (Valji 2003, 9). In addition, official reports from the Department of Correctional Services show that Nigerians constitute a small number of the prison population in South Africa. In the 2011 report, the prison population was 162,162. Foreign nationals only constitute 8580 inmates which had Zimbabweans and Mozambicans in the majority. Only 426 Nigerians featured in the list. Of these, 242 were still in the awaiting-trial category (Singh 2013).

Institutional Naijaphobia

In addition to stereotyping Nigerians as criminals, the group of migrants further faces discriminatory treatments at government institutions, especially at the Department of Home Affairs responsible for immigration-related services. One of the clear examples of this was the widely reported mass deportation of 125 Nigerians at the Johannesburg Airport over alleged possession of fake vaccination cards. The South African immigration officers were not ready to properly verify the authenticity of the vaccination cards presented by the Nigerian travellers who flew into the country in March 2012, and decided to send them back to Lagos on the same flight that brought them. For the Nigerian government, the action was unacceptable because it was a clear case of xenophobia targeting Nigerians. Given this, the government adopted a tit-for-tat policy by deciding to also refuse entry to South Africans coming to Nigeria. This created a major diplomatic row that was resolved after Pretoria tendered an official apology to Abuja.

The above incident might have caught the attention of the government and the public because of its wide reportage and the diplomatic row that attended it. There are many other discriminatory treatments Nigerians experience daily in governmental institutions because of the prevalent prejudices against them. In 2013, a group of South African women married to Nigerians under the platform of United Nigerian Wives in South Africa protested against the discrimination they receive at the Department of Home Affairs simply because of their marriage to

Nigerians. According to them, they wanted to use the opportunity to 'put an end to the current situation where those of us married to Nigerians are being called names such as "prostitutes", and insulted in the presence of our children, when we visit the immigration offices to renew documents for our husband' (Vanguard 2013). Furthermore, they complained that:

> …when our spouses having duly notified the Home Affairs department that they are travelling and are given assurance that they can travel with the TRP (Temporary Residence Permit) sticker they have, on return they are denied entry into South Africa. In some instances, South African Airways officials claim that they have been instructed not to board passengers with TRP stickers. (Vanguard 2013)

In a similar vein, a Nigerian tourist complained in an opinion piece about his harrowing experiences at the South African airport in 2008 and 2015. For him, the worst was his experience in 2008 when he was jailed under a false allegation of carrying a fake visa on his passport. The tourist insisted that he was treated that way because of his 'Nigerian green passport' since he was immediately suspected as a criminal even though he flew in from the United States (Enebi 2016).

In addition to the discriminatory practices at the Department of Home Affairs, Nigerians also encounter appalling experiences in the hands of the police. Nigerians are regular victims of extortion by the police and usually framed up for different crimes. For example, Justin Ejimkonye, a Nigerian migrant based in Johannesburg, decided to sue the South African government after he was shot in the leg by the police for refusing to pay bribe in 2012. According to *Brock* (2017) that reported the incident,

> One day, he says, police stopped him as he was driving his Toyota truck. They demanded 900 rand ($70), which he refused to pay. The police impounded his vehicle and charged him a fine to recover it. A few weeks later, on Feb. 25, the same police officers stopped him again, documents drawn up by both Ejimkonye and the police show. Ejimkonye says he told them he would not pay any bribes. At that, he says, police officer John Kichener Johnstone removed his police issue Beretta revolver from its holster and fired a 9 millimeter round into the back of Ejimkonye's leg.

For this reason, it has become a popular saying amongst Nigerians in South Africa that they are the 'ATM' (Automated Teller Machine) of the police and immigration officers.

Professional Naijaphobia

This category underscores the prejudices and discrimination Nigerians experience in their work environments. This pattern of Naijaphobia is largely under-reported by the victims because of a possible backlash at their workplaces which may involve dismissal. Indeed, there are numerous reports concerning the treatment of other foreign (African) nationals which demonstrates the extent of the problem of professional xenophobia in South Africa (Human Rights Watch 2007). A deeper conversation with the Nigerian employees reveals untold stories of open discrimination because of their nationality. In usual cases, it manifests in the employment process. Although it should be acknowledged that the South African system has a certain equity policy which understandably gives premium to the employment of the disadvantaged black indigenes and the female gender in order to address existing socio-economic inequality, this policy is usually, and deliberately, abused to exclude foreign migrants—especially Nigerians—from having access to job opportunities.

In a personal conversation, two Nigerian academics aiming for a job at some top universities separately narrated their similar experiences to me. With incredible Curriculum Vitae and impressive performance, the individuals were roundly accepted as suitable candidates at the interview stages. Surprisingly, their employment was refused by the Human Resources Department for undisclosed reasons. One of them said he only got an email from the Human Resources Department stating that: 'I regret to inform you that even though you were found appointable, you were not a recommended candidate for the position.' For them, these events could not be disconnected from the growing phenomenon of xenophobia against Nigerians in institutional places.

In a similar vein, a respondent (Zimbabwean) who was a teacher in a secondary school in KwaZulu-Natal, in a research, narrated an experience concerning a case of theft in her school. According to her, the principal simply concluded, without any investigation, that '…it must be the Nigerians who stole the laptops' (Manik 2013). It should, however, be acknowledged that this pattern of prejudice and discrimination may not be an isolated phenomenon, but a sad reflection of a deep-rooted problem of racism and xenophobia in workplaces in South Africa. A research conducted by Afrobarometer (2016) reports that 56% South Africans agree that employers discriminate on the basis of race. In the urban areas, six in ten people (59%) believe that unequal treatment on the basis of race is a prevalent practice amongst prospective employers.

Societal Naijaphobia

In addition to the above patterns, Nigerians further encounter different prejudices in their interactions with people in the communities. Increasingly, they found it difficult to be accepted in the society and face the problem of social integration. In an earlier research, Adeagbo (2013, 283) usefully observed that '[n]egative comments often follow when a Nigerian name is mentioned amongst South Africans, particularly black South Africans, because of what they have heard and learnt about Nigerians. This has affected and still affects the relationships of some Nigerians with South Africans in business, marriages and other areas in no small measure.'

In most cases, societal prejudices against Nigerians manifest when they attempt to consummate marriages with South Africans. They are subjected to severe suspicions and sometimes face total rejections from the families of their spouses. In a study, a South African woman married to a Nigerian stated that 'anytime I tell people (mostly black South Africans) that I am married to a Nigerian, you will see the shock in them and there is always a kind of stigma there…' (Adeagbo 2013, 284). In a similar vein, a Nigerian man married to a South African stated that:

> Initially my in-laws were not happy and my wife's mother nearly got a heart-attack when she heard of our relationship. Their perception was that I will lure her into drugs and other illegitimate activities, and my wife's sister has been the major antagonist of our relationship. She says all sort of things to their mother about Nigerian…

While Nigerian men go through a very tedious process before they can marry South African women, they further encounter another problem of labelling as women-snatchers by the black South African men. The claim is that Nigerians who have made some fortunes from crime use their riches to snatch girlfriends and for this reason young Nigerian men represent a major threat to their love lives. This is why Makashule Gana, a local politician associated with the Democratic Alliance (DA), appealed to his compatriots that '… I ask my fellow brothers from South Africa, if you want a woman please go speak up, don't go around and killing someone from Nigeria because they can speak up for themselves. Speak out because it is important' (PM News 2015).

Causes of Naijaphobia

State Failure

The array of analyses around the rising phenomenon of xenophobia in South Africa has featured prominently the failure of the state to respond to the needs of the citizens as a central problem. State failure has created an army of unemployed, frustrated and angry youths, who had great expectations of a post-apartheid state, and because of their poor understanding of the social circumstances of their fellow Africans, fail to accept the fact that migrants would come to their country and make fortunes while they live in squalor and abject poverty. This is compounded by the fact that the leaders employ anti-foreigners' narratives to shift blames and distract the people from their accumulated failures. With distressing statistics demonstrating that over half of the population live in poverty (55.5%), unemployment rate of 26.7% and one of the most unequal society in the world (www.tradingeconomics.com), there is a clear signal of the vulnerability of the state to social crises which manifest in various forms of violence including service delivery protests and xenophobic attacks. This has its roots in the failure of the post-apartheid leaders to fulfil their promises of addressing the underlying social problems inherited from the apartheid regime. Rather, corruption and patrimonialism have characterised the modern South Africa.

In addition, the escalated crime rate in South Africa has a lot to do with state failure. This is because the state has been unable to strengthen the police and criminal justice system, making the state one of the countries with the highest crime rates in the world. The 2017 crime statistics show that murder rates in the country rose by 1.8% and 52 murders were reported daily, while daily rape incidents stood at 109 daily. The murder rate was considered five times higher than Mexico's and ten times higher than that of India. The year recorded 46 hijacking on a daily basis and 57 business robberies daily (Pearson 2017). The sad picture graphically illustrates the enormous problem of crime and questions the capacity of the state to contain the problem. With yearly increases in the incidents, it can be argued that the government has failed in its duty of guaranteeing a secure state. Thus, criminalising a specific group of migrants is an escapist approach and a smokescreen for the inherent systemic failures, which are left to degenerate. It should be the responsibility of the state to block avenues for individuals—locals and foreigners—from engaging in criminal activities. The state should ensure that the country should be made unsafe for criminals.

Attitude of Nigerians

Without a doubt, Nigerians are by nature hardworking and ostentatious people. They believe in living an elaborate lifestyle to compensate for their hard work. This lifestyle goes with a belief that their presence has to be felt wherever they find themselves. David Jenkins (2013) writes that 'Nigerians all say they work hard and party hard, believe that they're better at anything than anyone else, collect PhDs like confetti and are intensely entrepreneurial.' Nigerians are categorised as one of the heaviest spenders in shopping cities including Dubai, London, Paris and New York. A special report on Nigerians in the United Kingdom, for example, states that 'Nigerian shoppers are also some of the capital's biggest spenders, forking out an average of £628 per purchase' (Jarvis 2015). In addition, an average Nigerian has an orientation of exceptionalism because of the idea that the people have the largest population of Africans and black people. Hence, it is believed that Nigerians should always play the leadership role in any gathering involving Africans. This idea gave birth to the 'Pax Nigeriana' adopted in its foreign policy in the 1970s (see Obadare 2001; Adebajo 2010).

For people who have a history of domination and subjected to very harsh treatment by migrants (white settlers), black South Africans find the attitude of Nigerians unacceptable as it has a tendency towards domination. Indeed, the claims that Nigerians are snatching their women and taking their jobs are rooted in their problem with the disposition of Nigerians. There is a feeling of complex and envy that lead to hatred and occasionally expressed violently.

Political Reasons

Nigeria and South Africa are two important countries in Africa, with both competing for leadership on the continent (Landsberg 2012). Since its independence in 1960, Nigeria has taken it upon itself—as the country with the largest population and economy in Africa—to commit huge resources for the promotion of peace, development and liberation in Africa. Thus, Afrocentrism has since represented a centre-piece of its foreign policy. Nigeria played important role in resolving conflicts in many countries including Liberia, Sierra Leone, Sudan, Cote d'Ivoire, Guinea

Bissau and Mali. It is argued that in West Africa only, Nigeria has spent up to USD 8 billion in peacekeeping operations (www.providingforpeacekeeping.org). In this spirit, Nigeria played a central role in the liberation struggles in the southern African region including in Zimbabwe, Angola, South Africa and Namibia (Akinboye 1999). Until the emergence of the new South Africa in 1994, the leadership role of Nigeria was not explicitly contested by any other country in the region.

Inheriting a massive infrastructure, typical of those in America and Europe, post-apartheid South Africa emerged on the scene with a great leadership potential and an open globalist agenda in its foreign policy. The nationalist leaders felt a moral responsibility to promote peace, human rights and democracy not only in Africa but the world as an expression of gratitude for the supports they received in their liberation struggle. Practically, the rise of South Africa, propelled by its thriving economy and increased investment in Africa, has seen the emergence of two regional powers competing for leadership on the continent. Clearly, this has set both countries on a somewhat collision course, although they manage it diplomatically. At the African Union, they both create opposing camps in voting and decision making. At the level of the United Nations, they both compete with each other on the slot for Africa's representation at the Security Council. The stiff competition has trickled down to the normal interactions between Nigerian and South African citizens. Thus, there is a perception of competition between them. Reinforced by leaders, there is a rising belief that Nigerians should not be looking for jobs and other opportunities in South Africa because of the capacity of their country. This became more intense when Nigeria became the largest economy in Africa. For an average South African, that should be a moment for Nigerians to return home and reduce the demands on their increasingly limited resources.

Conclusion

With increased Naijaphobia, it is safe to argue that Nigerians are fast becoming endangered species in South Africa. This has gradually caused a mass exodus of Nigerians in the country. Some have found alternatives in North America and Europe, while many others have returned to their country. Yet, a good number of those remaining in South Africa are making serious efforts to leave the country. Regrettably, most of those leaving fall into the category of highly skilled personnel who have the potential to contribute to the development of the country. Clearly, this is not a good sign for an economy plagued with a shortage of manpower. It cannot be over-emphasised that South Africa needs to address the lingering problem of xenophobia, and Naijaphobia in this case, by putting in place practical measures for re-orientation of its citizens about accepting other Africans. The media, most especially, must engage in responsible reporting and stop negative portrayal and stereotyping of other Africans in South Africa. The points of friendship and cooperation between Nigerians and South Africans identified by other contributors in this book may also be a good point for addressing prejudices against the former in the Rainbow Nation.

References

Adeagbo, O.A. 2013. 'We Are Not Criminals, We Are Just Victims of Circumstances': An Exploration of Experiences of Nigerian Immigrants' Men That Married South African Women in Johannesburg. *National Identities* 15 (3): 277–296.

Adebajo, A. 2010. Pax Nigeriana and the Responsibility to Protect. *Global Responsibility to Protect* 2 (4): 414–435.

Adejumobi, S. 1996. Adjustment Reform and Its Impact on the Economy and Society. In *The Political Economy of Nigeria Under Military Rule*, ed. S. Adejumobi and A. Momoh, 1984–1993. Harare: Sapes Books.

Adepoju, A. 2003. Migration in West Africa. *Development* 46(3): 37–41.

African Center for Migration and Society. 2012. *Nigerians in South Africa: Facts and Figures*. Johannesburg: African Center for Migration and Society and University of the Witwatersrand.

Afrobarometer. 2016. *South Africans Generally Tolerant but Report Racial Discrimination by Employers and Courts*. http://afrobarometer.org/sites/default/files/publications/Dispatches/ab_r6_dispatchno84-south-africa-discrimination.pdf. Accessed 7 Apr 2018.

Ajasa, F. 2016. Nigerian Trader Killed in South Africa. *Vanguard*, 15 September, https://www.vanguardngr.com/2016/09/nigerian-trader-killed-south-africa/. Accessed 10 Apr 2018.

Akinboye, S.O. 1999. Nigeria's Foreign Policy. *Elements of Politics*. Lagos: Malthouse.

Bangura, Y. 1994. Intellectuals, Economic Reform and Social Change: Constraints and Opportunities in the Formation of a Nigerian Technocracy. *Development and Change* 25 (2): 261–305.

Bernardo, C. 2017. Migration of the Nigerian Mafia. *UCT News*, 16 May. https://www.news.uct.ac.za/article/-2017-05-16-migration-of-the-nigerian-mafia. 15 Apr 2018.

Brock, J. 2017. In South Africa, Immigration Feeds Corrupt Officials and Race Hate. *Reuters*, 22 March. https://www.reuters.com/investigates/special-report/safrica-migrants-corruption/. 15 Apr, 2017.

Charman, A., and L. Piper. 2012. Xenophobia, Criminality and Violent Entrepreneurship: Violence Against Somali Shopkeepers in Delft South, Cape Town, South Africa. *South African Review of Sociology* 43 (3): 81–105.

Crush, J., and Dodson, B. 2007. Another Lost Decade: The Failures of South Africa's post-apartheid Migration Policy. *Tijdschrift Voor Economische En Sociale Geografie* 98(4): 436–454.

Daily Post. 2018. Nigerian Man Stabbed, Nearly Set Ablaze in South Africa. 16 February. http://dailypost.ng/2018/02/16/nigerian-man-stabbed-nearly-set-ablaze-south-africa/. Accessed 10 Apr 2018.

Danso, R., and D.A. McDonald. 2001. Writing Xenophobia: Immigration and the Print Media in Post-Apartheid South Africa. *Africa Today* 48 (3): 15–137.

Dodson, B. 2010. Locating Xenophobia: Debate, Discourse, and Everyday Experience in Cape Town South Africa. *Africa Today* 56 (3): 2–22.

Enebi, E.D. 2016. Why You Should Not Visit South Africa. *Guardian*, 27 October. https://guardian.ng/opinion/why-you-should-not-visit-south-africa/. Accessed 5 Apr 2018.

Essa, A. 2015. Is South Africa Taking Xenophobia Seriously? *Al Jazeera*, 1 May. https://www.aljazeera.com/blogs/africa/2015/04/south-africa-xenophobia-150430224826901.html. 5 April 2018.

Human Rights Watch. 2007. 'Keep Your Head Down': Unprotected Migrants in South Africa. https://www.hrw.org/report/2007/02/27/keep-your-head-down/unprotected-migrants-south-africa. 10 April 2018.

Jarvis, A. 2015. Rich, Urbane and Entrepreneurial: Meet Africa's New Super-Rich with a Taste for the London Lifestyle. https://www.standard.co.uk/lifestyle/london-life/rich-urbane-and-entrepreneurial-meet-africa-s-new-super-rich-with-a-taste-for-the-london-lifestyle-10308970.html. 8 April 2018.

Jenkins, D. 2013. The Nigerians Have Arrived... and London Is Paying Attention. 1 December. https://www.dailytrust.com.ng/news/others/the-nigerians-have-arrived-and-london-is-paying-attention/98758.html. 5 April 2018.

Labaran, B. 2010. Nigeria at 50: What Does Naija Mean? BBC, 1 October. https://www.bbc.co.uk/news/worldafrica-11447252#:~:text=Naija%20means%20a%20new%20beginning. 20 April 2018.

Landsberg, C. 2012. Nigeria-South Africa Tensions Leave African Leadership Gap. *World Politics Review* 18: 1–3.

Leggett, T. 2003. *Rainbow Tenement: Crime and Policing in Inner Johannesburg*. Pretoria, Institute for Security Studies. No. 78.

Manik, S. 2013. Zimbabwean Immigrant Teachers in KwaZulu-Natal: Count the Cost of Going Under the Hammer. *Alternation* 20 (7): 67–87.

McDonald, D.A., and S. Jacobs. 2005. (Re) writing Xenophobia: Understanding Press Coverage of Cross-Border Migration XE "Migration" in Southern Africa. *Journal of Contemporary African Studies* 23 (3): 295–325.

Misago, J.P. 2016. Responding to Xenophobic Violence in Post-Apartheid South Africa: Barking Up the Wrong Tree? *AHMR* 2 (2): 443–467.

Misago, J.P., I. Freemantle, and L.B. Landau. 2015. *Protection from Xenophobia: An Evaluation of UNHCR's Regional Office for Southern Africa's Xenophobia Related Programmes*. Johannesburg: The African Center for Migration and Society, University of the Witwatersrand.

Mosselson, A. 2010. 'There Is No Difference Between Citizens and Non-Citizens Anymore': Violent Xenophobia, Citizenship and the Politics of Belonging in Post-Apartheid South Africa. *Journal of Southern African Studies* 36 (3): 641–655.

Muhwava, W., and Chiroro, P. 2014. *Mapping of Nigerian Health and Education Professionals in South Africa*. Abuja: International Organization for Migration (IOM).

Nieftagodien, N. 2008. Xenophobia in Alexandra. In *Go Home or Die Here: Violence, Xenophobia and the Reinvention of Difference in South Africa*, ed. S. Hassim, T. Kupe, E. Worby, and A. Skuy, 65–78. Johannesburg: Wits University Press.

Obadare, E. 2001. Constructing Pax Nigeriana? The Media and Conflict in Nigeria-Equatorial Guinea Relations. *Nordic Journal of African Studies* 10 (1): 80–89.

Onyeche, J.I. 2004. As Naija pipo dey tok: A Preliminary Analysis of the Role of Nigerian Pidgin in the Nigerian Community in Sweden. *Africa and Asia* 4: 48–56.

Oshin, F. 2017. There Are About 30,000 Nigerians in South Africa? http://www.nigeriansinsouthafrica.co.za/2017/07/29/there-are-about-30000-nigerians-in-south-africa/. Accessed 20 Apr 2018.

Pearson, P. 2017. *Crime Statistics 2017*. Southern African Catholic Bishop's Conference.

PM News. 2015. Xenophobia: Nigerian Men Are Snatching Our Wives—South African Politician. 25 April. https://www.pmnewsnigeria.com/2015/04/25/xenophobia-nigerian-men-are-snatching-our-wives-south-african-politician/. Accessed 12 Apr 2018.

PM News. 2017. 2 More Nigerians Killed in South Africa in 48 Hours. https://www.pmnewsnigeria.com/2017/11/14/2-nigerians-killed-south-africa-48-hours/. 8 April 2018.

Premium Times. 2017a. 1 Nigerian Killed, Another Abducted in South Africa—Union. 1 January, https://www.premiumtimesng.com/news/top-news/219

383-1-nigerian-killed-another-abducted-south-africa-union.html. Accessed 10 Apr 2018.

Premium Times. 2017b. Again, Another Nigerian Killed in South Africa. 11 October, https://www.premiumtimesng.com/news/top-news/245734-another-nigerian-killed-south-africa-3.html. Accessed 11 Apr 2018.

Premium Times. 2018. Xenophobia: South African Mob Burns Another Nigerian alive. 23 April. https://www.premiumtimesng.com/news/headlines/265935-xenophobia-south-african-mob-burns-another-nigerian-alive.html. Accessed 12 Apr 2018.

Pulseng. 2017. 'We Don't Want Nigerians in Our Country'—South African Citizens. 3 January. http://www.pulse.ng/gist/racism-we-don-t-want-nigerians-in-our-country-south-african-citizens-id5985400.html. Accessed 8 Apr 2018.

Rydgren, J. 2003. Meso-Level Reasons for Racism and Xenophobia: Some Converging and Diverging Effects of Radical Right Populism in France and Sweden. *European Journal of Social Theory* 6 (1): 45–68.

Sahara Reporters. 2018. Another Nigerian Killed in South Africa. 13 April. http://saharareporters.com/2018/04/13/another-nigerian-killed-south-africa. Accessed 9 Apr 2018.

Salau, A. 2017. 116 Nigerians Killed in South Africa in 2 Years. *Daily Trust*, 7 February. https://www.dailytrust.com.ng/news/international/116-nigerians-killed-in-south-africa-in-2-years/184329.html. Accessed 15 Apr 2018.

Sekhotho, K. 2015. Zuma: I Doubt South Africans Are Xenophobic. EWN. http://ewn.co.za/2017/02/24/zuma-i-doubt-south-africans-are-xenophobic. Accessed 12 Apr 2018.

Singh, S.B. 2013. 'Voices From Behind Bars': Xenophobia and Foreign Nationals Incarcerated in a South African Correctional Centre. *Love Thy Neighbours* 215.

Steinberg, J. 2008. *South Africa's Xenophobic Eruption*. Pretoria: Institute for Security Studies Papers.

Tafira, K. 2011. Is Xenophobia Racism? *Anthropology Southern Africa* 34 (3–4): 114–121.

Tevera, D. 2013. African Migrants, Xenophobia and Urban Violence in Post-Apartheid South Africa. *Alternation* 7: 9–26.

The Nation. 2017a. Another Killing of Nigerian by South African Police. http://thenationonlineng.net/another-killing-of-nigerian-by-south-african-police/. Accessed 15 Apr 2018.

The Nation. 2017b. Another Killing of Nigerian by South African Police. 1 September 2017b. https://thenationonlineng.net/another-killing-of-nigerian-by-south-african-police/. Accessed 12 Apr 2018.

The Nation. 2018. Nigerians Attacked in South Africa, Houses Burnt. 20 January. http://thenationonlineng.net/nigerians-attacked-south-africa-houses-burnt/. Accessed 15 Apr 2018.

The News. 2018. 27-Yr-Old Nigerian Killed in South Africa. 19 January. http://thenewsnigeria.com.ng/2018/01/27-yr-old-nigerian-killed-in-south-africa/. Accessed 15 Apr 2018.

Vahed, Y. 2013. Crime, Fear of Crime, and Xenophobia in Durban, South Africa. *Alternation* 7: 197–214.

Valji, N. 2003. *Creating the Nation: The Rise of Violent Xenophobia in the New South Africa*. Unpublished Masters Dissertation. Centre for the Study of Violence and Reconciliation, Johannesburg.

Vanguard. 2013. South African Women Married to Nigerians in Protest. 22 March. https://www.vanguardngr.com/2013/03/south-african-women-married-to-nigerians-stage-protest-aganist-discrimination/. Accessed 18 Apr 2018.

Vanguard. 2017. S/Africa Police Kill, Abduct Nigerians. 1 January. https://www.vanguardngr.com/2017/01/safrica-police-kill-abduct-nigerians/. Accessed 15 Apr 2018.

Vanguard. 2018. Xenophobia: Nigerian Stabbed in South Africa. 17 February. https://www.vanguardngr.com/2018/02/xenophobia-nigerian-stabbed-south-africa/. Accessed 15 Apr 2018.

van Zyl, R. 2018. Drama After Foreign National Is Shot Dead in Roodepoort. https://citizen.co.za/news/news-cns/1888753/drama-after-foreign-national-shot-dead-in-roodepoort/. Accessed 18 Apr 2018.

de Villiers, J. 2017. Govt Can't Ignore Claims About Foreigners and Crime—Zuma. *News 24*, 2 February.https://www.news24.com/SouthAfrica/News/govt-cant-ignore-claims-about-foreigners-and-crime-zuma-20170224. Accessed 18 Apr 2018.

CHAPTER 5

Cyberspace Xenophobia in South Africa

Efe Mary Isike, Zainab Olaitan, and Christopher Isike

INTRODUCTION

According to Sander and Maimbo (2003, 10), an estimated 175 million people worldwide live outside their countries of origin, up from 75 million in 1965. This rapid increase in the global migrant population has been a cause of concern in many host countries including South Africa where relations between South Africans and African migrants have increasingly worsened since the end of the apartheid era. International migration, especially from Africa, has taken different forms in South Africa. At one end of the continuum is the highly regulated and formalized mine contract-labour system established between 1890 and 1920, which continues today. At the other end are various kinds of

---

E. M. Isike · Z. Olaitan (✉) · C. Isike
University of Pretoria, Pretoria, South Africa
e-mail: zainab.olaitan@tuks.co.za

E. M. Isike
e-mail: efe.isike@up.ac.za

C. Isike
e-mail: christopher.isike@up.ac.za

© The Author(s), under exclusive license to Springer Nature Singapore Pte Ltd. 2022
C. Isike and E. M. Isike (eds.), *Conflict and Concord*,
https://doi.org/10.1007/978-981-19-1033-3_5

informal or unregulated movements across borders (Crush 2000, 13). South Africa has received both kinds of migrants for decades, making it one of the major destinations for African migrants of all classes, professionals, students, tourists, businesspersons, etc. Indeed, following the end of Apartheid in 1994, the pattern of international migration took a new shape. The country attracted more Black professionals in large numbers as against the migrant labour stock it attracted during the apartheid period, prompting concerns of brain drain from African countries to South Africa. Democratization, a strong economy and South Africa's human rights regime also attracted a bulging number of asylum seekers, refugees, illegal immigrants, etc., leading to a relatively large migrant population in the country.

The increasing number of migrants in the country has elicited several reactions from South African citizens, both positive and negative reflecting both conviviality and conflict in the relations between South Africans and the Africans from the continent. On the negative side, South Africans have often used different platforms to openly express their discontent over the relatively large and increasing number of African migrants in the country in many ways. For example, this discontent has often been expressed through violent protests, looting and burning of African-owned shops and businesses, including maiming and killing African immigrants. Such anger and violence directed towards foreigners is only one manifestation of xenophobia which has also been rightly framed as "Afrophobic" because it is targeted at African immigrants. Expression of popular slogans such as "Zimbabweans are taking our jobs", "Nigerians are drug dealers" and "Somalians have run us out of our small businesses" are another manifestation of xenophobia/Afrophobia which point to the conflict from contact between both groups (Isike and Isike 2012).

This chapter therefore focuses on the conflictual aspect of contact between South African and African migrants and argues that there is a new space where Afrophobia is actively taking place in South Africa—the cyberspace. It contends that this space which encompasses all social media platforms such as Twitter, Facebook, Instagram and WhatsApp have been largely ignored in literature and policy as much of the focus has been on the private and public geographic spaces. This is even though the cyberspace is both a theatre of xenophobia itself and also a platform for mobilizing for and against xenophobia in South Africa. To make its argument, the chapter explored and thematically analysed the negative views of South Africans on issues that affect African immigrants expressed on Twitter and Facebook. While acknowledging that there are amicable interactions between South Africans and African immigrants on social media, the chapter focuses on the conflictual aspects of the cyber engagement of both identity groups.

THE POWER OF SOCIAL MEDIA AS PLATFORM FOR ENGAGEMENT

Conceptualizing Space

Globalization and technological advancement have enabled a cyber space, where interested parties engage various issues such as the contestation on belonging between African migrants and South Africans. Indeed, as scholars such as Jenkins have argued, with the advancement of cyberspace including social media, a new era of media democratization emerged where citizens are able to participate more through the media (Carpentier et al. 2014). This is significant given the agenda-setting power of the media and its role as a public watchdog that force governments to be accountable to their citizens, qualifying it as the fourth pillar of democracy (Saeed 2009).

What do we mean by the term social media? These include technologies that enable social interaction, collaboration and deliberations across various platforms and between people in the cyberspace (Bryer and Zavatarro 2011). Shrock (2009) similarly describes it as a "variety of different technologies" which go beyond one on one conversations to multifaceted means of communication and function. Elsewhere it is described as an online global forum through which people connect so as to create a cyber-community or network where exchanges of information and resources take place irrespective of the geographical barrier (Sokoya et al. 2012). Examples of these social media platforms include Facebook, Twitter, Instagram, YouTube, MySpace, Social Blogs, Skype, WhatsApp, among others. There have been numerous studies focusing on the role of social media in particular issue areas and sectors such as social media and organizations (Razmeritaa et al. 2014); social media and marketing (Heinonen 2011); and social media and political change (Nam 2012). However, very little has been done on the role of social media as a platform for engagement on migration issues of inclusion and exclusion. Therefore, this chapter analyses social media as a novel and fast growing space for engagement between African migrants in South

Africans which is used as a medium for expressing xenophobic sentiments and mobilizing xenophobic actions by the latter against the former.

Creating the Space

For engagement to take place, there must be a platform or space where the various opinions are exchanged. As Lefebvre (1991, 51) puts it, change cannot materialize without an "appropriate space". The public space has over time always been the most popular site of engagement between citizens on issues. This space is defined as the arena where members of society interact among each other and engage with societal issues (Sennett 2008). It connects human opinions and values with their physical environment (Hillier 2008). In fact, there is a connection between humanity, which is intangible, and social structures and objects, which are tangible. This nexus in most cases influences societal behaviour. For example, studies such as that of Hillier and Vaughan (2007) argue that the physical design and structure of cities (the public space) influence the nature of interaction of people and impact on the inclusion and exclusion. Simply put, the public space is not just one of the sites for contest of belonging but also influences the nature of that contest. A typical example in the South African context of this chapter is how the apartheid South African society propagated racial differences and discrimination, and the public space was designed and structured in a way that perpetuated racism. The cities were built and structured along racial lines, and this complimented the social behaviour of Whites towards Black South Africans. There were structures within the cities which Black people were not given access to, and spaces they could not enter as their movements were regulated through pass laws for instance. In this way, racist intentions that were developed and propagated in private spaces were enacted in public spaces.

In more recent times, a new space has evolved that cuts across the public and private space and this is the cyber space. It connects the private space with the public space without the physical sites and structures and this impacts on the nature of engagement that takes place. This does not downplay the importance of either spaces as the engagement that takes place within the public space is usually extended to the cyber space where they linger long after the public engagement. In many instances, cyberspace engagements over time tend to feed new engagements in the public space creating a cycle of mutually reinforcing relationship between these spaces. As part of the cyber space which this study is focused on, social media has become such an influential site of societal engagement that many governments in the world openly seek to regulate or control it. For instance, Uganda, China and North Korea have successfully restricted the cyberspace according to (Associated Press 2017; Okiror 2019). Ewang (2019) also asserts that Nigeria tried to pass a bill called "The Protection from Internet Falsehood and Manipulation Bill" in 2019, but this was greatly resisted by its citizens. Indeed, social media has become such an integral part of the twenty-first century as a new space for engagement and a tool to foster change. Grunig argues that in the past, non-governmental organizations and civil societies were main actors in advocating social justice and inclusion; but presently, the social media has become a fourth space where social movements are mobilized in the cyber world (Grunig 1978). It is important to note that social media does not in any way downplay the importance of the conventional media but rather complements it. As Jenkins argues, traditional media actually buttress the voices on social media, and this was evident in Egypt during the Arab spring, where positions on social media were highlighted on radio and television stations (Jenkins 2006).

Within the social media space, cyber communities have been developed around common interests and ideas which are harnessed to effect social change. Scott and Maryman (2016) contend that the use of social media has given birth to a connected age where relationships are developed through social media linkages. Inevitably, communities have evolved across and beyond geographical spaces to cyber space. These cyber communities may mirror other geographical communities except for its wider coverage and anonymity. They further state that cyber communities are inclusive because groupings go beyond country of origin, disability status, among other indicators of social stratification (Scott and Maryman 2016). This makes them a powerful platform to advocate for social change as when mobilized, they are known as cyber social movements. Cyber social movements are organized groups which operate in any of the social media spaces, and which have the ability to organize themselves sometimes with very limited resources but go a long way in attaining its objectives. For instance, the Arab uprisings that took place in Egypt and Libya were initiated by cyber social movements (Miladi 2016). In both cases, citizens were able to connect online and join voices to advocate for democratic change in their countries. Therefore, social media has been able to mobilize people with common ideas, values and interests into cyber social networks to communicate and pursue these interests.

Characteristics of Social Media

Social media has revolutionized communication and social engagement in the twenty-first century. Just as physical structures in the public space influence social behaviour (Hillier and Vaughan 2007), the specific characteristics of social media also influence the nature of engagement in that space, and one of these is unboundedness of communication among actors in social media networks. Wu and Atkin (2018) opine that the range of communication and networks is more global as a result of the unboundedness of social media. Second, the nature of communication differs from that of traditional media. According to McQuail (2005), one of these differences is in the level of engagement that takes place in the communication of actors within the social media space. Unlike the traditional form of communication that is basically one-directional, social media's form of communication is engaging and interactive. The effect of this is the development of virtual communities bound by common ideas and interests as a result of interactions and networks that are created in the cyber world. Abu-Shanab and Mushera (2015, 62) reiterate that it "allows its participants to connect with each other and build relations among people who have the same interests and activities". Impliedly, the strength of virtual communities is in their being able to permeate geographical and social boundaries.

Third, the anonymity factor of social media provides a measure of invisibility which enables marginalized groups and interests to come to the fore. As such, social media has become a strong tool for engagement used by marginalized and excluded groups to advocate for change (Miladi 2016). The geographical space where exchanges and advocacies take place is usually dominated by power (economic and political) elites. In essence, the voices of the poor, vulnerable and minorities are usually silenced through threats and violence. The lack of anonymity in this space makes it easy for these marginalized groups to be identified, persecuted and silenced. In this regard, the relative invisibility that social media provides allows these marginalized groups to express their views without the fear of immediate danger or being oppressed. Also, the sense of anonymity present in virtual networks makes it easier for the members to discuss and engage social issues more freely than in traditional face-to-face networks.

Therefore, the social media space empowers not only marginalized groups but encourages and strengthen the voices of those advocating for change, especially on issues that are sensitive such as the exclusion of African migrants in South Africa in the context of this chapter.

A fourth characteristic of social media is the development of virtual networks. Social media has become a strong tool for empowerment and voice for change through the organization of individual resources bound together in virtual networks that cost less than physical network spaces. Panteli (2009) argues that this low cost enables virtual networks and communities to achieve more than traditional communities in terms of coverage and networking. Again, the anonymity that social media gives members of cyber communities makes the nature of ties among members dynamic compared to traditional networks as it is more inclusive. Needless to say, the nature of interactions among members within such cyber networks or communities differs from the traditional networks (Hemsley and Mason 2013). This does not imply that virtual networks are totally different from traditional networks. There are certain similarities that both networks share. For instance, like the traditional networks, virtual networks provide support—emotional or social—to its members and also creates a conducive space for the exchange of information among its members (Dogruer et al. 2011). Scholars have in fact argued that virtual networks advocating societal change must necessarily complement traditional networks for them to be successful as social media does not work in isolation of other social agents of change. In fact, for effective transformation, social media and other agents of change must complement each other. This is what Penney and Dadas (2013) call a physical and virtual hybrid space. For Jordan (2009), social media has created a hybrid world where the boundaries between public and cyber spaces merge. According to him, in a hybrid world "cultural and social dynamics interact with demographic and technological trends…" (2009, 181). The hybrid feature of the social media may take different shapes in different countries as a result of the diverse cultural mix. However, one major effect that is common to all is the blurring of lines that transcends virtual to physical spaces. In fact, Jordan (2009, 182) describes this blurring as "the processes by which cultural practices, lifestyles and underlying ideologies are reshaped in relation to one another". In other words, these worlds, the virtual and geographical world, are not independent of each other but exist in a dynamic web where new identities and cultures are created.

Relating all these to cyberspace xenophobia, there has been contestation for economic space between African migrants and South Africans in post-apartheid south Africa which has over time built up negative sentiments towards the former. This has led to several violent xenophobic attacks against African migrants with the most notable and widespread being those in 1998, 2008, 2015 and 2019. These contestations which all took place within the public space were controlled by the South African Police Service including the military in some instances such as the 2019 one. However, these contestations have increasingly moved to another space that is less policed—the cyberspace. In most cases, this contest starts and lingers in the cyberspace long after it has ended in the public space. Thus, the next section discusses the theoretical framework employed to show and explain the role of social media in fuelling xenophobia by disseminating and propagating false information (fake news) that creates negative feelings and attitudes towards African migrants in South Africa.

False Belief Theory

This chapter uses the false belief theory as an explanatory framework to shed light on how the media generally, and social media in this context, is a driver of xenophobia. The theory was specifically chosen because it recognizes the role of the media as a space for engagement and explains how false information peddled against African migrants leads to xenophobia. The main argument of the false belief theory is that misinformation, untrue information or fake news propagated by the media and government are responsible for hostility towards foreigners in a country which manifests in anti-foreigner sentiments and actions including xenophobic violence against them. The theory was developed by Michelle Peterie and David Neil in their 2019 article titled *Xenophobia towards asylum seekers: a survey of social theories*, which was conducted in Australia. According to Peterie and Niel (2019, 24), "government and media discourses propagate erroneous information regarding the threat posed by asylum seekers and the legitimacy for their claims", and this false information over time results in anti-foreigners' sentiments, actions and violence. They substantiated their claim by contending that there is a strong correlation between false beliefs and negative attitudes towards asylum seekers; media and government officials' false information often spreads hate and thus leads to xenophobia. Their theory was based on what some researchers call the "propaganda model" and power of the media given its agenda-setting functions (Herman and Chomsky 1998). Klocker (2004, 14) drives home the central point of the theory arguing that "negative government and media representations of asylum seekers foster negative public perceptions and fears, which in turn provide justification, legitimation and electoral support for increasingly exclusive, harsh and deterrence-oriented asylum policies". In their seminal work, Peterie and Neil (2019) argue that the prevalence of these false beliefs stem from host communities' realization that they are also reinforced by "public comments made by the political leaders", giving the falsehoods more credence. The list of such legitimizers also includes thought leaders and public intellectuals. Two important points to note are: the role of the media and government/political leaders in the propagation of false beliefs, and two, the impact such falsehoods have on how citizens see and relate to foreigners.

In applying this theory to xenophobia against African immigrants in South Africa, we can see the actors that propagate false information and the channel through which these (false information/fake news) are disseminated. Using the false belief theory, we argue that that government officials, public intellectuals, opinion and thought leaders including social influencers in South Africa make inciting statements that largely contribute to the animosity towards African migrants in South Africa. These leaders use traditional and social media platforms to make careless public statements that start a discourse which goes viral on social media and then engaged in ways that build anti-African migrants' sentiments and attitudes. In extreme cases, the animosity stemming from negative attitudes that were informed by false beliefs lead to xenophobic acts of violence such as looting and destroying businesses owned by African migrants, maiming and killing them in extreme cases.

As aforementioned, social media is a novel and powerful space for engagement, which are both positive and negative, that cut across the public and private spaces. It has enabled engagements between African migrants and South Africans, and in the context of this chapter, served as a medium for expressing xenophobic sentiments and mobilizing xenophobic actions by the latter against the former. The false beliefs that drive these engagements thrive in the social media space largely because of the increased access to internet and devices. Also, as the literature on the power of social media shows, the unboundedness, lack of regulation and absence of fact-checking of the information that are shared within the social media space account for its high patronage. With the limitation on traditional media, social media presents itself as the new space for this form of engagement where discomfort, false beliefs and negative attitude towards African migrants can be expressed without repercussions. Much of the false beliefs are primarily economic-based centring around African migrants competing for and limiting opportunities for citizens. This is what informs the false argument that African migrants are the reason for the high unemployment rate of citizens which is fostered by popular slogans such as "they are taking our jobs" and "they are taking our local businesses". Another of such falsehoods is that all economic migrants, refugees and asylum seekers from Africa enter South Africa illegally. This enables the use of one brush to paint and taint African migrants as illegal aliens who must be flushed out. Other false beliefs revolve around social cohesion narratives such as "they are the cause of crime" and "they bring us disease". These falsehoods and the narratives they spew completely discountenance the fact of critical skill shortages in the country and employment equity laws which prioritize the employment of South Africans first before African migrants in terms of employment for example. African migrants only become the last option only when a South African applicant is not qualified or available for the position. Also, many African migrants create their own jobs and businesses which also employ South Africans as they do not qualify for social grants given by the state. They are business and personal taxpayers and generally contribute meaningfully to the economic growth and development of the Republic. Last, while there are several African migrants involved in criminal activities in the country, the failure to apprehend, prosecute and imprison and even deport them where necessary is that of law enforcement agencies who South Africans should hold responsible for unfettered crime instead of scapegoating African migrants through spreading falsehoods about them on social media. Unfortunately, top politicians and government officials have increasingly expressed these falsehoods openly and thus legitimizing them. This helps to fuel anti-African migrants' sentiments and violence expressed in both digital and physical spaces respectively. In this way, apart from being a platform of expressing Afrophobia, social media also becomes a platform for South Africans to mobilize for xenophobic marches and violence against African migrants in South Africa. This theoretical argument is tested in the remaining sections of the chapter.

METHODOLOGY

A qualitative research approach was used as the chapter was both an exploratory and descriptive study aimed at assessing the cyberspace as a theatre of xenophobia, and as a platform for mobilizing xenophobic action in South Africa. Primary data was collected from two social media platforms: Facebook and Twitter, using the search word "xenophobia in South Africa" between September 2019 and March 2020. Xenophobic/Afrophobic comments were gleaned from the posts that emerged. Out of 100 tweets and comments on both Facebook and Twitter during the period, 30 were gleaned and used as data for the chapter. The location of the tweets and comments searched was restricted to only South Africa to exclude Twitter and Facebook comments from users in other countries. Both Twitter and Facebook have user IDs that remain permanent even when users change display names. They also have location settings that can enable a researcher to identify the location where a post was made depending on the privacy settings of the user/account owner. The researchers set a location for the kind of content they wanted to access and view and cross-matched the Twitter and Facebook accounts with each other to confirm they belonged to the same account owner/user ID, and all 30 were positive matches. Such methodological firewalling in data collection was necessary to ensure that the tweets and comments were indeed made by South Africans to allow for data validity and reliability. From the user IDs, it was clear that the comments were made by people across gender and race. Additionally, a September 2020 news publication by Patrick (2020) in the *Sunday Times* which gave a detailed account of xenophobic Twitter campaigns orchestrated by a former South African soldier against Nigerian migrants was used as primary data source to signpost the growing trend of cyberspace xenophobia in South Africa. Together, these tweets, Facebook comments and analysis helped underscore the argument that the cyberspace is a theatre of xenophobia in South Africa and a space for mobilizing South Africans for xenophobic actions against African migrants in the country.

The thematic analysis technique was used to analyse the comments and tweets which were organized under specific themes in line with the objectives of the chapter. The dataset was first organized and the themes that emerged were analysed as stipulated by Braun and Clarke (2006). Despite firewalling and cross-matching locations of comments and tweets to confirm user accounts, we note a limitation in terms of ascertaining the identities of the Facebook and Twitter account owners given the anonymity factor which permits users to hide their real identities while being able to express controversial view. However, we are positive that these accounts are owned by South African users as the comments and tweets are consistent with those made regularly on the feeds of the researchers' personal Facebook and Twitter accounts by South African friends who follow them and those they follow. Besides, this anonymity helps in mitigating any ethical concern on protecting the identity of users and copyright violation concerns. We also note that a sample of 30 Facebook comments and tweets is not large enough to draw conclusions from, but our purpose was to draw attention to the cyberspace as an emerging space of citizenship engagement on migration issues which needs to be studied further.

PRESENTATION OF XENOPHOBIC COMMENTS

As aforementioned, "xenophobia in South Africa" were used as search words to unearth 100 social media comments on Facebook and Twitter out of which 30 with gender and race representation were used for the chapter. These 30 comments, presented in Table 5.1, were collapsed and paraphrased as views to anonymize and thus mitigate ethical and copyright concerns.

ANALYSIS OF XENOPHOBIC COMMENTS ON CYBERSPACE

This section undertakes a thematic analysis of the xenophobic comments to underscore two points: first, that social media has become a new space for engagement on African migration issues in South Africa, and that this space is used by South Africans to freely express and propagate falsehoods and fake news about African migrants which fuel hostilities towards the latter. Second, contrary to the widely held belief that only a certain socio-economic class (poor, illiterate and the street urchins) exhibit xenophobic attitudes and hostilities towards African migrants in South Africa, the phenomenon cuts across all classes. Overall, this section lends credence to the argument that conflict is an outcome of contact between South African and African migrants.

Table 5.1 Paraphrased xenophobic views expressed on Twitter and Facebook between September 2019 and March 2020

That Foreigners (African migrants) get into South Africa illegally, commit crime and when they are called out, they fight back in ways that make locals wonder whether they will not be chased out of their own country one day by foreigners

That "foreign nationals from Africa" pose more danger to South Africans than the other way round; therefore, resisting them is "for South Africa's survival, not xenophobia". Therefore, the term "xenophobia" should not be misused for those fighting for their legitimate survival as citizens of South Africa

That most African migrants come from corruption-ridden countries and their presence in South Africa is affecting the country negatively, so they should leave. They are "damaging the country more than the whites did during the apartheid regime"

That no country in the world has as many illegal migrants as South Africa who do not positively contribute to the economy, and are rather draining the country's resources. According to a view, there is a city in South Africa that is 80% foreign nationals and this needs to be addressed

That the government compromises the lives of South Africans as for example, the Department of Home Affairs does not do proper screening of "amakwerekwere[1]" who they believe "act lawlessly, falsify documents, commit fraud, human and child trafficking and other crimes" with impunity

That it is time to punish "amakwerekwere" like Nigerians who commit crimes with impunity. South Africans should not allow criminals to evade accountability because of the fear of being labelled "xenophobic"

That "foreigners from Africa" want to take over South Africa and therefore anyone advocating for the removal of borders in Africa is a traitor

That South African Members of Parliament whose parents are not fully form South Africa are not considered as patriots because they are "offspring of illegal aliens" and thus labelled as "kwerekwere"

That African migrants support their fellow country people involved in drug-dealing, prostitution, human trafficking and fake pastors so they will not get sympathy they are attacked and left to "burn in hell"

(continued)

[1] Amakwerekwere is a derogatory slang used to describe African foreigners. Therefore, it is used as identifier for a Black person who cannot demonstrate mastery of local South African language, and one who hails from a country assumed to be economically and culturally backward compared to South Africa. According to Nyamnjoh (2012: 70), the term is also stereotypically used on local South Africans with dark skin as "the more dark-skinned a local is, the more likely s/he is to pass for makwerekwere, especially if s/he is in articulation Setswana. BaKalanga, who tend to be more dark-skinned than the rest, are also more at risk of being labelled makwerekwere. In general, the le-/ma- (sing./pl.) prefix in Setswana usually designates someone as foreign, different or outside the community".

Table 5.1 (continued)

That South Africans are proud of being labelled "xenophobic" so long as African migrants leave them in peace to enjoy their country. African migrants are seen as accessing state benefits, sometimes more than citizens and that the law works for them than the citizens

That the government should close the borders and deport all illegal migrants and their countries should cover the cost of the deportation

That the service delivery system in South Africa is collapsing due to the influx of African migrants and South Africans cannot continue to condone illegal migrants "simply because they are Africans like us"

That the education and health systems are collapsing and government must "save South Africa from migrants! Send all of them home whether legal or illegal"

That most unskilled labour jobs in retail stores and restaurants are now done by immigrants from mainly Zimbabwe who accept low pay and poor working conditions "because they are forced by conditions to accept slave-like working conditions"

That African migrants want to turn South Africa into their run-down countries as they are desecrating the townships with filth. For example, Sunnyside and Arcadia have been destroyed by Nigerians who also engage in all kinds of illegal acts which South African citizens can no longer tolerate

Social Media as a New Space for Propagating Xenophobia in South Africa

Generally, as shown in the literature and theoretical review, the media is a powerful tool that shapes social reality through media bias and propagation/dissemination of misinformation or outright false information. For instance, Hyden and Leslie (2002, 2–3) assert that the "media have a powerful effect in shaping social reality through framing images of reality in a patterned and predictable way". Bringing this home to the context of this chapter, Smith et al. (2001) asserts that it is important to dissect and analyse the role of the media as creators of perceptions on and about African immigrants. Thus, it will be useful to show how social media is being used to construct a false reality that perpetuates hostility by South Africans towards African migrants. As aforementioned, the emergence of social media platforms such as Facebook, Twitter and Instagram has shrunk the physical space for public engagement on societal issues. While several people argue that the negative impact of social media among the populace outweighs the positive impact, social media continues to be relevant in today's world. By virtue of the fact that the emergence of this space has led to a widening of platforms for social engagement, social media has positioned itself as an important landmark in the twenty-first century. While traditional media is still largely the main source of disseminating news, social media is the space where news are being discussed and interpreted both before and after it is reported by traditional media. In the process, realities are constructed, reconstructed and disseminated opening the gap for the distribution of fake news. According to Grunig (1978), social media has become a fourth space where social movements are mobilized in the cyber world, thus making it relevant to this discourse on cyberspace xenophobia.

As Table 5.1 shows, South Africans take to social media to express their views on the migration crisis South Africa is facing. This is in a bid to either influence others or to simply spark a conversation. Sparking these conversations fosters a sense and form of community; cyber-community of members articulating and solidarizing around common interests. This emboldens them (members) to voice their opinions on issues that are raised giving a sense of social belonging and worth. While in most cases, these communities go beyond nationality, ethnicity, gender and age, in this case, the South African nationality is a single common denominator which is used to appeal to nationalism. Often, there is a denial that their comments amount to xenophobia as most of them believe they are only defending themselves from the threats posed by African migrants by speaking up against crime and other illegalities allegedly perpetuated by the migrants. However, the reality is different as is shown in the table above which illustrates clear xenophobic/Afrophobic views.

Also, many of the views paraphrased in Table 5.1 are based on falsehoods about African migrants. Some of these include the falsehood that foreign nationals make up 80% of a city in South Africa, that foreign nationals have more rights in South Africa than citizens, or that African migrants are the only one dealing in drugs and perpetuating crime. To be clear, there is no city in South Africa with 80% foreign nationals as occupants, African migrants do not have access to hospital beds that citizens do not have access to, and laws do not work for African migrants more than they work for South Africans. On the contrary, there are specific laws in place such as the Employment Equity Act 1998 that prioritizes the employment of South Africans over foreign nationals. Also, the Amendment Act 2014 of the Broad-Based Black Economic Empowerment (BBEE) Act, Protection of Investment Act 2015, the Competition Amendment Act 2018, and the National Small Enterprise Amendment Bill of 2020 are some of regulatory efforts designed to protect South

Africans from foreign domination and exploitation in small and big business. Often, these online engagements, and the xenophobic views and comments they spew are either a reaction to news about a foreign national committing a crime in the country or a response to a dog-whistle statement by a politician about ridding the country of migrants to combat crime such as the reported cases of opposition politician Herman Mashaba, former Mayor of Johannesburg and leader of the Action SA party as well as Bongani Mkongi, former Deputy Minister of Police[2] (see Okeke-Uzodike et al. 2021; Fabricius 2019). Relatedly, upon news for instance, that a Member of Parliament was of Malawian descent, there was a flurry of comments on both Facebook and Twitter which showed intolerance of a South African born of non-South African parents who held public office. Apart from the profiling, using such derogatory words as "kwerekwere" to qualify a South African citizen because she has Malawian blood is a classic example of how some South Africans view Africans from the continent—as aliens (Nyamnjoh 2006, 38–39).

Social Media as a Platform for Mobilizing for Xenophobic Action on the Ground

Xenophobic engagements on social media sometimes get exported into the public and private space where they are enacted. In the case where the comments made online gain traction or large number of responses such as likes, shares and retweets, it sparks a controversy in the public space showing that engagements in the cyberspace can also influence action on the ground. Recognizing the utility of social media as an effective platform for mobilizing anti-foreigners action, many South Africans have latched on to it and used it as such. For example, they used social media to mobilize citizens to take part in xenophobic actions such as protest

---

[2] Mkongi, while as Deputy Minister of Police in 2017, made controversial remarks during a press conference that it was "dangerous that one whole South Africa city is now 80% foreign nationals. If South Africa did not debate that problem, the whole of South Africa could one day become foreign and the future president of South Africa could be a foreigner" adding that "we are surrendering our land". Although he was made to recant and repudiate these comments in 2019 after they went viral and used to incite the 2019 xenophobic incidents in parts of South Africa (Fabricius 2019), they were still popular used by commentators up to March 2020 as recorded in Table 5.1.

marches and violent riots characterized by sporadic looting and destruction of businesses belonging to African migrants. It is in this light that comments such as "I am not going to feel sorry (migrants) when you all burn" and "Save SA from migrants; send them home" in Table 5.1 should be viewed as "a call to action". Similarly, views expressed calling on government to respond are also a form of sustaining African migration on the public policy agenda and *ipso facto*, pressuring government to act.

Another example of this growing trend of using the cyberspace to organize xenophobic action against African migrants under the guise of combating crime is cases of the #NigeriansMustGo and the #PutSouthAfricansFirst campaigns of 2020. It started 20 September 2020 on Twitter by groups such as *Action for Change* movement calling for a march to the Nigerian Embassy in Pretoria to protest the alleged involvement of Nigerians in human trafficking. They sent the following message which made the rounds on various social media platforms between 20 and 23 September 2020: #SaveOurChildren, their lives matter too. No to GBV. No to human trafficking. We can't be silenced anymore. We plead to all South Africans to come and join us as we do a demonstration protest on the Nigerian Embassy.

This messaging was used to mobilize support of South Africans by *Action for Change* and another interest group called the *Only One SA* for a march to the Nigerian and Zimbabwean embassies in Pretoria to protest against crimes such as child trafficking and drug trafficking alleged to be perpetrated by especially Nigerians. Some members of the Khoisan Revolution Party's 1st Nation Organization in relation to the protest stated that their organization will join the protest and that they are not against Nigerians but against "bad elements in the Nigerian community" (Patrick 2020). Relatedly, a march to "cleanse Johannesburg" of African migrants on September 23 was orchestrated and amplified by #PutSouthAfricansFirst, a movement that coalesced around the social media persona of one Sifiso Jeffrey Gwala, a former Lance Corporal with the 121st Infantry Battalion of the South African Defence Force in KwaZulu-Natal. He was uncovered by the Digital Forensic Research Lab as the person behind the "anonymous" Twitter account previously known as @uLerato_pillay, which has been accused of inciting xenophobic tensions in South Africa. According to a Daily Maverick report, "Mr Gwala used the @uLerato_pillay account to incite his more than 60,000 followers against foreign nationals and refugees living in South Africa, usually under the guise of one of several nationalist pro-South African hashtags" (Le Roux 2020). A careful study of hashtag movements involved in planning and executing xenophobic activities aimed at "riding South Africa of crime and criminals" on 23 September 2020 shows a connection between these three groups: *Action for Change, Only One SA* and #PutSouthAfricans-First. This indicates that it was a well-orchestrated prejudice against African migrants that was effected through social media to stoke hatred and galvanize support for possible violent action against the victims of this prejudice that is based on falsehoods. Without verifying the information peddled around, some South Africans utilized the cyberspace to push an anti-Nigerian agenda in what analysts have referred to as "social media abuse" (Ekambaram 2020).[3] This is one of the many actions by some South Africans that sow divisions and violence against African migrants which end up portraying all South Africans as xenophobic.

Xenophobic Attitudes and Socio-economic Class

One theme that emerged from the data is the link between socio-economic class and xenophobic attitudes and behaviours. Another false belief narrative about xenophobia that is propagated by the media and government in South Africa is that it is perpetrated by people in the lower economic class and poor masses. This is with a view to justify the characterization of xenophobia as acts of criminality occasioned by poverty. Indeed, popular explanations for the xenophobic attacks and attitudes to African migrants argue that the perpetrators of this act are mostly unemployed and illiterate South Africans who are transferring aggression to African migrants they feel are taking their opportunities and thus better off economically (Singh 2019). This frames xenophobia as a purely class and education issue that tilts responsibility for it towards the masses at the bottom of the socio-economic ladder. The evidence of this claim is usually in videos of media reporting including viral social media pictures and videos which show South Africans looting foreign-owned shops, burning their businesses and properties as well as assaulting, maiming and sometimes killing their victims. While this argument may be true to an extent, cyberspace xenophobia turns it on its head as it shows us

---

[3] Sharon Ekambaram of the Refugee and Migrants Rights programme during an eNCA interview on 23 September 2020.

xenophobia is perpetrated by people across classes including the educated. This is because people on social media platforms, particularly Twitter, are often regarded as literate and middle class because unlike Facebook that accommodates everyone, Twitter is perceived as more elitist as it is more technical and requires some level of literacy to navigate. We have seen from Table 5.1 that these individuals also voice xenophobic comments engaging in false belief narratives that frame and blame African migrants for everything that is wrong with South Africa. For example, over 60% of the Twitter and Facebook comments blame African immigrants for the high unemployment rate, high crime rate, gender-based violence and poor service delivery in housing, education and public health care.

This scapegoating of African migrants and the xenophobic behaviour it produces is held not only by ordinary citizens but also by top government officials such as influential opposition politician, Herman Mashaba. As Okeke-Uzodike et al. (2021) argue, Mashaba has severally echoed these sentiments in both the public and cyber spaces especially on Twitter where he has over 100,000 followers (Okeke-Uzodike et al. 2021, 286). Some of his vitriol against African migrants in South Africa which echo the falsehoods of the xenophobic views presented in Table 5.1 include the famous tweet Mashaba made in 2018 after his citizen's arrest of an African migrant pushing a butchered cow head in a trolley in the Central Business District of Johannesburg. According to him, "we are not going to sit back and allow people like you people to bring us Ebola in the name of small business. Health of our people first. Our Health facilities are already stretched to the limit" (Okeke-Uzodike et al. 2021, 286).

Also, in October 2019, Mashaba wrote "a series of tweets about crimes committed by African migrants in the City of Johannesburg under the hackneyed hashtag #WorldCupOfCrime" (Bornman 2019). Other such public xenophobic statements made by the former mayor include "Nigerians are drug dealers" and "African foreigners must leave our country". According to De Vries (2020), although Mashaba clarified in a statement during the September 2020 anti-foreigners demonstrations that he does not condone violence, he has been supporting the #PutSouthAfricans-First movement and his party's selling points are aligned to the movement's objectives of the seeking to amend the "broken" immigration laws and enforcement methods currently in place. Similarly, social influencers and celebrities in South Africa "have also thrown their weight behind the PutSouthAfricansFirst movement with musician Lvovo being one of the recognizable figures. He even changed his Twitter name to #PutSouthAfricansFirst" (De Vries 2020).

The conclusion we draw from these is that xenophobic sentiments, attitudes and behaviour are not limited to the lower classes of society, but are also held and expressed across class, social status, gender, age and even race in South Africa. Wade Pendleton (2008)'s conclusion in this regard is still relevant in 2022:

> a rise in intolerance and animosity towards migrants has been observed in South Africa, right across all social classes, regardless of social status. In other words, the poor and the rich, the employed and the unemployed, the male and the female, the black and the white, the conservative and the radical, all express remarkably similar attitudes. This poses a significant problem of explanation because it runs counter to the more general belief that certain groups in a population (usually those who are or who perceive themselves to be threatened) are more prone to xenophobic attitudes than others.

Clearly then, although not all South Africans are xenophobic, xenophobia is a present and fast growing phenomenon in South Africa and it is not peculiar to the unemployed, poor, illiterate or Black South African.

Concluding Remarks

Beyond the usual private and public geographic spaces where contestations between African migrants and their host communities take place in South Africa, the cyberspace has become a prominent third space of engagement. It is fast becoming a strong platform for many South Africans across all levels of society to advocate for change or in the least have their say. In this way, South Africans are increasingly popularizing the use of the hashtag# as a social mobilization tool for change in government stance and or policy on African migration. Behind such social media platforms as Facebook and Twitter for instance, people become emboldened to express their views on all kinds of issues in an unfettered manner. In many instances, cyberspace engagements over time tend to feed new engagements in the public space creating a cycle of mutually reinforcing relationship between these spaces. This leads us to our second conclusion that social media is a veritable platform for mobilizing xenophobic action on the ground such as protest marches. A number of interests groups have severally used social media as a platform to coalesce around common interests that are interrelated such as "African migrants must leave" and "South Africans first". Social media is also used organize anti-African migrants protests that include looting and destroying their businesses, violently assaulting perceived African migrants and even killing a few in the process as was the case in 2015 and 2019. Finally, our analysis of the Facebook and Twitter comments of South Africans on African immigrants in South Africa has shown serious anti-African migrants prejudice that cuts across class, social status, gender and age.

REFERENCES

Abu-Shanab, Emad, and Frehat Mushera. 2015. The Role of Social Networking in the Social Reform of Young Society. *International Journal of Technology Diffusion.* https://doi.org/10.4018/IJTD.2015010104.

Associated Press. 2017. North Korea's Internet Is as Weird as You Think It Is. *Fox News*, November 9.

Bornman, Jan. 2019. Mashaba's Xenophobic Legacy. *Mail & Guardian*, November 7.

Braun, Virginia, and Victoria Clarke. 2006. Using Thematic Analysis in Psychology. *Journal of Qualitative Research in Psychology* 3 (2): 77–101.

Bryer, Thomas A., and Staci M. Zavattaro. 2011. Social Media and Public Administration: Theoretical Dimensions and Introduction to Symposium. *Administrative Theory & Praxis* 33 (3): 325–340.

Carpentier, Nico, Peter Dahlgren, and Francesca Pasquali. 2014. The Democratic (Media) Revolution: A Parallel History of Political and Media Participation. In Audience Transformations: Shifting Audience Positions in Late Modernity, ed. Nico Carpentier, Kim Schroder, Lawrie Hallett, pp. 123–141. Routledge, London: Routledge Studies in European Communication Research and Education.

Crush, Jonthan. 2000. Migrations Past: An Historical Overview of Cross-Border Movement in Southern Africa. In *On Borders: Perspectives on International Migration in Southern Africa*, ed. David A. McDonald. New York: St. Martin's Press.

De Vries, Gilmore. 2020. Foreigners Fear Xenophobia as 'Clean South Africa' #Sidikiwe Campaign Hots Up. https://savannanews.com/foreigners-fear-xenophobia-as-clean-south-africa-campaign-hots-up/.

Dogruer, Nazan, Ramadan Eyyam, and Ipek Menevis. 2011. The Use of the Internet for Educational Purposes. *Procedia-Social and Behavioural Sciences* 28: 606–611.

Ewang, Anietie. 2019. Nigerians Should Say No to Social Media Bill: Proposal Would Criminalize Criticism of Government. *Human Rights Watch*, November 26.
Fabricius, Peter. 2019. Government Agrees to Censure Deputy Police Minister for Remarks About Foreigners, Say African Ambassadors. https://www.dailymaverick.co.za/article/2019-04-02-government-agrees-to-censure-deputy-police-minister-for-remarks-about-foreigners-say-african-ambassadors/.
Grunig, James E. 1978. Defining Publics in Public Relations: The Case of a Suburban Hospital. *Journalism Quarterly* 55 (1): 109–118.
Heinonen, Kristina. 2011. Consumer Activity in Social Media: Managerial Approaches to Consumers' Social Media Behaviour. *Journal of Consumer Behaviour* 10: 356–364.
Hemsley, Jeff, and Robert M. Mason. 2013. Knowledge and Knowledge Management in the Social Media Age. *Journal of Organizational Computing and Electronic Commerce* 23: 138–167.
Herman, Edward S., and Noam Chomsky. 1998. *Manufacturing Consent: The Political Economy of the Mass Media*. New York: Pantheon Books
Hillier, Bill. 2008. Space and Spatiality: What the Built Environment Needs from Social Theory. *Building Research & Information* 36: 216–230.
Hillier, Bill, and Laura Vaughan. 2007. The City as one Thing. *Progress in Planning* 67 (3): 205–230.
Hyden, Goran, and Michael Leslie. 2002. Communications and Democratisation in Africa. In *Media and Democracy in Africa*, ed. G. Hyde, M. Leslie, and F.F. Ogundimu, 1–27. New York: Routledge.
Isike, Christopher, and Efe Isike. 2012. A Socio-cultural Analysis of African Immigration to South Africa. *Alternation* 19 (1): 93–116.
Jenkins, Henry. 2006. *Convergence Culture*. New York: New York University Press.
Jordan, Brigitte. 2009. Blurring Boundaries: The "Real" and the "Virtual" in Hybrid Spaces. *Human Organization* 68: 181–193.
Klocker, Natascha. 2004. Community Antagonism Towards Asylum Seekers in Port Augusta South Australia. *Australian Geographical Studies* 42 (1): 1–17.
Lefebvre, Henri. 1991. *The Production of Space*. Malden, MA: Blackwell.
Le Roux, Jean. 2020. Lerato Pillay Uncovered: Xenophobic Twitter Campaigns Orchestrated by a Former South Africa Soldier. https://www.dailymaverick.co.za/article/2020-09-23-xenophobic-twitter-campaigns-orchestrated-by-a-former-south-african-soldier/.
McQuail, Denis. 2005. *McQuail's Mass Communication Theory*. London: Sage Publications.
Miladi, Noureddine. 2016. Social Media and Social Change. DOMES: *Digest of Middle East Studies* 25 (1): 36–51.

Nam, Taewoo. 2012. Dual Effects of the Internet on Political Activism: Reinforcing and Mobilizing. *Government Information Quarterly* 29: 90–97.
Nyamnjoh, Francis B. 2006. *Insiders and Outsiders: Citizenship and Xenophobia in Contemporary Southern Africa*. New York: Zed Books.
Nyamnjoh, Francis B. 2012. Intimate Strangers: Connecting Fiction and Ethnography. *Alternation* 19 (1): 65–92.
Okeke-Uzodike, U., C. Isike, and Iloh E. 2021. *The Political Economy of Migration in Africa*. Enugu: Afriheritage Institute.
Okiror, Samuel. 2019. This Is Intended to Create Fear: Ugandans Fear New Online Laws Designed to Stifle Dissent. *Independent*, November 24.
Panteli, Niki. 2009. Virtual Social Networks: A New Dimension for Virtuality Research. In *Virtual Social Networks*, ed. Panteli Niki. London: Palgrave Macmillan.
Patrick, Alex. 2020. Nigerians Fear Xenophobia and Violence in March on Crime. *Sunday Times*, September 20.
Pendleton, Wade. 2008. Migration and Xenophobia in Southern Africa. *Journal of Adult Education and Development* 70: 35.
Penney, Joel, and Caroline Dadas. 2013. (Re)Tweeting in the Service of Protest: Digital Composition and Circulation in the Occupy Wall Street Movement. *New Media and Society* 16: 74–90.
Peterie, Michelle., and David Neil. 2019. Xenophobia Towards Asylum Seekers: A Survey of Social Theories. *Journal of Sociology* 56 (1): 23–35.
Razmerita, Liana, Kathrin Kirchner, and Thierry Nabeth. 2014. Social Media in Organizations: Leveraging Personal and Collective Knowledge Processes. *Journal of Organizational Computing and Electronic Commerce* 24 (1): 1–34.
Saeed, Saima. 2009. Negotiating Power: Community Media, Democracy, and the Public Sphere. *Development in Practice* 19 (4): 466–478.
Sander, Cersten, and Samuel M. Maimbo. 2003. Migrant Labour Remittances in Africa: Reducing Obstacles to Developmental Contributions. Africa Region Working Paper Series No. 64. Washington, DC: World Bank.
Scott, Taylor, and J'Vonnah Maryman. 2016. Using Social Media as a Tool to Complement Advocacy Efforts. *Global Journal of Community Psychology Practice* 7 (1): 1–22.
Sennett, Richard. 2008. *The Craftsman*. New Haven: Yale University Press.
Shrock, Andrew. 2009. Examining Social Media Usage: Technology Clusters and Social Networking Site Membership. *First Monday* 14: 1–5.
Singh, Kaveel. 2019. South Africans Are Not Xenophobic; They Are Hungry—Chief Justice Mogoeng Mogoeng. *News24*, September 12.
Smith, Jennifer K., Donald P. Green, and Laurence H. McFalls. 2001. Hate Crime: An Emergent Research Agenda. *Annual Review of Sociology* 27: 479–504.

Sokoya, Abiola, Fehintola Onifade, and Adefunke Alabi. 2012. Establishing Connections and Networking: The Role of Social Media in Agricultural Research in Nigeria. http://conference.ifla.org/ifla78.

Wu, Tai-Yee, and David Atkin. 2018. To Comment or Not to Comment: Examining the Influences of Anonymity and Social Support On One's Willingness to Express in Online News Discussions. *New Media & Society* 20 (12): 512–4532.

CHAPTER 6

From Paradise Gain to Paradise Loss: Xenophobia and Contradictions of Transformation in South African Universities

Samuel Ojo Oloruntoba

INTRODUCTION

The call for transformation has become one of the main issues of public discourses and intellectual engagements in contemporary South Africa. This call is premised on what decolonial scholars refer to as coloniality of power, being and knowledge in which despite the official end to apartheid, structures of colonialism continue in various forms (Ndlovu-Gatsheni 2018). In the case of South Africa, coloniality continues in the hegemony of white minority population on the economy, land ownership and education. In other words, the expected gains of freedom in form of equitable access to resources, opportunity for social mobility and

S. O. Oloruntoba (✉)
Institute of African Studies, Carleton University, Ottawa, ON, Canada
e-mail: samuelojooloruntoba@cunet.carleton.ca

acquisition of knowledge that reflect the local peculiarities of the black majority population are yet to be realised. This chapter focuses on the call for transformation in the higher education sector in terms of curricular review, mix of faculty and how this is unwittingly leading to a revised apartheid in the form of discrimination in employment and conditions of work against those considered as the others that is the African Academic Diasporas (AAD) in South Africa.

Using personal reflections, and responses from four African diaspora academics from two African countries in South Africa, which were purposively selected for this study, as well as objective analysis of existing literature, this chapter interrogates how transformation is affecting job placements and careers of African diaspora academics working in South Africa. I argue that contrary to the spirit of the Freedom Charter (1955), which recognises that South Africa belongs to those who live in it, political rhetoric, increasing resort to populism, militant labour union aristocracy and a facile idea that the university can be used as a source of employment generation for all comers have resulted in a situation in which there is a deliberate policy to turn African diaspora academics into causal labourers through exclusion from permanent positions, and administrative posts in South Africa. These suboptimal turn in the experiences of AADs in South Africa is a negation of the spirit of inclusiveness and search for excellence that informed recruitment of faculty from far and wide post-1994. Many of these academics are from other African countries, who have made immense contributions to research productivity in South Africa. As Jansen (2019) argues in response to the xenophobic attacks on certain African nationalities in 2019, African academics and professionals contributed immensely to building local capacity at the end of apartheid in 1994.

From various accounts, Swapan in South Africa is the leading country in Africa in terms of research outputs (Patra 2019). This is not because of the population of the country as several other African countries such as Ethiopia, Egypt, Nigeria, Ghana has more population but because post-1994, the country welcomed academics from different parts of the world. The policy of attracting talents from other parts of the world, particularly Africa, created a promise of another American dream in Africa. This dream is what I call paradise gain in South Africa in the context of this paper. It is a dream that created opportunities for talents who can contribute to the development of an emergent nation, regardless of race or country of birth. While the call for transformation is imperative, it is currently being implemented in relations to appointment of scholars from other African countries in ways that suggest a replication of the old apartheid system of exclusion, discrimination, and worse, exploitation. While many are left untenured and unpromoted, some AAD scholars have remained permanent postdoctoral fellows as they move from one university to another in search of livelihood. Those who could not secure any positions are left with doing menial jobs such as e-tutoring. Others had no option but to leave the country for other countries.

The hash socioeconomic conditions in the home countries of some of these African diaspora academics made going back unattractive. Some unscrupulous academics in South Africa have taken advantage of this situation to invite academics from other African countries to the country but end up exploiting them through unethical practices of using the latter to publish. There have been cases where local academics who invited postdoctoral fellows from other African countries intimidated the latter into writing papers and putting their names without contributing anything to such papers. Some scholars from other African countries have also faced threat of deportation or being reported to the Department of Home Affairs by their hosts. I argue that these threats are meant to force such African diaspora academics into servitude. The expectation of fairness, professionalism and mutual respect that are supposed to define relationship among professionals in citadel of learning have been compromised by some hosts. In reaction to these challenges, some scholars from other African countries have been forced to leave for other countries in Europe, Asia or North America, where their talents are valued and appreciated. The forced exodus of such AAD from South Africa is a contradiction to the foreign policy objectives of South Africa, which is anchored on Pan-Africanism and African renaissance (Umezurike and Ogunnubi 2016).

While it may serve the immediate desire of nationalists who are championing the slogan of South African first in the university system where diversity ought to be the defining feature, the long-term implication is the loss of quality, global rating and recognition that have been the defining features of South African university system since 1994. This is the paradise loss. What are the drivers of the current transformation efforts? How is the transformation affecting scholars from other African countries in South Africa? How can the government turn the tide of discrimination to concord or accommodation of talents from other African countries?

The rest of this paper proceeds as follows. The second section contextualises the legacy of apartheid in the higher education sector in terms of its exclusion and subjugation of indigenous knowledge systems. The third analyses the core issues within the call for transformation such as decolonisation of curriculum and diversification of faculty to reflect the demographics of the country. In the fourth section, I establish the link between the call for transformation and the reverse apartheid that is being meted to African diaspora scholars in the country. This section also includes an analysis of the contradictions of a democratic country, which seeks to derive benefits from the global commons but has unwittingly been complicit in the *otherrisation* of fellow African nationals in spaces where the latter can add value. Empirical cases are presented as examples of how nationalist or nativist approaches to critical institutions such as universities have led to reduction in quality and global importance. Section five concludes with recommendations on how transformation can be implemented without undercutting the essence of what a university should be. This section also amplifies the imperative of reconstruction of African identity beyond the confines of colonial borders, as a bulwark against downward path to deepening ethnic and tribal contestations over spaces. In other words, without a deliberate policy of redefining citizenship and humanity beyond the confines of colonial borders, the current onslaught against other African scholars may further cascade into provincialisation of university system in South Africa in the long run, where recruitment of faculty members will be determined not by the quality of their academic pedigrees but the ethnic group that they belong to. I conclude that to avoid this path to self-erasure, thought liberation and critical consciousness of African place in the global capitalist system and the need to rethink and strategise for inclusive transformation is imperative (Oloruntoba 2018; Nyamjoh 2006).

APARTHEID AND THE POLITICS OF EXCLUSION IN THE HIGHER EDUCATION SYSTEM IN SOUTH AFRICA

Like in many African countries, the South African encounter with colonisation started as far back as 1632 (Terreblanche 2002). Colonialism fosters the assumption of direct political and administrative control over the natives. As Mamdani (1996) argues, the subjugation of the natives in contemporary South Africa, especially those of the Khoisan in Cape Town and the Zulus was not without resistance. Indeed, over century wars were fought before the colonialists were able to defeat the natives and instituted formal control. The idea of university came into being in 1910 with the establishment of University of Cape Town, which was in fact established for the British white South Africans. The institutionalisation of apartheid policy by the Nationalist Party in 1948 exacerbated the challenge of racial inequality and creation of access to quality education for the black majority population. According to Albertus and Tong (2019), these practices continue to define the higher education sector in South Africa in contemporary times and are directly responsible for the protests that rocked this sector in South Africa in 2015. Placing the call for transformation into historical contexts, the authors note that,

> the apartheid system created social and economic inequalities through overt racist policies. Central to the apartheid system were two important legislations: The Group Areas Act of 1950 and the Bantu Education Act of 1952. The first determined where and how Non-Whites lived and work, and the second ensured that Non-Whites received a substandard education to perpetuate the social and economic inequalities. (Albertus and Tong 2019, 3)

Under apartheid, the discrimination against the black majority population in terms of the quality of education that they received was informed by racism and the assumption of superiority of the European settlers over the black majority. Like in other colonial systems, indigenous people could have western education only to certain level. This limit to educational attainment was a deliberate ploy by the colonial authorities to keep indigenous people subservient to their colonisers socially, economically and politically. As Albertus and Tong (2019) further argue, the Bantu education was racist both in intention, structure, content and practice. They note that,

> This policy determined the content and level of education with the goal of institutionalising racial inequalities by preventing access to higher education and entry into occupations requiring more than basic skills. The apartheid legislation stipulated educational opportunities for each racial grouping. Compulsory schooling was required for all Whites from age seven to sixteen, for Asians and Coloureds from seven to fifteen, and for Blacks from age seven to thirteen, while institutions of higher education were reserved for Whites. (Albertus and Tong 2019, 4)

The differentials in quality of education across spatial divides (urban and rural), and the limit to the extent to which indigenous people can aspire to in the level of education that they can attain, have implications for economic and other social opportunities in post-apartheid Africa.

The history of higher education in South Africa is complex and diverse as it has passed through various forms of transformations. Randall (1998, 165) puts the series of changes in this sector this way:

> Any study of South African universities is complicated by their diversity. Three major groupings may be discerned: the older English-language universities (Cape Town, the Witwatersrand, Natal and Rhodes), sometimes called the 'liberal' universities; the Afrikaans-language universities (including Stellenbosch, Pretoria and Potchefstroom), which until fairly recently supported strict segregation; and the newer so-called 'ethnic' universities created in the 1960s in terms of apartheid policies for the different 'non-white' population groups (Zululand for the Zulu, Western Cape for Coloureds, Durban- Westville for Indians etc.). In addition, there are two distance universities (the very large University of South Africa or UNISA, and Vista) and the bilingual (English and Afrikaans) University of Port Elizabeth.

At the foundational phases, these universities were established to fulfil various objectives in the service of coloniality. As the author notes, the Afrikaans-language universities until recently supported racial segregation. Of greater importance is the content of the courses on offer in these universities as well as the make-up of the faculty members. Given the denial of African knowledges that pervade Eurocentric epistemology (Oloruntoba 2014), the curricula of universities in the country were suffused with European thoughts, knowledges, theories and methods. In what Ake (1979) refers to as social science as imperialism in the book of the same title, courses offered in these universities produced and to a significant extent continue to produce knowledges that are irrelevant to the development challenges that confront the country. The history of economic inequality also ensures that the white minority have access to universities that are well-resourced. In other words, South Africans from poor households suffer from double jeopardy of lack of access to quality education from elementary through high school to university as well as possibilities of social mobility that could result from acquiring quality higher education. The high cost of acquiring higher education post-1994 significantly maintained this structure of exclusion. Although the government has made some money available through the National Student Financial Aid Scheme (NSFAS), many black students could not meet the conditions required to access this fund. It was in the context of the challenges with access to quality higher education, static curriculum and undiversified faculty that the call for transformation took the centre stage from 2015. The next section examines the contours and forms of the call for transformation.

Transformation in Higher Education in South Africa: Issues and Debates

The high expectations that black majority democracy will bring about transformation in South Africa have remained illusory too much of the black population; we continue to carry the baggage of the past policies of exclusion. In what he calls South Africa; s suspended revolution, Habib (2013) established a causal link between the manners of negotiations that the African National Congress (ANC) had with the apartheid regime. Habib (2013) correctly identifies the changing international environment that pervaded during this time, in which neoliberal capitalism had assumed a hegemonic status with little or no alternative ideological counterpoint, from the defeated communist Union of Soviet Socialist Republics (USSR). The hegemony of capital, the dwindled fortune of the apartheid economy and the increased violence created conditions under which the negotiations that the ANC leadership had with the apartheid regime limited the extent of radical transformation that could have reduced poverty and inequality in the country. It was the sense of exclusion, alienation from the gains of freedom, choicelessness and lack of timely responsiveness from the state and the institutions of higher learnings in the country that forced the 'born frees' (South Africans born after 1994) to make them champion the cause of transformation in the sector, and to some extent in the economy. 'As Albertus and Tong (2019) further argue, for young activists, staying silent while observing the slow pace of transformation across key sectors of South African society, has had the effect of deepening their anger and frustration'.

The anger and frustrations of the born-frees were set against the difficulty in access to quality higher education, employment and better livelihood. Thus, in March and October 2015, students (mainly blacks) from institutions of higher learning who have met brick wall from both the government and university management resorted into violent protests under what is now regarded as 'fee must fall' and 'Rhode must fall' protests. The protests were violent with attendant destruction of school properties in different parts of the country. As it has been the characteristic feature of many of the states in post-independent Africa, law enforcement agents were deployed to quell the legitimate protests. Leaders of the protests were arrested, tried and hounded into correctional centres. While violent protests are condemnable in all ramifications, nevertheless, the protests served a useful purpose as the Zuma led administration set up the Heher Commission of Enquiry to Higher Education on 13 November 2016 to examine the feasibility of scrapping fees in higher education in the country. The Terms of Reference of the Commission include the following:

> The feasibility of making higher education and training (higher education) fee-free in South Africa, having regard to:
> - The Constitution of the Republic of South Africa, all relevant higher and basic education legislation, all findings and recommendations of the various presidential and ministerial task teams as well as all relevant educational policies, reports and guidelines.
> - The multiple facets of financial sustainability, analysing and assessing the role of government together with its agencies, students, institutions, business sector and employers in funding higher education and training; and
> - The institutional independence and autonomy which should occur vis-à- vis the financial funding model (The Presidency, South Africa, 2017).

The Commission several recommendations but fell short of requesting the government to provide free education to university students. Rather, it recommends that all undergraduate and postgraduate students studying at both public and private universities and colleges, regardless of their family background, be funded through a cost-sharing model of government guaranteed Income-Contingency Loans sourced from commercial banks.

Although President Zuma announced full and free funding for university students at the twilight of his administration, several issues that warranted the protests such as the imperative of decolonisation of the curriculum and diversification of faculty members, remain till today. The next section provides a theoretical and empirical analysis of how the transformation in terms of diversification of faculty is being carried out and how this process affects scholars from other African countries as well as its likely effects on the future of higher education in South Africa.

(Mis?) Transformation in South African Universities and Job Conditions of African Academic Diasporas

The transformation of the higher education sector in South African universities has assumed a xenophobic and exploitative dimension through casualisation of the AAD. It must be noted though, that there are instances where South African citizens are left as contract workers for years in contravention of the Labour Act of South Africa. The difference is while the latter have a prospect of being appointed to permanent positions at some point, in the current situation, the former rarely have such prospects in this era of nationalistic transformation. Before analysing the responses from the AADs interviewed for this study, I will present a theoretical underpinning of the larger historical and contemporary manifestations of otherness and exclusion, to which African scholars in South Africa are currently subjected. Mihize (2019) provides a useful theoretical entry point to the discussion of why xenophobia or more properly put, and Afrophobia pervades the South African society, more than two decades after apartheid. Using the concept of coevality, he argues

> that grappling with xenophobia, for instance, is not about coming to terms with what's gone "wrong" with South Africa. Rather, it is about reckoning with something internal to the logic of the country's construction and the ongoing negotiation of its history and contradictions.

Borrowing from Edwards (2003) and Fabian (1983), Mihize (2019) explicates on the articulation and disarticulation of differences, otherness and politics of (un)belonging that characterise the narratives, nuances and the emergent policy of exclusion of AADs in South Africa. The construction of identity around a South Africa that is different from other African North of Limpopo and the social bifurcation into insiders and outsiders have been a subject of scholarly discussion (Oloruntoba 2018; Nyamjoh 2006). In Mihize's (2019) view, sporadic attacks against other Africans in South Africa should not be construed as an accidental event. Rather, these incidences flow from both intellectual and political construction of otherness-the others being foreign Africans who were labelled as Makwerekwere-people with unintelligible language. The derogation that this labelling implies continue to shape the attitude of an average South African to other Africans in the country. And this is regardless of the professional status or social standing of such foreign Africans. In an attitudinal survey of the perception of South Africans about African foreigners in South Africa, Gordon (2015) argues that there are deep-seated resentments against the latter. He notes that even though the dominant narrative has been that concerns over limited economic opportunities have created conditions for the general resentment and subsequent attacks, this is an incomplete analysis. Given the utterances of the political leaders, the complicity of the Police in the various attacks, the resentment against other Africans living in South Africa is borne out of political tolerance (Chigumaozi 2019). Notwithstanding the condemnation of xenophobic attacks, there are other comments from political leaders in the country that appear to justify the direct and indirect attacks on other Africans in the country.

The above background provides the basis for the subsequent parts of this section and how labour unions and university management, especially in historically black universities have instrumentalised transformation in excluding and discriminating against AADs in terms of appointments to faculty positions in the universities in the country.

Starting with personal reflections of this writer, the agitation for diversification of faculty members has been interpreted as exclusion of foreign African academics. Although this writer was head-hunted from his country of origin to contribute to building a new institute in one of the historically black universities, first under a Postdoctoral arrangement and later as a Contract Senior Lecturer and Associate Professor, all attempts to secure a permanent position proved abortive. Even though the writer met and surpassed requirements for various positions in his discipline, he has been shut out of the system because he was deemed unappointable due to his status as a foreign African scholar. This is even more confounding when one considers that the writer in question is not only a Permanent Resident of the Republic but a scholar who is rated by the National Research Foundation of South Africa and who has secured over a million Rands in research grants from external sources. It is the case that contract workers lack pension or other incentives such as medical insurance that permanent academics are entitled to. The lack of respect for labour rights of foreign African scholars is symptomatic of the larger society, where rights of migrants are severally infringed (Gordon 2015). The rest of this section analyses the responses from four of the ten foreign African scholars that were purposely selected for this study. While three of them are from the same country, Nigeria, one is from Zimbabwe.

Analysis of Data from Primary Sources

First Respondent

The first respondent who completed Ph.D. in Nigeria and secured postdoctoral fellowship in a historically black university in South Africa narrates the experience of exploitation, silencing and intimidation. This respondent started by commending the idea behind what he refers to as ethnocentric studies of the experiences of scholars who are engaged as postdoctoral fellows. Further, the respondent notes how the expectations that a postdoctoral training will provide additional skills for the researchers' areas of interest is different from the reality. This is because rather than being supervised by his host to work in advancing knowledge in his chosen field of specialisation, he has been forced to work on the research agenda set by the host. He narrates his experiences in the following ways,

> My experience so far proves that widespread practice of a Host-Postdoc Fellow productivity often is negated and unproductive to building future sound scholar out of me. In my experience, I have learned that Hosts see their positions as an opportunity to "colonize" the intellectual abilities of the fellows for personal gratifications in terms of having their names compulsorily appended to researches they practically did not make any input in. To a great extent, this tendency of Hosts can explain the cold inter-personal relationships that usually persists with postdocs.

The use of the word *colonise* above constitutes a critical point in this paper. It speaks to the abuse of privilege and violation of labour rights of foreign African scholars in the country. To further buttress his point, the respondent continues thus,

> Worse still, my Host is never interested in promoting my maturity in other key areas of academic life like pedagogy/lecturing relevant

courses/modules to me, involving me in planning conferences and encouraging me to co-supervise postgraduate thesis in political science topics. My Host typifies the self-interested personality that thinks like one on a colonizing mission. He usually reminds me that: "your life is in my hands as long as I am the one signing for your quarterly bursary and continued visa". I need to quickly add, that my host treats me like I am his "clerk" and not a colleague with a PhD degree as him. This unfortunately is the common treatment many postdocs experience where I am.

These experiences contradict the ideal of what transformation should be in a university. Apart from negatively impacting on the productivity of the postdoctoral fellow, such experiences leave the postdoc with the feeling of otherness, discrimination and degradation. Questions arise as to the possibility of reporting such Hosts to the university management. However, as it is always the case with those who suffer from oppression, the fear of deportation and other denial of rights could keep the victim of such abuse from talking, preferring rather to suffer in silence.

Second Respondent

The second respondent provides a more general assessment of the state of universities in South Africa and how the exclusion of AAD has led dwindling in quality of higher education in the country. In his words,

> South African higher education is very expansive with higher quality than what are obtainable in other African countries. However, there has been a downward spiral in the last decade, particularly since 2014, due to subtle xenophobia that have accounted for the dwindling quality that characterized the contemporary University system. While every country has adopted economic protectionism, the need to maintain high quality of knowledge generation, expansion and dissemination in the Universities has 'compelled' many countries to seek human capacity, irrespective of the nationality of the professionals. The height of xenophobia in the country is unimaginable. And it seems both the political and educational elites do not care about maintaining higher standard, as long as jobs are reserved for unqualified local citizens in the quest for 'affirmative action'.

The idea of university is engagement with global knowledge. In the context of transformation in South African universities, the students would gain more from exposure to faculty members from outside the country. While one agrees with the respondent that foreign African scholars do bring quality to research productivity in South African universities, this does not preclude the reality that South African citizens are also adept in producing quality research. The point being made by the respondent is the extent to which foreign African academics are excluded, regardless of the level of expertise. The reference to emerging protectionism is also very critical. Although the global turn in populism is making many countries to shut their borders against the so-called unwanted others, these countries still create room for skilled manpower regardless of their countries of origin. In this regard, countries like the United States of America, Canada and Britain put in place various programmes to attract global talents. Britain and Canada have policies in place that allow graduate students at Masters and Ph.D. level to obtain work permit and work after completing their programmes. Paradoxically, this is not the situation in South Africa. Whereas the Government of South Africa provides funding for many international students to complete Ph.D., many of these students are left without jobs after their studies, The respondent puts this dilemma this way,

> It became so paradoxical that despite the enrollment and the conferment of Doctoral Degrees on many foreign nationals, at no or reduced costs, they are forced out of the system due to restriction of opportunities. Indeed, no country can record excellence in the University system by relying on locally generated brains, 'universal' brains are very important and inevitable. The government should rethink the political economy of xenophobia, and how the country has missed out on the opportunities presented by foreign nationals to contribute to the development of the country's educational system. They should learn from the US.

Flowing from the above is that the current transformation agenda in the universities is undermining value for money as well as stifling increase in research productivity in South African universities. In other words, when those who are trained with government or donor money and who are willing to stay back to contribute to the growth of the university system are not allowed, this constitutes a loss in technical and financial values to the university system and the economy in general.

Third Respondent

The third respondent puts the contradictions of transformation and exclusion of foreign African academics as well as the ongoing challenges in the university system. The respondent narrates this point in the following ways,

> Despite acknowledgement of the shortage of skills and the resolve to accommodate and possibly employ scarce skills professionals, this is becoming mere rhetoric in the context of academics as vacant positions are re-advertised when no South African qualifies despite applications from qualified foreigners. Attitudinal xenophobia is pervasive across South African universities. This is evident in anti-immigrant comments, exclusionary relationships, and the denial of certain privileges. In extreme cases, foreign academics are frustrated out of the university system. This has resulted in several foreign academics in the country migrating to other countries.

The respondent also contextualises the transformation agenda in the university and noted the following,

> Most, if not all, South African universities pay lip service to transformation. There have not been any conscious and comprehensive attempts to transform South African universities in terms of the composition of academics (whose top echelon is still largely dominated by white Professors) and curriculum (which still largely reflects Western epistemology). While it is important for South Africa to seriously consider internally constructed strategies such as the development and use of indigenous languages in classrooms, it is equally germane for these institutions to draw lessons from the transformation efforts of other African countries such as Nigeria, Ghana, Tanzania, Uganda and Kenya, and African American studies in the United States.

The point raised by the third respondent in terms of diversification of faculty to reflect the demographics of South Africa as well as decolonization of curricular are at the root of the Rhode must fall protests organised by students of higher education in South Africa in October 2015. This point was made by Cornell and Kessi (2017). Using experiences of students in university of Cape Town as case studies, these authors note that The Rhode Must Fall Movement created awareness for institutional racism at University of Cape Town and demanded for transformation. As in other white dominated universities such as Wits, Stellenbosch and Pretoria, the study shows how students remain dissatisfied with the low number of black academics as well as the dominant Eurocentric curricular in the various departments at UCT. Although the students want to see more black academics, the intellectual elites and government officials in South Africa have stringently sought to ensure that only South African blacks are seeing as academics in these spaces. As the third respondent further notes above, the need to ensure that only South Africans are appointed to faculty positions is responsible for many academic vacancies that remains unfilled in some of the universities in the country today. Keeping those positions unoccupied because there are no South Africans qualified to fill them runs counter to the spirit of transformations in ways that can satisfy the yearnings of the students.

The Fourth Respondent

The response from the fourth respondent is similar to the previous respondents in terms of the suboptimal way in which transformation is being carried out in South African universities, the exclusion of non-South African blacks from faculty positions and the contradictions that these pose to the country. He summarises his responses in this way,

> The South African policy seem to promote the advancement of the indigenous population such that, to compete as an African scholar, one has to work and achieve several times more. As a PDRF, job security is not imaginable. Acceptance into permanent and contract employment seem closed. The future as an African scholar in South Africa is bleak, notwithstanding academic outputs. As an African scholar the scope for securing an opportunity for growth and development is unavailable, even though the ability and capacity to share knowledge is evident.
>
> My sense is that job opportunities ought to be availed in terms of qualification and performance to allow for inclusiveness, productivity, and global competitiveness in the Universities. Without doubt, the production of PhD in various fields, of individuals from across the continent is applauded. But the exclusiveness with which employment is accorded is un-African and adds no value besides reducing opportunities of transformation in scholarship as well as for Africa as a continent in general. Currently, as an African deploys him/herself in knowledge accumulation and development, the preoccupation is quite frequently the quest to secure alternative

employment elsewhere. This reduces commitment by African scholars who feel unwanted and rarely acknowledged. For an African scholar, one word that squarely describes their circumstance is – insecurity.

The feelings of exclusion breed insecurity. Although an average foreign African scholar is generally committed to productivity, the lack of building a future in South Africa will continue to keep them on the move to the detriment of the contributions they could have continue to make to the growth of the university system in South Africa. The concluding section presents some recommendations that may be considered for retooling the transformation agenda in ways that can ensure that merit and productivity are not sacrificed on the altar of providing employment for locals who may not even be interested in an academic career.

Conclusion and Recommendations

This chapter has examined the challenges with transformation in South African universities and how this process has reinforced exclusion of foreign African academics in the country. I argue that although transformation is necessary on issues such as decolonization of curricula and diversification of faculty members, the ways in which this is being carried out could have a long-term suboptimal outcome. Despite its wide appeal within the university system, the exclusion of the AADs in appointment to faculty positions on permanent basis reflects the politics of nationalism and xenophobia. Whereas AADs have contributed significantly to building capacity in early days of black majority rule in South Africa, with some even holding top administrative positions, this has changed (Jansen 2019). Granted that from 1994 there have been increase in the number of South African citizens who have obtained doctoral degrees and indeed working in the sector, several academic and management positions remain unfilled due to non-availability of locals. While there are justifications for hiring locals, who meet the requirements to be appointed to positions, there is no justification for keeping positions unfilled when there are available talents from other parts of the continent and the world in general, that can fill those positions. I also argue that the casualisation of foreign African academics in South Africa has become a new normal. This has resulted in many Ph.D. holders becoming permanent postdoctoral fellows. Beyond the allure of nationalistic and populist feelings that inform the ongoing exclusion of many AADs from getting permanent positions in South African universities, lessons from other African countries like Nigeria, Ghana and Uganda that adopted indigenisation policies in the early days of their independence, in ways that excluded other nationals show that development and quality were stifled rather than enhanced. South Africa should learn from these unwholesome experiences.

In concluding this paper, the following reflections are necessary:

First, the transformation agenda must be divorced from the preponderance of nationalist populism that is rooted in the politics of the ruling African National Congress. As Mihize (2019) argues, the otherness and exclusion of foreign African scholars in South Africa can be located in the politics of identity and belonging in the country. By seeing South Africa from the prism of exceptionalism and difference from other African countries, there are rhetoric of xenophobia, which is responsible for the increasing exclusion of African diaspora academics in South Africa. Changing this narrative will require a fundamental shift in mindset and a re-engagement with Pan-African ideals, which underpinned the solidarity that South Africa received from other African countries during the struggle for independence.

Second, the transformation of higher education in South Africa should be sustained in ways that provide more access to previously disadvantaged groups and addressing their concerns such as decolonization of curricula and diversification of faculty. It is precisely in carrying out these aspects of the transformation that African diaspora academics in South Africa remains critical. Apart from filling the capacity gap, these group of Africans can bring experiences and Afrocentric theoretical perspectives from different parts of the continent. Thus, creating a level playing grounds for these categories of academics through appointment to permanent positions, where applicable, is critical.

Third, as in many countries, migrant professionals are motivated by various factors to work harder on average than locals. Consequently, ensuring that African diaspora academics are appointed on permanent basis with pensions and medical insurance could create further incentives for them to publish more and increase the research profiles of the respective departments and universities.

Fourth, despite the growth in the numbers of South African citizens that are currently working in the university system, there is still need for mentoring and developing future local talents. African diaspora academics have been providing mentoring and could do more if the right environment is created for them through appointment into permanent positions.

Fifth, despite the increasing resort to exclusion, the South African government has done well in providing scholarship for graduate students from other African countries. Creating rooms for these students to be integrated into the university system beyond working as permanent post-doctoral fellows or contract staff would be a way of recouping the money spent on training them.

Sixth, to ensure increasing competitiveness of the university system, the transformation agenda should borrow from best practices from other countries such as the United States of America, Canada, Germany and the United Kingdom to mention but a few. These countries have increasingly leveraged on international students who came to study to recruit critically needed skills in various sectors through the provision of various visa regimes.

Seventh and lastly, the transformation of the university system should be guided by ensuring quality in faculty recruitment and promotion. Notwithstanding the crisis of unemployment in the country, the university should not be an institution for employment generation for job seeking people who may not be interested in research and innovation. Examples from other African countries such as Nigeria, Kenya, Uganda and so on have shown that complete indigenisation of the university system has led to decline in research productivity, capacity and outputs. It does not serve any development purpose for South Africa to travel the path of self-erasure that has undermined the development potentials of other African countries. Regaining the paradise loss in the university system in the country will require a new approach to the ongoing transformation, in ways that will ensure that while South African citizens are given prime consideration in employment to faculty positions, African diaspora academics who are in the country with keen interest in contributing to building research capacity should be treated with fairness and be accorded constitutionally guaranteed labour rights of permanent appointment, without consideration to their countries of birth or origin.

REFERENCES

Ake, C. 1979. *Social Science as Imperialism: The Theory of Political Development.* Ibadan: University of Ibadan Press.

Albertus, R., and K. Tong. 2019. Decolonisation of Institutional Structures in South African Universities: A Critical Perspective. *Cogent Social Sciences* 5 (1): 1620403.

Chigumaozi, P. 2019. Afrophobia Is Growing in South Africa. Why? Its Leaders Are Feeding It. *African Arguments.* https://africanarguments.org/2019/10/08/afrophobia-is-growing-in-south-africa-why-its-leaders-are-feeding-it/. Accessed 10 Oct 2020.

Cornell, J., and S. Kessi. 2017. Black Students' Experiences of Transformation at a Previously "White Only" South African University: A Photovoice Study. *Ethnic and Racial Studies* 40 (11): 1882–1899.

Edwards, H. 2003. *The Practice of Diaspora: Literature, Translation and the Rise of Black Internationalism.* Cambridge: Harvard University Press.

Fabian, J. 1983. *Time and the Other: How Anthropology Makes Its Object.* New York: Columbia University Press.

Gordon, S. 2015. Xenophobia Across the Class Divide: South African Attitudes Towards Foreigners 2003–2012. *Journal of Contemporary African Studies* 33 (4): 494–509.

Habib, A. 2013. *South Africa's Suspended Revolution: Hopes and Prospects.* Ohio: Ohio University Press.

Jansen, J. 2019. Jonathan Jansen to Nigerians: 'I Apologise for the Reckless Generalisations'. *Timeslive*, September 12. Available: https://www.timeslive.co.za/news/south-africa/2019-09-12-jonathan-jansen-to-nigerians-i-apologise-for-the-reckless-generalisations/. Accessed 15 May 2020.

Mamdani, M. 1996. *Citizen and Subject: Contemporary Africa and the Legacy of Late Colonialism.* Princeton: Princeton University Press.

Mihize, K. 2019. South Africa and the Politics of Coevality. *Scrutiny* 24 (1): 73–91. https://doi.org/10.1080/18125441.2019.1651386.

Ndlovu-Gatsheni, S. 2018. *Epistemic Freedom in Africa: Deprovincialization and Decolonization.* London: Routledge.

Nyamjoh, F. 2006. *Insiders and Outsiders: Citizenship and Xenophobia in Contemporary Southern Africa.* Dakar and London: CODESRIA and Zed Books.

Oloruntoba, S.O. 2014. Social Sciences as Dependency: State Apathy and the Crisis of Knowledge Production in Nigerian Universities. *Social Dynamics* 40 (3): 338–352.

Oloruntoba, S.O. 2018. Crisis of Identity and Xenophobia in Africa: The Imperative of a Pan-African Thought Liberation. In *The Political Economy of Xenophobia in Africa*, ed. A. Adeoye. New York: Springer.

Patra, S. 2019. Science and Technological Capability Building in Global South: Comparative Study of India and South Africa. In *Innovation, Regional Integration, and Development in Africa: Rethinking Theories, Institutions, and Policies*, ed. S. Oloruntioba and M. Muchie. New York: Palgrave Macmillan.

Randall, P. 1998. From Orthodoxy to Orthodoxy: The Study of Education at the University of Cape Town, South Africa, 1910–1980. *Paedagogica Historica* 34 (sup1): 163–173. https://doi.org/10.1080/00309230.1998.11434882.

Terreblanche, S. 2002. *History of Inequality in South Africa: 1652–2002*. Durban. South Africa: KwaZulu Natal University Press.

The Freedom Charter. 1955. Available at: http://www.historicalpapers.wits.ac.za/inventories/inv_pdfo/AD1137/AD1137-Ea6-1-001-jpeg.pdf.

The Presidency, South Africa. 2017. Release of the Report of Commission of Inquiry into the Feasibility of Making High Education and Training Fee-Free in South Africa. Available at: http://www.thepresidency.gov.za/press-statements/release-report-commission-inquiry-feasibility-making-high-education-and-training. Accessed 7 May 2020.

Umezurike, S., & Ogunnubi, O. 2016. South Africa's Africa Renaissance Project: Between Rhetoric and Practice. *Socio-economica—The Scientific Journal for Theory and Practice of Socio-economic Development* 5 (10): 263–278.

CHAPTER 7

Language, Being, Belonging, and Non-belonging in South Africa

Ivan Katsere

INTRODUCTION

I ~~think~~ speak therefore I am. (Kohlenberg 2006, 1)

We don't want to speak like in Shona. We speak Shona like when we, when we, when there are no Zulu people that's where we speak Shona, but when we are like with them, we speak Zulu. Because sometimes when we speak Shona, when they are around us, those Zulu people, sometimes they laugh at us, they say that we don't understand what you are saying this and that, so it makes us sometimes to fear to speak our language, so we are forced to speak that Zulu.—Nosy Tinashe, Participant.

The function of language in social life is very implicit but its impact is immediate and pivotal to every interaction. Language is the best and most

I. Katsere (✉)
Capte Town, South Africa
e-mail: ikatsere@yahoo.com

efficient way we use to communicate and get acquainted with each other. In this chapter, I attempt to highlight that in communication, language also carries with it, markers that communicate who belongs and who does not belong ('Us' vs 'Them'). Through these markers, and specific to the South African context, language has played and still plays a pivotal role in transferring information and communicating the politics which serve to initiate and maintain boundaries of who belongs and does not belong to social spaces.

To understand language within South Africa, the historical lens of the context which shapes the existing perceptions and ideologies that characterize language in South Africa are used in this section to explore how these also impact on the politics of belonging and 'policing' of Black African bodies by Black South Africans.

In this chapter, I contend that through language, people are thought of as belonging to a space and get the privileges of occupying that space, and the access is granted or denied merely through language. Language is the key signifier and identifying quality of non-belonging and anyone marked as an African outgroup in South Africa has the risk of losing any privileges, be discriminated against or worse be violated. The loss of the humanness of the African outgroup the discrimination and labeling, also carries with it the potential provision of non-human treatment, traumatic Afrophobic attitudes, and in some cases, discrimination which might lead to physical attacks.

In terms of methodology, this chapter benefited from a Master's research study that focused on narratives of children who translate for their parents and family members in Johannesburg. The data were collected using semi-formal narrative interviews with the family pairs made up of a parent and a child who served as a language broker. The total sample size of the study 9 participants consisting of 6 parents and 3 children interviewed in 3 batches composed of 2 parents and 1 child each with no pairing family member (Katsere 2016). All the interviews were conducted by the author who interviewed each parent and the child separately; a measure put in place to enable a discussion of sensitive issues that are hard to communicate in family settings. Ethical approval for the study came from the University of the Witwatersrand in Johannesburg, and all ethical considerations and protocols were observed.

Overall, an analysis of the data shows that the 'othering' of Black bodies in South Africa embodies Black self-hate or the hate of 'blackness' and Black bodies which culminates in traumatic experiences of violent xenophobia by African migrants. Language in its current form in South Africa mobilizes the politics of belonging and ignites identification of ingroups and outgroups, a conscious reality which guarantees security or potentially places one at risk in Black South African spaces.

Talking South African

South African history uniquely combines various historical and social factors that we need to pay special attention to in understand the progression of language. These multi-layered intersections which include tribal pride, racism, and class are the background on which South African society is formed, operates, and can be understood. In some cases, these intersections form the spark that ignites various forms of conflict. Reality in South African spaces is formed through the ideological prism of 'race' (Alexander 2011).

This reality is lived through social interactions and navigation of social spaces which bring these ideologies to life. Attacks on African migrants have served as evidence that language functions to identify Black non-South African bodies and further label them with undesired traits including but not limited to criminality. This exemplifies one of the many cases in which perception as stated by Alexander Neville morphs into or is a reality which builds up and erupts into a moment of violence we experience as xenophobic attacks matted out specifically to Africans who are not able to communicate in local languages.

These multiple layers that form the reality of South African spaces bring to reality the ways language functions as an identity and combines with the color of one's skin to create an imagined reality, an 'ideological prism' through which one's behavior is not only expected but punished if the expectation is not met. If the reality is this challenging for each South African that identifies as Black or Colored, one can only imagine the social and ideological trials stacked against Black migrants. Survival when navigating South African spaces becomes imperative not only for migrants, but also South Africans who have to always have their linguistic resources in check when they leave their houses.

Seroka (2011) exemplifies taxis as a space where one has to speak the right language or face discrimination or worse as he refers to the taxi drivers and people in general as, unwilling to accommodate other people and commonly respond with the phrase 'Khuluma isintu' (literally meaning 'Speak human') (Seroka 2011, 2). Such statements function to give language power to either label one as a human or non-human based on the language they speak. In the same frame of thought, it also functions to take away one's humanness or dehumanize anyone who speaks any other language. This signifies the embodying of the taxi as a space that is shaped by language. And the language you speak gains you access or keeps you out of that space.

> You can't speak Shona in a taxi. It's like a dog barking in a taxi. They will wonder where the dog has come from...you are not welcome. You feel inferior and you cannot answer your phone. (Hungwe and Gelderblom 2014, 86)

Survival in these spaces for all people Colored or Black becomes about adapting and being buffered all language 'amour' that an individual might have gathered. For local South Africans, this takes the form of using the right language and the right use of colloquialism to gain acceptance. This is a mask that most people wear and in most cases are unconscious of this contrived identity that has to be 'worn' from one space to the next. Failure to follow these rules entails discrimination or worse for Black and Colored bodies.

This discrimination and dehumanization are matted in the form of names and words that serve to exclude and control any behavior that, through language, departs from the norms of the group. The use of English for Black South Africans entails departing from these norms and is accompanied with being tagged a 'coconut' or 'oreo' (Rudwick 2008). For Nonku Dijam (21), a Zimbabwean student in South Africa, departing from these norms warranted her being labeled a 'snob' and rejection in her school:

> When I learnt 'tsotsi tal' I could get back at them like, "Hai wena uyangijwayela khabi" that typa thing then Lord I pray he doesn't follow me or I'm gonna freak out ((Laughs))... It helped because, tsotsi tal is a mixture of I think, I think it's a mixture of broken English and Zulu. So when I was learning, it would make it easier, coz they would think, "Ahhhh, she is such a snob trying to act all gangster." And tsotsi tal comes from the gangster side, so they will be like, "She so snobbish but she is trying to act all strong, and she so chilling." So it was a cover up for a lot of things for me. So you would find in a scenario that I was probably scared, then I'd go on that 'tsotsi tal' vibe, wana be gangster, reckless and crazy while speaking English too, and broken English at it. And, it helped because I

learnt few words, I learnt few tricks then I learnt isiZulu kahle then I learnt other languages, so it was like. (Katsere 2016, 88)

Her armor in warding off discrimination or being called a 'coconut' was adapting through learning local languages and colloquialisms governing English and Zulu at her school.

Language and Power—Resistance Politics of Language

Language and the 'politics of language' are best understood and viewed by the need for people to interact with each other rather than the actual interaction. Apart from interacting with each other, through language, we create an identity which is shared by us and 'others' within our group. This is important, as it is the starting and defining process of belonging. Language serves as a marker of who belongs and who does not belong. In South Africa specifically, a 'Hello' is a statement that carries more weight than just a greeting. Included in the word are devices of belonging which help to locate the other person with geographical connections and inheritance through dialects, pronunciations and even colloquialism. 'Hello' in South African languages asks who you are, if you are part of my group, and can I interact with you. It is a word used to gauge if one belongs in that space or not.

Language through the greeting and other words especially in colloquial language does the 'dirty work' of boundary creation and maintenance. This is the separation and partitioning of society according to and by markers of language. These markers which include a proper response to 'Hello' and/or the use of a language in accordance to the social rules gains one access into a social group or denies them access into the groups. Language functions as the key to access these social and formal spaces, and in the absence of this key, one runs the risk of bringing 'othered', dehumanized or face worse consequences. One of the participants, Edmore Kure aged 39 stated:

> We had a challenge… I had a challenge on taxis, sometimes you fax a CV to where you don't know, those guys can reply, say you have to come for an interview but for you to get ehhh that place, it will be a challenge, because you can get to a taxi rank where those guys who control taxis they can tell you that no If you are speaking English, I am not in London, I can

answer you (laughs)... when you are in the taxi also they... they speak in their language in terms of money, the driver when you are speaking with English they cannot even like to you, unless even maybe for him to drop you, he acts as if he is not understanding you.

In addition to Achebe's notion that introduces the 'racial arrogance' of the English language, Rudwick (2008) further stipulate the perception of power encapsulated in the English language and other languages in South Africa. According to their view, South Africans perceive English and other languages which are introduced in addition to the 11 local languages as efforts to appear superior or contaminating their efforts of preserving their languages. The resistance of other languages and specifically the resistance of the use of English by other Black people may be steps at preventing a 'language genocide' (Kamwangamalu 2000).

Viewing Black people in above way suggests that any Black body which does not perform in expected and normed ways is going against this project. English and other languages introduced to South Africa after colonialism are perceived as having the power to wipe out or replace local languages, killing the valued identity of South Africans and therefore they are resisted. The perceived attempt to dominate and the efforts to preserve one's identity therefore combine to elicit the resistance experienced in South Africa. This is also evidenced in making rules of the language and combining it with local language to form a colloquial which is controlled and 'owned' by the people who created it.

Languages are closely tied to and inseparable to bodies. This has an impact on how these entities are expected to behave and the spaces that they are expected to occupy. Black bodies are expected to sound a certain way and occupy certain spaces, and the language follows the body and the space.

Black bodies have to perform language based on the rules governing the spaces that they occupy, a 'decorum' only reserved for Black and Colored bodies in South Africa. White bodies, on the other hand, are also expected to sound a certain way and to occupy certain spaces. 'Decorum' is less expected for White bodies in South Africa as their bodies are not expected to perform any other way. Significant to this notion though is the fact that White bodies who do not perform according to expectation are met with celebration, a signifier of progress and seemingly an effort that is unattainable. Contrary to this, a Black body which sounds the way it is not expected (Communicates in English) is subjected to attitudes and behaviors that are contrary to these celebratory tones. Rather these bodies are discriminated against, dehumanized, or worse.

Translanguaging which is 'the ability of multilingual speakers to shuttle between languages, treating the diverse languages that form their repertoire as an integrated system' (Canagarajah 2015, 2). The differences between this and code-switching is explained by Garcia and Werci (2014, 63) as 'Translanguaging differs from the notion of code-switching in that it refers not simply to a shift or a shuttle between two languages, but to the speakers' construction and use of original and complex interrelated discursive practices that cannot be easily assigned to one or another traditional definition of language, but that make up the speakers' complete language repertoire'.

The unconscious power and politics of translanguaging simply put is to take the power of various languages used by multilingual speakers and dilute them with other languages, to introduce a new language with markers from the various languages which form the rules of how to speak the new language. Although the speakers identify themselves with one or a few of these languages, their identity within their own spaces is through this newly formed language. Translanguaging gives power to the speaker by taking power of a historically superior language and giving it rules which are diluted by a historically inferior language. In the same moment, this is not only happening to the language, but also the speakers of the language. Speaking English or Afrikaans in these spaces, also carries all the connotations which are associated with the languages being associated with the person.

Mechanisms of Survival

Any perception of colonial or racial arrogance/association breeds hostility in South Africa. Any perception of economic superiority also breeds hostility. Any Black person who does not perform according to the set rules is guaranteed of hostility. The reality and awareness of these hostilities in some families have necessitated children to serve as language brokers, who translate, mediate, and speak in efforts to ward off attacks against themselves and families because of their language. As the *lingua franca*, English is spoken throughout most of South Africa; and therefore, there would be ostensibly less need to translate and for children to broker in English.

Language in South Africa creates barriers to social and formal access, the conflict, through language surpasses formal and informal spaces. One of participants explained how they have been helped by their child (6 years) in explaining their legal status in South Africa at a traffic stop. As much as the father tried to explain their situation in English, the policeman adamantly used isiZulu to respond. The 6-year-old had to intervene for the father and the family in this situation, and the father recognizes this as a moment they were saved by the child from potentially being violated or potentially spending the night behind bars.

Language brokering is dominant among migrant families as they transition spaces and is a necessity for their safety, a clear indication of how they always exist near possible conflict. English is the language of economy in South Africa, so why is this necessary? The role of English as a *lingua franca* is foregrounded by the politics of language and an increasing awareness of the 'necessity to revalorize or replace the indigenous languages and a strong tendency to select the colonial language, English as the lingua franca' (Kamwangamalu 2000, 63). Not only does the English language carry a history of racial arrogance and prejudice as highlighted by Chinua Achebe (2006) it is also perceived as the 'killer language' responsible for 'language genocide' (Kamwangamalu 2000) of local languages.

LANGUAGE AND AFROPHOBIC CONFLICT

As humans, we have the need to locate ourselves and others within social spaces. Categorizing ourselves and others help us to navigate social spaces and predict behavior due to someone's category. Whether this assessment and predictions are true/valid is a conversation for another day. The one side of this is the stereotypes, attitudes, and prejudices that can originate from this need. This, however, is not harmful as these are cognitions with the potential to inform conflict but cannot yet be referred to as conflictual. The other side of this need to survive and predict behavior is language functioning as an act to discriminate, dehumanize, and actively create demarcations between people. Creation of the African Other, Mobilization of nationality, Dehumanization of the Africa Other, 'Us vs. Them'.

Creation of the African Other

Language in South Africa has played a pivotal role in informing how we relate to each other. The media, politics, and social validation have combined in creating a discourse that has been acceptable, framing the unacceptable and unwanted and wanted 'Other' on South Africa. The wanted 'Other' plays a role in highlighting what characteristics are wanted in South Africa, in the same instance, clarifying those that are unwanted. The discourse that characterizes the European and American 'Other' significantly is welcoming and their presents more beneficial, warrantying protection as they cannot do any harm. From the media to the politics, Europeans and Americans are viewed as expats, who are a resource needed by South Africa. Their arrival in South Africa through the airports is viewed as a positive indicator of the country's success and much more needs to be done to increase their visits to South Arica.

Contrary to this, the discourse that characterizes African migrants is different from this. The media stereotypes them as drug dealers, fraudsters, and criminals who are a menace to society, the 'Other' who is flocking the border and needs tighter reactions to be kept out. Nationality is mobilized by the media as an indicator or validator of the crime being reported. Many crime stories have been reported in South Africa and the criminals have been identified as 'Some of these were Zimbabweans or Nigerians'. Nationality in such stories does not serve any other use than attempting to validate the genuineness of the stories by activating any stereotypes that are related to any migrant as being associated with crime, illegal activity, or stealing some resource belonging to South Africans.

Politics has also contributed to the strengthening of this discourse by blatantly blaming African migrants for all social ills and crime in South Africa. Although the contribution of African migrants to the current state of South African communities (just like any other person existing in South Africa) cannot be denied, the constant pairing of nationality and negative connotations sparks any underlying stereotypes and is the switch that transforms this into the act of Afrophobia. Validated stereotypes find life in discrimination, and invalidated stereotypes can be changed and can be transformed through disproving them, which is the pivotal role the media and politics should start occupying.

The igniting of these stereotypes is not hard to find in South African spaces and because of these, the conflicts that are pervasive could actually be thought of as a natural flow. The discourse is taken and used in social spaces in the way it has been carried out or pervaded in the media or political spaces. Zanefa Ngidi, a prominent *maskandi* artist was taken to court for lyrics which pervaded and serve as evidence of the Afrophobic conflict activated through 'validated' stereotypes. The song Abahambe Osbari [Foreigners must go!] Langa (2015) creates a representations and perception that migrants in South Africa are not earning an honest living and are a source of criminality in societies. The song creates and affirms the African 'Other' who is defined through stereotypes of criminality.

This criminal 'Other' is perceived by society and people in formal spaces. The police have been known to use this discourse of criminality to label African migrants and justify searching them based on the stereotypes of engaging in criminal activity or being in South Africa illegally. Language is also used by police in these random stops to identify who is a foreigner and who is native. The inability to speak in local languages in this case is enough to attach criminal connotations on an individual who is in the 'safety' of their house causing no harm to any individuals.

Nationality and names that depict the African 'Other' are hugely mobilized in South Africa. Tafira (2011) argues that we should do away with the discourse of xenophobia and address how this is a construction of a racialized 'African Other' based on racial categories which include, but are not limited to terms like makwerekwere—'speakers of a "strange" language with unusual phonetic sounds – bearers of an alien speech. The phonetic sound goes like "kwerekwerekwere" hence the name makwerekwere' (Tafira 2011, 114). This derogatory term means that their language(s) sounds like animal sounds. Other racial categories that are also created are: Magrigamba, Maforeigner, Abantu BakaMugabe (Mugabe's people), and MaZimbabwe (Tafira 2011). Narratives of children who serve as language brokers also highlight that these terms even stretch to the playground in schools. Richard Kure, a 15-year-old participant, tells us of how names are used in schools to depict him as belonging to an outgroup:

> This one is from Mugabe, he speaks Shona, he is not a South African…Yah, this other boy called Munashe from my school, we used to be in the same class, now he went out because they were calling him names, they actually called him "Mugabe" he is dark like Mugabe, so they gave him a title "Mugabe" so whenever like they are calling on Assembly, like "Munashe" then the children will say say "Mugabe" "Mugabe" "Mugabe" "Mugabe!" so the whole school even teachers started calling him "Mugabe".

Naming an individual Mugabe, for Zimbabweans, may seem to be relatively neutral or even positive, given that he was the president of the country and has been considered an African hero by some. However, for some, Mugabe was considered as a failed leader whose failures largely led to 'his people' ending up in South Africa. The name Africa is another term that has been used to refer to African migrants in the media and social spaces. The use of the term Africa, does not imply either national or continental pride, rather carrying racist and colonial connotations of places that are backward, challenged, of an inferior nature, backward culture or not fit for human survival (Katsere 2019).

Dehumanizing the African 'Other'

The creation and the maintenance of the African 'Other' gives life to their existence and validates their difference through a European/American and a South African 'Other'. After these groups have been created and successfully categorized, the politics of belonging dictates the interaction between the groups and any negative interaction leads to conflict. Based on citizenry, South Africans are categorized as the people who belong to the context, and through their language, have access to resources and social relations. In the same manner, Europeans and Americans alike through their citizenry, skin color, and language are categorized as people who are an accepted 'Other', and honorary member of the society. Although they are not South African, by their economic and political value, they are a group that belongs to South Africa by their guarantee of access, welcome responses and spaces in society that are reserved for them.

Apart from these two boundaries, an African 'Other' is also created as stipulated in the above sections. What is unique about this group though is the fact that, through a combination of language and nationality perceived by race, they are categorized as the people who do not belong to the context. Language for them, serves as an agent for social exclusion (Hungwe and Gelderblom 2014). Belonging, as explained above, is associated with rewards and access to resources. Not belonging, on the other hand, is associated with a lack of access and punishments through various agents which are conflictual in nature. The need to belong and avoid any punishment emanating from being excluded marks the politics of language and the use of mechanisms of survival exemplified by migrant children serving as language brokers for their African families and friends.

All this conflict is summed up in Afrophobia, which is a daily challenge and reality for African migrants. The imperative step after the creation of the African 'Other' is the starting point of the conflict, which goal is dehumanizing the 'Other'. Dehumanization, through language functions, has the basis of communicating who the 'Other' is through identifying them, and subsequently, discriminate the African 'Other' through dehumanization.

Dehumanization functions on 2 different levels; on the first level, dehumanization is a tool used to detach one from human beings and rob them of any qualities associated with humans. The same act also attaches human qualities to these people, which allows for them to be perceived as less or non-humans. The second level seems to serve the 'dehumanizer'. This level seems to serve to reduce any perceived superiority associated with race, mostly embodied in the language (English) and any historical connotations the language is perceived to carry. The latter dehumanization seems to be a response to the Politics of Language as displayed in the sections above.

> So these guys were saying ahhh ehhh this guy is not a South African guy so he is a Zimbabwean. So of which I was the only Zimbabwean, the foreigner there, so they were saying "No!", they don't want foreigners here, "a foreigner we treat him like a rat, if you leave one rat in the house, it will call out the other rats… we have to fumigate all the rats out in order for us not to have all the rats in the company because if you let the rats, they will call the other ehhh rats and they will destroy the company then all of us will run out of work because of them because they do the work" that was the main issue with these guys.

The above narration by one of my research participants provides evidence of the African 'Other' being identified and the beginning of the conflict through dehumanizing them and the potential harm that can be associated with this. Dehumanizing people by equating them with animals or vermin is not a new phenomenon, especially for the Black population in South Africa. Amagundwane (rats), 'Grigambas' (Dung Beetles), and 'Makwerekere' are some of the various derogatory terms used to dehumanize Africans in South Africa (Neocosms 2010).

Conclusion

African migrants in South have for long been called *amagundwane* and the conflict marked by actions which follow the naming shows that like scabs; African migrants are blamed for stealing jobs and other limited resources, which justifies their 'fumigation' in the same instance desensitizing any ill-treatment as they are not looked at as human. These dehumanizing names carry a strong and intentional language of purposefully and urgently 'cleansing' themselves of the unwanted and dangerous elements which eat the fabric of society and destroy it. This destruction of society is viewed as 'feeding' through the economy, criminality, and taking away South African women. Similar sentiments were echoed in the Rwandan genocide where the word 'cockroach' was used by the Hutus to dehumanize the Tutsis. Belman (2004) highlights how important it was in this situation that one group be identified as an outgroup and non-human, drawing the lines for conflict, ethnic cleansing, and the eventual genocide that was experienced. Once the Tutsis were identified as cockroaches or *inyenza*, they were detached from humanity and were no longer perceived as humans. This not only provided justification for their killings, but also led the government to not intervene in protecting this minority group.

Naming in South Africa plays a pivotal role in highlighting the drawing of boundaries, but also, in a lot of ways, the inception of conflict between locals and African migrants. Through naming, dehumanization is made lighter and sensitivity to the humanness of the individual is removed. As evidence to this, languages spoken by African migrants can also be an originating point of conflict in South Africa. Unlike European languages which are associated with a sense of pride and sophistication when spoken by English and Europeans, African languages are considered as unwanted sounds and noises that mimic the sounds made by animals.

Ultimately, the consensus of all the highlights of my assertion creates an ongoing problem that continues to divide Africans against each other. This relegates African migrants to an inferior place and detaches South Africans from an African stereotype to a more advanced place separated from Africa thereby creating a perceived 'superiority'.

REFERENCES

Achebe, C. 2006. *The African Writer and the English Language.* Durban: University of Kwazulu-Natal.

Alexander, N. 2011. After Aprtheid: The Language Question. In *The Second Decade*, ed. I. Shapiro and T. Kahreen. Virginia: University of Virginia Press.

Belman, J. 2004. A Cockroach Cannot Give Birth to a "Butterfly" and Other Messages of Hate Propaganda. Retrieved January 9, 2021, from http://gseweb.harvard.edu/t656_web/peace/Articles_Spring_2004/_Belaman_Jonathan_hate_propaganda.htm.

Canagarajah, S. 2015. *Translanguaging in the Classroom: Emerging Issues for Research and Pedagogy*, September. Retrieved September 15, 2015, from Aplpied Linguistics Review: http://www.enca.com/southafrica/foreigners-report-maskandi-muso-hrcFrontline.

Garcia, O., and L. Wei. 2014. Translanguaging and Education. In *Translanguaging: Language, Bilingualism and Education*, 63. London: Palgrave.

Hungwe, C., and D. Gelderblom. 2014. Understanding the Social Exclusion of Zimbabwean Migrants in Johannesburg, South Africa. *Journal of Community Positive Practices* 14 (1): 75–91.

Kamwangamalu, N.M. 2000. *Languages in Contact*. In Webb Vic & Kembo, Sure, *African Voices: An Introduction to the Language and Linguistics of Africa.* Cape Town: Oxford.

Katsere, I. 2016. *Narratives of Zimbabweah Children and Parents: Language Brokering in Johannesburg.* Johannesburg: University of the Witwatersrand, Department of Psychology. Unpublished Masters. Retrieved December 5, 2021, from https://wiredspace.wits.ac.za/bitstream/handle/10539/21895/Ivan%20Katsere%20%202016%20Research.pdf?sequence=2&isAllowed=y.

Katsere, I.M. 2019. Dehumanising the Other: The Language of Black-on-Black Racism. *Daily Maverick Op-Ed*. Retrieved November 13, 2021, from https://www.dailymaverick.co.za/article/2019-09-09-dehumanising-the-other-the-language-of-black-on-black-racism/.

Kohlenberg, R.J. 2006. *I Speak, Therefore I Am: A Behavioral Approach to Understanding Problems of the Self*, July 5. Retrieved January 22, 2020, from https://www.functionalanalyticpsychotherapy.com/i%20speak.pdf.

Langa, J. 2015. *Daily Sun*. Retrieved October 4, 2015, from https://www.dailysun.co.za/news/entertainment/2015-09-17-maskandi-singer-taken-to-hrc-for-xenophobic-lyrics.

Neocosms, M. 2010. From 'Foreign Narratives' to 'Native Foreigners': Experiencing Xenophhobia in Post Apartheid South Africa. Retrieved October 6, 2015, from www.codesria.org.

Rudwick, S. 2008. "Coconuts" and "Oreos": English Speaking Zulu People in a South African Township. *World Englishes*, 101–116.

Seroka, R. 2011. *My Thoughts*. Retrieved April 14, 2015, from R. Seroka, Producer, and (Blog Post), September. http://ronnie-seroka.blogspot.com/2011_09_01_archive.html.

Tafira, K. 2011. Is Xenophobia Racism? *Anthropology South Africa* 34 (3 & 4): 114–123.

CHAPTER 8

Beyond Xenophobia: Migrants-Locals in Socio-Economic Spaces in Cape Town, South Africa

Godfrey Maringira and Rosette Sifa Vuninga

INTRODUCTION

Research on migration has largely paid attention to the conflict which characterise immigrants, mostly African nationals on the continent, in particular their everyday experience in South Africa in post-1994 (Neocosmos 2010). Such conflicts include the incessant xenophobic attacks against immigrants which include discrimination in both formal

G. Maringira (✉)
Department of Anthropology, Sol Plaatje University, Kimberely, South Africa
e-mail: gmaringira@gmail.com

Department of Anthropology and Development Studies, University of Johannesburg, Johannesburg, South Africa

R. S. Vuninga
University of the Western Cape, Cape Town, South Africa
e-mail: rosettesifa@gmail.com

© The Author(s), under exclusive license to Springer Nature Singapore Pte Ltd. 2022
C. Isike and E. M. Isike (eds.), *Conflict and Concord*,
https://doi.org/10.1007/978-981-19-1033-3_8

and informal work and social spaces (see also Landau 2008; Neocosmos 2010). Of importance and central to this chapter is the idea that immigrants are never waiting nor passive in the process, rather they employ their social and economic agency to deal with xenophobic attacks. This chapter focuses on the ways in which Zimbabweans and Congolese migrants create, 're-make' and re-produce socio-economic spaces of interactions with local South Africans. Hence the chapter argues that migrants are not only victims of xenophobia but they are also actors within these socio-economic spaces which they themselves re-create and re-produce overtime. This chapter focuses on spaces such as barber shops, saloons, street and train station vending among others.

In terms of methodology, the authors draw on an ethnographic study in immigrants' most frequented spaces business spaces, including open markets, and hair salons, among others in Cape Town, South Africa where most Zimbabweans and Congolese do businesses. In these spaces, the authors observed and interacted with Zimbabweans and Congolese as well as local South Africans within those spaces. Most of these sites were familiar to the researchers because they have previously conducted research in these places (Vuninga 2014, 2021). The familiarity of the field also contributed to the ways in which the researchers were able to surmount ethical dilemmas in the field (Ansoms et al. 2021). Thus, in order to understand the everyday social engagements between migrants and locals, the authors reveal the ways in which both migrants and locals act, behave and talk about their lives. The major finding across these spaces reveals that migrants and locals co-exist as a community, with migrants emerging as *abangani* meaning friends in IsiXhosa, the language spoken by the majority of 'black' South Africans in Cape Town. The research contributes to our understanding of immigrant networks and how they contribute to their everyday integration in South Africa (Owen 2015; Amisi 2006) paying particular attention on how on how migrants co-exist with local South Africans in socio-economic spaces.

MIGRATION IN SOUTH AFRICA

Migrants often practice what Landau and Freemantle refer to as 'tactical cosmopolitanism', which denote migrants' willingness to belong to South Africa (Landau and Freemantle 2010). However, it is important to note that migrants do not seek and or have a desire to 'tactically' belong to South Africa, rather the sense of belonging is real and is characterised by the realities of co-existing in South Africa, especially among black African migrants. We examine the socialities of living together as part of the everyday practices. Of importance is to note that migrants possess different skills, and they work in varying capacities and in different cities across South Africa, formally and informally. They range from lowly skilled, semi-skilled and skilled migrants (Steinberg 2005). They live in different areas, townships and very posh suburbs in South Africa. These varying statuses point to the complexities associated with studying migrants' everyday life in South Africa. Thus, while those who live in South African townships like Alexander in Johannesburg are viewed as being at risk of xenophobic and other forms of violence, posh suburbs migrants also live in gated/walled communities, a clear testimony of the pervasiveness of criminal violence in South Africa. However, it is not the purpose of this chapter to explore all these issues as other scholars have done this in other texts (see e.g. Crush 2008; Everatt 2011). But, an interesting issue is how the South African government and civil societies have responded to migrants' socio-economic concerns overtime. According to Polzer, the response to migrants has been largely fragmented (Polzer 2010). In situation where the government respond to migrant needs, the response is often delayed and indeed fragmented (Landau 2009). This is seen from the most basic things such as acquiring immigrant documentations in South Africa, especially for asylum seekers to getting protection during xenophobic attacks as observed, for example, in 2008 and 2015 (Neocosmos 2010). This is mostly behind scholars of migration in the post-apartheid South Africa have often represented migrants as victims of social and structural injustices in South Africa. Although that is true to a considerable extent, research should also pay attention to immigrants' agency in ways, despite the hostilities they endure as immigrants, they have managed to forge social, economic and spiritual ties with the South Africans they share various spaces within the community. The main question there this chapter endeavours to answer is: How have migrants been able to live in close proximity with local South Africans and to forge relations beyond the known violence in the townships in which they reside?

The above analytical question is pertinent in at least two ways: it invokes the existing socio-economic pathways in which migrants live-by and with local South Africans. Secondly, it pushes our understanding that living with local South Africans does not always involve violence, but it is also characterised by social and economic intimacies coupled with a sense of humour. We therefore discuss the socio-economic interactions and relations forged and maintained between immigrants and locals in and beyond salons, barber shops, street and train station vending, and which prove a conviviality beyond xenophobic practices, actions and violence.

MIGRANTS-LOCALS IN STREET AND TRAIN STATION VENDING

The informal economies have become a livelihood source for both migrants and local South Africans. In these spaces ordinary migrants and locals often share the social knowledge related to survival through informal economy often involving small businesses such as selling food, fruits, vegetables and some wares. In these spaces, the streets and train station vending, migrants find and interact with local South Africans. This is also the case with local South Africans who also do small businesses around the train stations and public transport centres and who rely on migrant as their customers, who often became their 'clients'. This has extended to sharing food recipes between South Africans and immigrants who also sell cooked food in these spaces. For example, the local South Africans know that the Zimbabwean staple food is *pap* referred to as *sadza* (thick maize-meal porridge). The IsiXhosa women have learnt to cook *sadza* the Zimbabwean way, making it even thicker, prepared alongside with vegetables known as *rape/covo*. They cook and sell on pathways to the train station and free markets nearby in places like Parow and Bellville in Cape Town.

This reveals to us that the spirit of living together harmoniously spans from the home spaces to streets spaces where what the local women had learnt in the home is transposed to the street context. Local women often share living spaces, rent together with migrants, and it is also in the home space where they had been taught the best way to prepare *sadza*. While train stations are known to be crowded and filthy spaces, women are selling on these spaces and make them home to their customers. When the first author asked how the Xhosa women learnt to cook *sadza* the Zimbabwean way, the response was twofold: they were taught by their Zimbabwean boyfriends and Zimbabweans they shared the house with or befriended. While the majority of the local IsiXhosa people prefer spinach vegetables, Zimbabweans prefer *covo/rape* and Congolese like cassava leaves prepared with peanuts and palm oil. IsiXhosa women who worked in a Congolese restaurant in Parow explained she learned how to make casava leaves from sharing the house with Congolese and perfected it and other Congolese dishes through working with mama Leki—a Congolese shop owner in Parow, Cape Town. Other Congolese dishes the South African participants were familiar with include *makayabo*, meaning salty dried fish, *mikebuka* (smoked fish) which they eat with *bugali ya muhogo*, meaning cassava pap. The *muhogo* sold in Congolese food stores is imported from Zambia, Mozambique, and as far as Malawi. This is often another basis of network formations across nationalities in market places.

In Cape Town, Congolese work in both skilled and lowly skilled sectors often despite having degree from their country (Steinberg 2005). Congolese are employed as security guards in malls, nightclubs, residential complexes, farms, construction sites etc.), car guards (in mall parking and busy commercial streets) and waiters in restaurant outlets. As Owen noted, Congolese migrants in South Africa, survive by all means, relaying on their home country habitus, which include fending for oneself (*se débrouiller*) (Owen 2011; Amisi 2006; Gondola 1999). Similarly, Williams reveals that Congolese and other francophone Africans make a living in the city-centre's commercial streets such as Long street in Cape Town (Williams 2015). This implies that migrants are active agents within a specific setting in South Africa.

Other Congolese migrants prefer to work for fellow countrymen who own barbershops, hair salons, restaurants, clothing shops, African food shops, internet cafés, agencies of sending money and other goods 'home'. Some of them are self-employed as tailors, shoe-makers, wedding organisers and other informal businesses. Through these activities, whether modest or fancy, Congolese find ways to interact with local South Africans, as customers and or employees. Thus while during attacks on migrants' shops, Congolese interacted with revealed that not everyone was attacked by locals, instead some South Africans intervened to rescue them especially when they knew them. South Africans have often also intervened when the Metro police harass migrants in market spaces because of conducting business with no licence or permit to do so. Other participants testified about being rescued by South Africans when they were about to be arrested for not carrying their immigration documents or for not having one altogether. What is more interesting about market spaces, however, is that in situations where immigrants are denied permits or licence to run business in some spaces, local South Africans who easily get these permits often share their stands or shops with migrants. This points to the fact that both foreigners and locals share the frustrations associated with social injustices in South Africa and often stand together in overcoming them. African beliefs and Christianity are among the shared ways through which both immigrants and South Africans in shared spaces such as markets interpret their everyday socio-economic hardship. Thus churches and traditional spiritual spaces such as *sangoma* (traditional physical and spiritual healer) house are also important spaces for both immigrants and local South Africans.

Locals in Migrant Churches

immigrants-led churches have often attracted South Africans because of their 'healing', miracles, deliverance and their prosperity gospel Nigerians, Zimbabweans, and Congolese are the nationals who lead the most popular charismatic churches in South Africa (Muzondidya 2008; Núñez 2015). Examples include Gospel Ramah Church, World of Life, Come and See, Repentance Pentecostal Churches, Synagogue Church of All Nations, with branches in Johannesburg, Cape Town and Durban in South Africa. Local South Africans not only are important and sometimes, majority in these churches, but they also occupy important position in these churches' ministries, as well as other migrants attends, here we only focus on Congolese and Zimbabwean led churches where locals are also found. On Congolese churches we had an observation on Pentecostal churches in the townships.

Like many of the Pentecostal churches, the Congolese pastors talk more about prosperity and miracles for healing and deliverance. These are issues affecting the majority of both locals and migrants. What is interesting is that migrant pastors are often viewed as 'powerful' in the healing and deliverance ministry, and this includes the majority of Nigerian pastors too. The local IsiXhosa people attending these services believe the pastors do attend to their predicaments in a profound way. Of interest is how the locals also participate in the church choir, present and worship and as ushers as well. This reveals that they are not only members of these migrant led churches but they are part of it. In order to accentuate that locals are part of the church, the migrant churches sing local songs in IsiXhosa, an issue which welcome and legitimate the presence of locals.

The locals do participate in church activities such as outreach to and other township community members, inviting them to join them for prayers in mid-week services and on Sundays. Migrant pastors speak about living together as a community, and in situation where any of their members encounter a social problem, whether a local or migrant, they converge in their numbers to help-out. Thus, the notion of brotherhood and sisterhood extend beyond the church. This is the spirit of the church, 'love your neighbour as you do yourself'. In this case your neighbour might be a migrant or a local, the love is extended to each other despite their social and economic status. So in other words, the ways in which church members live with other community members are viewed as a prerogative for the holiness as sons and daughters in the eyes of the Lord. This preaching is of significance because it helps members to transfer this kind of relationship to other community dwellers. The locals also participate in church practices such as: thanks giving, tithe and offerings which are viewed as supportive actions to the growth of the church. In contributing to the church activities, this is viewed as belonging to the same 'body of Christ'. The body here is understood in its metaphorical sense, i.e. it is a point of contact and engagement for all members of the church which includes local IsiXhosa people.

Apart from these Pentecostal churches, Zimbabwean Zionist churches have been points of contact between locals and other migrants as well. The Zionist provides healing and deliverance but often in ways which are seen to be different to and from Pentecostal churches. The people visit the Zionist at the holy shrines, often known as *masowe*, where they are given a word of prophesy and given *muteuro* i.e. symbolic prayer often three small stones, which they would mix with water and bath as a way of cleansing *umnyama* meaning bad luck. At *masowe*, local IsiXhosa people are also found in the queue to receive their own *muteuro*. An observation at *masowe* revealed that one of the IsiXhosa women who had visited the Zimbabwean woman prophet was married to a Zimbabwean. The two had marital problems, and the IsiXhosa woman had come to the Zimbabwean Zionist Prophet for *muteuro*. What was fascinating is the way in which the Prophet resolved the problem: both prophetically and in more humane way. The IsiXhosa woman was told that her problems would soon be her past. She was given *muteuro* of three stones which she was to put in water in a small bottle. She was also instructed to put very little water in the pot at home and the cook *sadza* with her Zimbabwean husband. They would then eat together. In this case, eating together would be a symbol of togetherness, love and being romantic in the home. An overall observation revealed that, the women at the *masowe* were testifying that, *muteuro* works very well especially on marital problems. In situations where they are given *munamato* meaning prayer and *muteuro*, and how they will bath with it to cleanse their *umnyama*, the prophetic explanation will be in one of Zimbabwean local languages Shona. So interestingly, other Zimbabweans will then translate it from Shona to the local IsiXhosa language. In townships where the Zionist prophets live, they are respected, people pass-by just to greet them. However, though the greeting maybe be viewed as one which is characterised by power relations, it reveals to us that, this is also a form of recognition of what migrants are doing in their respective townships. Even the Xhosa taxi drivers are found at these Zionist places of residence and holy shrines, seeking divine help in their work places.

BARBERSHOPS AND SALONS

Barbershops and saloons are also important space of interaction presents to us the different ways in which migrants forge particular social and economic relations with locals. Congolese hair salons are well-reputed in being the best in all African hair styles ranging from bradding with synthetic fibres to all kind of natural hair styling. Participants also added that Congolese hairdressers are preferred over other nationals and even South Africans because their hairstyles last longer. This is similar to barbershops in which Congolese haircut is the preferred one by the local South Africans including the 'coloured' men as observed in the townships such as Kayamandi, Phillipi, Gugulethu, Nyanga and Delft in Cape Town.

In a conversation with Helen, a Congolese hairdresser in Bellville (Cape Town), she explained that she owned a hair salon in Nyanga Township and her South African neighbours were her first clients. They did not see her as a foreigner, but as a hairdresser and they chose her because she was good at her work. Helen is also fluent in IsiXhosa, the local language South African language which she learned from her South African customers and neighbours. This has enabled Helen to engage in more social chats with her regular and new customers. Helen also testified that the 2008 xenophobic attacks did not affect her business because her South African neighbours and local customers promised that 'they will not let anyone touch her or her business'. Helene is also a respected member of her neighbourhood because of her kindness. For example, she explained that when her landlord's daughter lost her job as a cleaner, Helen offered her employment as a trainee hairdresser in her salon. Helen trained her on how to make hair 'Congolese hairstyle', like most of her customers who are South Africans preferred it.

The ability to train and employ local South Africans reveals to us that foreigners are not only doing business and establishing social and economic relations, it also points to the fact that migrants do also engage in capacity building and economic empowerment in their host community.

Marriage, Clothing and Other Ways Life

It is worth to note that considering the years that migrants have stayed in South Africa, they have in some way brought in their way of life among the locals with whom they live in close proximity to each other, either at work and or at home. The locals have also influenced migrants' ways of life, i.e. the cloth they wear, food they eat, the music they listen to and importantly the choices of marriage partners in some way.

The migrants, whose voices are presented here, knew their fellow foreigners who had married to local IsiXhosa women. Marriage is out of intimate love which had in some way grown overtime. The issue of migrants-locals' marriage is very common in South Africa, for example, Nigerians have successfully done this. The married women would even visit the husband's family in his country of origin. South Africa allows foreigners married to local South Africans to apply for citizenship. Among Congolese and other migrants, the issue of documentation has always been a thorny in their lives. For Congolese, the problems of legal documentation and *ngunda* (refugee or asylum seeker permits in Congolese slang) are one of the most common ones associated with living in South Africa. But, when asked how foreigners got to marry local South Africans, the majority of our respondents revealed that, the very fact that they live in close proximity to each other makes relations develop. However, the majority of men who married local women bring them into migrant socialities. Women therefore learn the social life of their husbands, who are migrants. The social life learnt varies and span from food they eat how to cook it as well as clothing styles.

One of the clothing styles for Congolese is known as *pagne*, meaning a wax-print cloth. *Pagne* is believed to be an African clothing which brings with it dignity, belonging and identity of an African woman. In terms of dignity *pagne* is believed to be a form of dressing which is 'respectful' in some way. For the participants once a local South African is married to a Congolese man, they usually have one or two *pagne* outfits. This gives them a sense of belonging to a Congolese community especially when they meet for social gatherings. They are identified as Congolese rather than as locals. So what is interesting with *pagne* is that it re-makes issues of belonging and identity in profound ways.

An interesting practice among Congolese men is, *la sape*, i.e. a practice of buying and wearing expensive clothing even if one is poor. So the assertion is that Congolese men always want to look good, to present an impression of a professional and business man. The participants revealed that, if you meet a Congolese man, you will just think he is the Mayor of the city, and or he is coming from a business meeting. For our participants, Congolese men always want to be presentable but if you go to their houses or places of residence then it is something different. The participants revealed that this is common among Congolese men and even in Congo. However, what is interesting is how such practices are transposed in local South African townships, especially the ways in which such a practice is inculcated into the mentality of local South African women. We are interested into how *pagne* practice forges a particular way of life in and among locals, especially women married to Congolese.

The Congolese ways of life is also reproduced in Congolese homes where they own illegal shebeens known as *nganda* in Congolese language. While shebeens exists and still flourish in South African townships, Congolese have opened up these sociality spaces in which they sell beer, as well as Congolese food. What is interesting is that, even though Congolese owns *nganda*, local South Africans also visit them as customers and neighbours. But, within *nganda*, the spaces are also sociality spaces in which Congolese and locals interact. Interestingly, the beer is cheaper at Congolese *nganda*. This therefore brings in locals as well as other migrants.

Conclusion

This chapter has revealed that migrants are not always victims of xenophobic violence in South Africa rather they have capacities and agencies to establish both social and economic relations with local South Africans. Our findings reveal that, scholarship needs to unpack these everyday lives of the many migrants as well as locals, on what they do within those proximity spaces with foreigners. Life as a migrant and as a local is not always characterised by violence of the other, but it is one which is also characterised by love, romance as well as collegiality. So what our chapter does was to tease out the lives lived in certain spaces especially where locals and migrants engage each other. These spaces such as train station vending, barbershops, hair salon, as well as *nganda* create and re-produce positive interactions which often go unmentioned by researchers on the field of migration in Africa. Hence, our suggestion is that we need to move beyond studying xenophobia as an object of our focus because in doing so, we keep on reproducing a particular discourse which does not always reflect a whole some life lived in the everyday.

Acknowledgements Rosette Sifa Vuninga's contribution is extracted from her PhD research. She therefore acknowledges the National Institute for the Humanities and Social Sciences, in collaboration with the Council for the Development of Social Science Research in Africa, the University of the Western Cape's Centre for Humanities (CHR)'s Andrew W. Mellon Flagship Doctoral Fellowship, and to the Social Science Research Council's Next Generation Social Sciences in Africa: Doctoral Dissertation Completion Fellowship whom so far have funded her PhD programme.

References

Amisi, Baruti. 2006. *An Exploration of the Livelihood Strategies of Durban Congolese Refugees*. Geneva: UNHCR.

Ansoms, A., Bisoka, A.N., and Thomson, S. (eds.). 2021. *Field Research in Africa: The Ethics of Researcher Vulnerabilities*. Woodbridge: Boydell & Brewer.

Crush, J. 2008. *The Perfect Storm: The Realities of Xenophobia in Contemporary South Africa*. Africa Portal on 01 Jan 2008. https://www.africaportal.org/publications/the-perfect-storm-the-realities-ofxenophobia-in-contemporary-south-africa/ Accessed on 09 June 2008.

Everatt, D. 2011. Xenophobia, State and Society in South Africa, 2008–2010. *Politikon* 38 (1): 7–36.

Gondola, C.D. 1999. Dream and Drama: The Search for Elegance Among Congolese Youth. *African Studies Review* 42 (1): 23–48.

Landau, L.B. 2008. Attacks on Foreigners in South Africa: More than Just Xenophobia? *Strategic Review for Southern Africa* 30 (2): 1–23.

Landau, L.B. 2009. Living Within and Beyond Johannesburg: Exclusion, Religion, and Emerging Forms of Being. *African Studies* 68 (2): 197–214.
Landau, L.B., and I. Freemantle. 2010. Tactical Cosmopolitanism and Idioms of Belonging: Insertion and Self-Exclusion in Johannesburg. *Journal of Ethnic and Migration Studies* 36 (3): 375–390.
Muzondidya, J. 2008, June. *Survival Strategies Among Zimbabwean Migrants in South Africa*, 9–11. (International Conference on the Political Economies of Displacement in Zimbabwe, University of the Witwatersrand, Johannesburg).
Neocosmos, M. 2010. *From Foreign Natives to Native Foreigners. Explaining Xenophobia in Post-apartheid South Africa: Explaining Xenophobia in Post-apartheid South Africa: Citizenship and Nationalism, Identity and Politics*. African Books Collective.
Núñez, L. 2015. Faith Healing, Migration and Gendered Conversions in Pentecostal Churches in Johannesburg. In *Healing and Change in the City of Gold*, 149–168. Cham: Springer.
Owen, J.N. 2011. *"On Se Débrouille": Congolese Migrants' Search for Survival and Success in Muizenberg, Cape Town*. Doctoral dissertation, Rhodes University.
Owen, Joy. 2015. *Congolese Social Networks: Living on the Margins in Muizenberg*. Cape Town: Lexington Books.
Polzer, T. 2010. Silence and Fragmentation: South African Responses to Zimbabwean Migration. In *Zimbabwe's Exodus, Crisis, Migration, Survival*, ed. J. Crush and D. Tevera. Cape Town: SAMP.
Steinberg, J. 2005. A Mixed Reception: Mozambican and Congolese Refugees in South Africa. *Institute for Security Studies Monographs* 2005 (117): 45.
Vuninga, R. S. 2014. *Théâtres and mikilistes: Congolese Films and Congolese Diasporic Identity in the Post-Mobutu Period (1998–2011)*. Doctoral dissertation, University of the Western Cape.
Vuninga, Rosette Sifa. 2021. Establishing Kinship in the Diaspora: Conducting Research Among Fellow Congolese Immigrants of Cape Town. In *Field Research in Africa: The Ethics of Researcher Vulnerabilities*, ed. Ansoms An, Bisoka Aymar Nyenyezi, and Thomson Susan, 63–84. Woodbridge, Suffolk, (GB); Rochester, NY, (US): Boydell & Brewer.
Williams, J. 2015. Poor Men with Money: On the Politics of Not Studying the Poorest of the Poor in Urban South Africa. *Current Anthropology* 56 (S11): S24–S32.

CHAPTER 9

Foes, Friends or Both? Looking Beyond Hostility in Relations Between Congolese Migrants and South Africans in Empangeni

Christopher Isike

INTRODUCTION

This chapter is drawn from a study that aimed to examine and explain the full nature of interactions between Congolese migrants and South African citizens in Empangeni town of Umhlathuze Municipality in KwaZulu-Natal province by analysing the social network ties that connect them. Conducted in 2016, the study sought to investigate the extent to which relations between African migrants and their South African hosts go beyond xenophobic, and the ways in which African migrants are able to integrate into the societies in they live in through specific kinds of engagement with South Africans. This was motivated by the fact that the literature on the relations between African migrants and South Africans in

C. Isike (✉)
University of Pretoria, Pretoria, South Africa
e-mail: christopher.isike@up.ac.za

South Africa is overshadowed by hostility reflected in xenophobic sentiments popularly expressed on a daily basis by a good number of South Africans and in violent attacks targeted mainly at African migrants across the country. This begs the question of whether there are other aspects of the relationship between both groups beyond hostility and exclusion which are understudied.

To answer this question, this chapter examines the nature of dyadic (two-way) relations that exist between Congolese migrants and South Africans in the small town of Empangeni. It examines the nature of the linkages/ties between both groups and contends that beyond the hostility/xenophobia discourse, there is a conviviality/integration reality which should also be presented in literature with a view to giving a much more balanced discourse on the relations between African migrants and South Africans in general. To foreground this argument, this chapter used data generated from a social network method which was used to interview 8 Congolese immigrants and their close South African ties (making a total of 16 respondents) in Empangeni for the 2016 study. Out of these 16 respondents, 4 (2 Congolese migrants and 2 South Africans) were selected for a biographical examination of their dyadic relationships in line with the objectives of this chapter. This chapter thus presents and discusses a detailed treatment of findings from the lived experiences of 2 of the Congolese migrants; Jean-Pierre, and Felicity, and their South African ties; Zungu and Ntombi (all not real names), respectively. The 2 Congolese migrants who were biographically analysed for this chapter had both male and female as well as middle- and working-class representations. This sub-sample was purposely selected for two reasons. First, their stories/experiences capture many aspects of the complex web of relations that exist between Congolese migrants and South Africans. Second, they portray a dynamic picture of migrants' diverse paths towards integration better than the others in the study sample.

Their biographical accounts and the analysis that follow show that intergroup contact in varying spaces created an enabling environment for interaction between Congolese migrants and South Africans which produce concord or discord depending on certain prevailing conditions such as socio-cultural stereotypes and class. They also show that relationships can be positioned at many points along the conflict and concord spectrum which include hostility, exclusion, cosmopolitanism, hybridity, assimilation and entanglement and conviviality. Generally, the findings show that there are various spaces where intergroup contact takes place and this creates an enabling environment for positive relations between Congolese migrants and South Africans, which is mutually beneficial not just for both groups in this case, but also for the Empangeni economy and society as a whole.

METHODOLOGICAL NOTE ON SOCIAL NETWORK THEORY AND METHOD

A study that investigates the relationship between African migrants and South Africans requires methodological flexibility to produce a nuanced understanding of this phenomenon. Bearing in mind its descriptive and exploratory nature, this study therefore combined a qualitative research approach with social network methods to examine the nature of dyadic relations and linkages/ties between Congolese migrants and South Africans in Empangeni.

Social network methodology is rooted in social network theory which originated in the early twentieth century and was used in the fields of anthropology and psychology. Hatala (2006) notes that in 1934 Moreno used sociograms[1] to map out the relationships between various individuals and to describe the nature and characteristics of their relationships. Moreno sought to examine whether the psychological state of people within a network is influenced by social relationships among members of the network (Tesson 2006). Similarly, Cartwright and Harrary in 1956 used the graph theory to mathematically measure the relationships between members of a network using points and lines that signified like and dislike (Hatala 2006, 48). More recently, Scott and Davis (2006) adapted social network theory to explain group ties and relations beyond group characteristics which previous studies focused on. Following the evolving development of social network theory, scholars have variously defined social networks. For instance, Mitchell (1973) defined a social network as "the actual set of links of all kinds among a set of individuals" while Wasserman and Faust (1994) defined social networks as "the set of actors (individuals) and the ties (relationships) among them". Going a bit further, Kadushin (2004) describes social networks in quantitative terms by contending that a network contains a set of objects/nodes

---

[1] A diagrammatic representation of the relationships between people in a social group.

and a mapping or description of relations between the objects or nodes. We can therefore summarise social network as a social relationship or connection between an individual and another or on a broader scale, among groups of individuals; a social connection or bridge between two or more nodes.

Social network theory[2] emphasises connections and ties between various nodes in intergroup relationships unlike social identity theory which focuses on differentiations between groups. It is more interested in the nature of the relationship created than in the individual agents themselves. In this way, social relationships become a predictor of social behaviour of the person or group under study (see Mitchell 1973; Wasserman and Faust 1994). The links and connections that are created are regarded as a reflection of the social behaviour of the object of study. For de Nooy et al. (2005), a social network analysis will help researchers better understand and interpret social behaviours that can be used to explain the nature of relationships that connect people within intergroup networks. This is based on the assumption that people enter into and build networks to pursue varying interests. The networks formed could be formal or informal and irrespective of the strength of the relationship, a network enables those within it to access resources and information that they may not be privy to if they were not connected to it (Jack et al. 2010). Network ties could be between two individuals (dyadic) or across levels between individuals and their ties with other groups (Katz et al. 2004, 308). Another assumption of social network theory is the interdependence of nodes or actors within a network. Wasserman and Faust (1994) reiterate that nodes within a network are interdependent and should not be regarded as autonomous individuals/actors but as social individuals interacting with others within a network. Since this is the case, the theory is not interested in the node in isolation but rather in the relationship between various nodes. Therefore, as Katz et al. (2004, 311) contend, the best way to understand group behaviour is to explore their ties or networks. This is because, as social networks studies have shown, people's traits and attributes are a reflection of their relationships and as such focus should be on these relationships (Monge and Contractor 2002, 441). According to Katz et al. (2004, 312),

---

[2] Social network theory describes the actors within the network as nodes, and the relations are described as linkages or flows (Martino and Spoto 2006, 53).

people's behavior is best predicted by examining not their drives, attitudes, or demographic characteristics, but rather the web of relationships in which they are embedded. That web of relationships presents opportunities and imposes constraints on people's behavior. If two people behave in a similar fashion, it is likely because they are situated in comparable locations in their social networks, rather than because they both belong to the same category.

As social beings, people interact and develop ties with others both within and outside their social groups, and the ties they form influence their behaviour. Therefore, exploring people's social attributes will not necessarily provide a complete picture of the reason why people act the way they do. This does not mean that social attributes and demographic data are not necessary, but that analysing them in isolation of social ties will not give the full picture of group relations. Therefore, to get a full picture of the relations between migrant and host groups in a society such as between Congolese migrants and South Africans in this study, it is helpful to use a social network method to analyse the relations between both groups. As Jackson (2011) argues, "the people with whom we interact on a regular basis, and even some with whom we interact only sporadically, influence our beliefs, decisions and behaviors". People's behaviours are usually a reflection of the type of relations between members of their network, irrespective of the nature of the tie.

There are different types of social networks such as the socio-centric network, open-system network and ego-centric network. A socio-centric network focuses on a group of people and how they relate to one another. Kadushin (2012, 17) describes it as a social network in a box. Open-system networks on the other hand are not as closed as socio-centric networks. According to Kadushin (2012, 8), they "are networks in which the boundaries are not necessarily clear, they are not in a box – for example, the elite of the United States, or connections between corporations, or the chain of influencers of a particular decision, or the adoption of new practices...., and they are also the most difficult to study". Then, there are the ego-centric networks which is the type this study is concerned with. Ego-centric networks, also referred to as personal networks, are those with ties that are connected to a single node (Kadushin 2012, 17). They are called ego-centric or personal networks because the focus of analysis is on a single node or person and how the nature of the ties with other members of the network impact on the ego.

Egos are the main actors in the network, while alters are those the egos have ties with within their network. An ego-centric network "comprises an ego, or individual node in a network, and nodes that are closely related to the ego along with all edges between those nodes. An ego-centric network describes the local view of an ego in a network" (Harrigan et al. 2012, 563).

Sample Population and Places of Interaction Studied

As mentioned earlier, the data analysed for this chapter was drawn from a 2016 social network study of Congolese migrant relations with South Africa in Empangeni. A random sampling technique was employed to select respondents from a sample drawn from the Congolese Community of Empangeni (COCOE) which has more than 48 registered members that were part of the Congolese immigrant community residing in the area. Eight members of the association were randomly selected using the lottery sampling technique.[3] In line with research ethics, pseudonyms are used to protect the respondents' identity. The 48 members of COCOE were segmented into two class groups (middle class and working class), and 12 (6 males and 6 females) were randomly selected from each of class these groups for the 2016 study. These 12 Congolese were then asked to name one South African they considered a closest tie they are connected to through work, friendship or marriage. The 12 South Africans named were also interviewed to test for reciprocity making a total of 24 respondents. Out of these 24 respondents, 4 (2 Congolese migrants and 2 South Africans) were then selected for a biographical examination of their dyadic relationships in line with the objectives of this chapter.

The spaces of interaction identified and analysed for the presence or absence of friendship and conviviality include *workplaces*, *religious* and *neighbourhood* settings. According to Amin (2012, 79), workplaces and religious settings are sites that enable potential interaction of host members and "unknown strangers" and are "the sites for coming to terms

---

[3] Before the lottery was done, all 40 members were divided into two groups; A and B representing the middle class and working class, respectively, then each group was further sub-divided into male and female. These categorizations were made on the strength of the information gleaned from COCOE's membership database. The classification of class and the equal representation of gender was done to determine if class and gender are predictors of the relationships between the Congolese immigrants and South Africans in Empangeni.

with ethnic difference" (Amin 2002). However, as we will see, not all contact or interactions within these spaces led to friendship, conviviality and concord lending support to the ambivalence or paradoxical effects of contact; that it can also lead to hostility and exclusion (Durrheim et al. 2014). In this case, Congolese migrants had various experiences with their South African alters that shaped their perceptions of South Africans and the nature of the network ties that were formed. The findings from their interviews were analysed thematically in line with the study objectives and are presented under the following themes: reason for migrating to South Africa, neighbourhood settings, workplace ties, friendship ties, kinship ties and most important South African tie.

Presentation and Discussion of Findings

As previously indicated, the 2 Congolese migrants whose stories were selected for a biographic analysis for this chapter are Jean-Pierre Kalumba, and Felicity Nzamwita and their South African ties are Zungu Ndlovu and Ntombi Dlamini, respectively.

Jean-Pierre Kalumba (Interviewed 13/09/16)

Migrating to South Africa

Jean-Pierre is a 48-year-old male from Tshopo Province in the Democratic Republic of Congo (DRC). He is a medical doctor working in a Public Hospital in Empangeni and was sampled as middle class. He is married to a South African woman (Nelisiwe) from KwaMashu in KwaZulu-Natal Province, and they have 3 children. Jean-Pierre studied medicine at the University of Lumumbashi in the DRC and migrated to South Africa in 2004. In 2005, he passed the medical board examinations in South Africa after which he obtained a licence to practice and has since then been working as a family medicine doctor, starting in Durban before moving to Empangeni in 2010. According to him, "I migrated to South Africa because of the development crisis in the DRC which did not give him much hope for the future, and with information from my senior sister who had migrated to South Africa I decided to also move here to work as a doctor and to start a family of my own".

When asked why he choose to come to Empangeni, Jean-Pierre who had previously lived in Durban, where he met his wife, said he relocated to Empangeni because of his sister and other relatives from the DRC who were well settled there. In his words, "my family members told me South Africans in Empangeni were more accommodating than those in Durban, so it was an easy decision for me especially since I had family there here in Empangeni".

Living Arrangements
Jean-Pierre owns a home in an upmarket residential area in Empangeni just 22 kms from Ngwelezane Hospital where he works. He considers his South African neighbours very welcoming, friendly and genuinely good. According to him:

> I feel a sense of community and belonging here as I socialise freely with all my neighbours both Black and White. My wife is friends with several other neighbours' wives, and we do a lot of exchange visits. We are almost like family with everyone and sometimes I wonder if I could have experienced such good neighbourliness at home in Congo.... During the 2015 xenophobia violence in Durban, there were rumours that it was going to spread to Empangeni, and some foreigners were actually killed in their business premises in Station. The rumour also had it that they would come house to house to fish out foreigners and even though I trusted that my neighbours would protect me, I stressed about whether they would really help because during a home owners meeting in 2014 I had a serious disagreement with a South African on our street who didn't like my position on replacing our security company which was owned by a Black South African. He felt I was not supportive of Black business because I was a foreigner so he told me to 'pack and go back to Congo if you can't support us here'. It was really hectic then and the others chastised him immediately. However, my worries were put to rest when other neighbours came together to assure me that I am safe and should never feel alone. This was very reassuring for me. (Interview with Jean-Pierre, 13/09/16)

Jen-Pierre's living arrangements reflect intergroup contact that fostered both concord and discord as his relationships with his South African neighbours showed both convivial and conflictual relations. He describes an instance of a neighbour who was quite unfriendly with no interaction irrespective of the spatial proximity between them. In sum, Jean-Pierre acknowledges that the relationships with his neighbours are mostly friendly and cordial although this is limited by the demanding nature of his work which makes him see and interact with his neighbours less than he should. However, we note that the friendliness Jean-Pierre enjoys from his neighbours may also have a lot to do with his occupation as a medical doctor considering the universal goodwill doctors enjoy wherever they are.

Workplace Ties
In terms of workplace interactions, Jean-Pierre also paints a mixed picture of concord and conflict which is not uncommon. According to him, "the hospital is where I spend more than two-thirds of my time daily, and it has become like a home and family of colleagues and patients, and as you know, even in the family there is peace and conflict, good and bad, ups and downs, such is life". When prompted further to talk about the "good" and "ups" of his workplace interactions, Jean-Pierre said:

> Oh, plenty of the good you know. I have been working at this hospital for more than 6 years now and I have come to establish friendships with different colleagues; doctors, nurses, lab technicians and other support staff including even the cleaners and security people. These relationships are crucial to my work daily and without them I will not be able to function properly. I am nice to them and they are also nice to me...Some of the work relationships have even developed beyond the hospital as we sometimes visit each at home other and organise braai during festive periods when I am not taking my family away from Empangeni or South Africa. Apart from workplace wellness, these relationships also help me deal better with my patients. For example, apart from my wife, my nurses have taught me a lot about Zulu culture and belief systems which help me interact better with my patients. Generally, I can tell you I mix better with my Zulu colleagues (especially doctors) than I mix with my fellow African brothers who are doctors in the hospital. But like I said it before, there are also not so good aspects of the workplace relationships and interactions. (Interview with Jean-Pierre, 13/09/16)

Highlighting the conflictual aspects of his workplace interactions, Jean-Pierre contended that:

> I have had more instances of frictions related to xenophobia from my seniors (hospital managers) who are South Africans than from my colleagues on the same level with me or those below me. I am really not sure if it was just jealousy or insecurity but some of them have openly reminded me of my migrant origins when work related disagreements get tense. These are frequent....I won't mention names or give details now

but the most recent was about 2 years ago when the Consultant (South African) who I report to queried me for an issue that other doctors don't get queried for. I explained what happened but later asked her wondered why I had to be queried for such an issue, and I was quickly told if I don't like been reprimanded, I must go back to Congo! My interaction with patients is ok as its mostly professional but sometimes I develop friendship with a few regular ones, and they even invite me to attend important family events. I also invite them for braai at home sometimes.

At Jean-Pierre's workplace, contact with colleagues, which was both vertical and horizontal, evolved from the formal/professional to friendship that went beyond the workplace, while in some instances, it was hostile. This reflects the paradoxical effect of contact (Durrheim et al. 2014). In terms of the types of ties identified in his workplace, these include state and event ties. The state ties include relationships with his colleagues, while the event ties are those with patients he sees less frequently. He describes the nature of his state ties with his colleagues and regular patients as formal and friendly with minimal hostility. This is consistent with Pettigrew (1998) assertion that intergroup contact that is frequent and results in informal relations usually evolves into cordial and more intimate relations. Similarly, Miguel and Tranmer (2009, 16) find that frequent and unavoidable interaction between migrants and members of the host community would ultimately lead to the development of mutually supportive relationships. In many ways, these kinds of interactions blur social boundaries between both groups which then fosters integration.

Friendship Ties
In terms of friendship ties, although Jean-Pierre belongs to COCOE (local community association of Congolese in Empangeni), he has more South African than Congolese friends and in fact indicates that his closest friends are South Africans. According to him, "my marriage to a South African woman and close relationships with colleagues at work has made me to lean closer to South Africans than Congolese. I know many; both South Africans and my fellow Congolese would expect this, but it is my truth and it is known only to me". Despite this, Jean-Pierre asserts that it is all not rosy even with his close friends as there are incidences that sometimes remind him of his roots as a Congolese:

…There are times I get the feeling I am not truly appreciated because of where I come from. I feel many of my south African friends are fiends with me because of my position as a doctor and what they can get from me. Whenever we have disagreements with some of them, I hear the snide comments they make about my Congolese worldview and how it is so different from the South African worldview hence I can't understand. This frustrates me a lot as I feel I am giving my best but it's like I am never going to be understood deliberately because I am seen to be different… but this is with very few individuals who have also shown to be very self-centred even in their relationships with other fellow South Africans we are common friends with, so I have accepted it as more to do with their individual character traits than something used against me alone.

From Jean-Pierre's network, we can see that cultural differences do dissolve as a result of interaction and assimilation over time. This implies that contact can break cultural boundaries between diverse groups such as those in migrant/host relations. We see that in spite of belonging to COCOE and having Congolese community to choose from as close friends, Jean-Pierre chooses to have more South African close friends. According to Macy et al. (2003), the more frequently diverse people interact, the more similar they are perceived to be, and this leads to a sense of homogeneity. It is instructive that Jean-Pierre explains the challenges of his friendship with some of his close South Africans as more to do with individual personality differences than nationality differences. He in fact clarifies this further by explaining how cultural diversity can be an asset for integration and not a tool of division. According to him:

I started with myself by acknowledging that I also have my own biases based on what I assume are differences between us. Once I accepted that, I decided to be open to learn about Zulu culture, and to also teach my friends my Mbanga culture starting with my wife and children who are part Congolese and part South Africans. I have also learnt the Zulu language which I speak well. I must tell you that this has helped me in building very good relationships with the Zulus… Many of my friends have also learnt to eat Congolese food, enjoy Congolese music and I actually have a patient turned friend who gave his children Congolese names just to celebrate me in their lives.

As can be seen in this case, contact enables both groups to learn about and understand each other better Pettigrew (1998), and this knowledge fosters an understanding that produces conviviality between Jean-Pierre and his South African friends and host community at large. However, as he mentioned earlier, there were instances where Jean-Pierre's own biases and feeling difference as a Congolese impacted on some of his friendship ties. Even though he claims to have overcome them by seeing them as personality issues of the individuals involved, this has not made him to dispel all of his own personal beliefs on certain issues. For instance, "as a devout Catholic, I do not believe in traditional cultural practices that involve sacrificing animals to ancestors for spiritual cleansing. I have running problem with my in-laws and some close Zulu friends because I don't participate in these ceremonies".

In this situation, contact did not bridge the "us" and "them" divide; instead, it sparked discord in some aspects of the relations between migrant and host. Cultural differences have a dual effect on Jean-Pierre's relationships with his family and friends. On the one hand, they have impacted negatively on his friendship with South Africans. And on the other hand, cultural differences were bridged through mutual openness to learn aspects of culture, language, food and dressing which helped to grow friendship. For example, Jean-Pierre learnt the Zulu language, learnt to eat Zulu food, wear Zulu clothes, and his Zulu friends also learnt to eat Congolese food, enjoy Congolese music and one even gave his children Congolese names. Also, while Jean-Pierre has assimilated Zulu culture somewhat, he is also conscious of certain differences between Zulu and his Mbanga culture that do not sit well with him, and this indicates selective assimilation.

Kinship Ties

Jean-Pierre's kinship relationships revolve around his wife, children and his wife's family (in-laws). Shedding light on his relationship with his wife, he said:

> I first met Nelly when I was practising in Durban. She was a nurse at the hospital and I first worked at in 2005 and then I got a job as a Medical Officer in another hospital and I moved. We met again at an end of year function at my new hospital and that was when we really started the relationship. A year or so later we became serious and you know, I proposed to her. She was a very decent lady and she was not narrow at all in her views about people and culture so I didn't have a problem deciding to marry her. Anyway, she agreed to marry me and the rest is history...Of course initially there were challenges with her family (my in-laws). They were not sure her

marrying a foreigner was a good thing and some of them really gave us problems but eventually they agreed and the lobola was done and we have not had any major problem since then. Her parents were very supportive especially her father who has now passed on. We are happy together, we have 3 beautiful children, her family is happy, my family is happy, and we are still happy together.

The intimate nature of the contact between Jean-Pierre and his in-laws over time helped to foster convivial relations. In the case, marriage was a tool used as bridging social capital. As Granovetter (1983) explains, this is necessary in ties characterised by relative trust among strangers. Marriage has been described as an indicator of interactive integration, where migrants are included in the primary relationships of the host society (Bosswick and Heckmann 2006, 10). Jean-Pierre's case shows marriage fostered migrant integration as eventually he was accepted into his wife's family as one of their own.

Jean-Pierre also has three children who form part of his kinship ties. These children represent a hybrid[4] of two cultures; Congolese and South African, and this indicate blended acculturation of both cultures producing a cosmopolitan two-in-one (partly Congolese and partly South African) identity.

Most Important South African Tie

In terms of his most important South African tie, Jean-Pierre mentioned Zungu who is a colleague at the hospital he works. He explains that he and Zungu started work the same day as young medical officers at Ngwelezane hospital and they from that day struck an acquittance which evolved into a friendship that has lasted till date. Reiterating his closeness to South Africans, Jean-Pierre described Zungu as his best friend and that their relationship is indeed an example true friendship that transcends family affinity. In his words,

> Zungu is both a friend and a brother. You know you can have a brother who you are not friends with and you can have a friend who is not your brother, but Zungu is both to me. I am actually closer to him than my two brothers, although they are in Congo. It's only been 8 years since

---

[4] Hybridity is a process that involves the blending or interaction of two different cultures such that diversities merge into one in ways that lead to the creation of a new hybrid culture and identity.

we met but it's like I have known him forever. Our families know each other and we both attend family functions together. He is my number one teacher of Zulu culture and he has really helped me to understand and embrace Zulu culture. Apart from my wife, he has really been helpful in getting acceptance into my extended family here. He is also a culturally open person because he has learnt French from me and he also knows a lot about our national culture in Congo. Last year (2015) he accompanied me on a visit to my family in Congo and he was very welcomed, he loved it because it was his first visit to another Africa country.

From Jean-Pierre's account of his friendship with Zungu, we can see the presence of reciprocity in cultural exchanges between them and in mutual dependence for social support towards their separate journeys to acceptance and belonging. For Jean-Pierre, his relationship with Zungu is valuable for his integration in South Africa both at the familial and societal as Zungu is central to his learning Zulu culture, interfacing with his in-laws and for meeting his social belonging needs.

Zungu Ndlovu (Jean-Pierre's Tie Interviewed 20/09/16)

Zungu is a 50-year-old male and hails from Newcastle in KwaZulu-Natal province of South Africa. He is a medical practitioner at Ngwelezane hospital. He confirms that he has known Jean-Pierre for about 8 years and that they resumed work at the hospital the same day and became friends immediately. He also confirms that the relationship has grown since then into what he describes as "beyond blood relations" because "he is closer than a brother that one! He is actually my best friend now". When probed further about the nature of their relationship Zungu said:

> I never imagined I would have a best friend that is not South African. Don't get me wrong, I have been around a bit and I have had good friends right from university days that are not Zulu or even South African, but JP was just different. Over time, we became very close and now we are closer than brothers so and he is now my best friend. Although I am a bit older than him, I talk to him about very difficult things you can only talk to family about. I have learnt a lot from him. He is a good man with a good soul that one.

This clearly shows that Zungu values the relationship just as Jean-Pierre does. For example, he says he has learnt a lot from their friendship and depends on Jean-Pierre as a confidant and adviser. That they both value the relationship and mutually benefit from it in varying ways indicates a symmetry that is characterised by reciprocity and mutuality in the tie. Also, the cultural differences between them did not hinder the formation of ties, but instead fostered a cultural exchange that made them both cosmopolitan; open and accommodating of cultural diversity. For example, according to him,

> I have learnt to speak French because of JP, I have been to the DRC and although I assumed before then that we were different, my trip to the DRC taught me that Africans have a similar worldview, and there are many similarities in our culture. I have also developed taste for new cuisines such as *Moambe*.[5] Instead of thinking proudly South African, I now think proudly African, and that is very fulfilling for me as an African.

Finally, Jean-Pierre's and Zungu's tie also shows how intimacy of contact fosters conviviality and concord between diverse peoples and groups.

Felicity Nzamwita (Interviewed 14/09/16)

Migrating to South Africa

Felicity is a 41-year-old female who hails from Katanga Province in the DRC. She holds the equivalent of a matric certificate and is a hair salon owner where she also sells hair and beauty products, and her income bracket put her in the working class, category of the sample for this study. Felicity migrated to South Africa in 2001 to join her husband, a high school teacher in one of the public high schools in Empangeni. They have 2 children. Expanding on why she migrated to South Africa, Felicity said:

> I came to South Africa to be with my husband. As a family, we decided he should come first, and he left Congo in 1998 to look for a job because things were very bad in Congo. He got a job as a teacher in 1999 because he could speak English and in 2000, I joined him with our daughter.

---

[5] A traditional Congolese dish made with chicken or fish and cassava leaves, hot pepper sauce, bananas, rice, peanuts and palm nuts.

Felicity claims her husband started as a teacher in a private school in Pietermaritzburg and was retrenched after 5 years there in 2004. Two years later (in 2006), she had to move again, this time with a second child, when her husband eventually got another position in a public high school in Empangeni. As at the time of interview, she had been living in Empangeni for 10 years during which she re-established her hair saloon business. In essence, Felicity is one of the many women who are forced to migrate because of marriage.

Living Arrangements
Felicity and her husband own a two-bedroom apartment in a block of flats close to the Central Business District (CBD). Although they would prefer a bigger apartment in a stand-alone property, the apartment was the best they could afford, and its location was good for her business as it made hers save on transport given its proximity to the CBD where her salon is located. According to her,

> Staying in the flat is the best we can do for now because houses are very expensive now. If we had more money, we would move to a bigger house place because this flat is a too small...you can see. There is too much noise in the evenings and people smoking Dagga (marijuana) every night. Last time we complained about the noise it ended in a fight between us and one of the neighbours, and her husband called us *Makwerekwere*. But there are other neighbours on our floor that are very good to us *nje*[6] so we are not scared. But generally we are not very close with all the neighbours. Everyone minds their own business. We are friendly, we know each other, we greet each other on corridor but we are not close... we don't visit each other. The good thing is some of them come to make their hair in my salon, and they buy my hair products also. I try to be friendly because of my type of business but there are too many issues in our neighbourhood so we try to mind our business with each other.

Felicity's relationship with her neighbours is more cordial than friendly and sometimes cold and hostile. Her response to the question on the nature of interaction with her neighbours shows that she adopts some sort of self-exclusion towards her South African neighbours by minding her business. However, when pushed to talk about "other good neighbours", she indicated that she had a more friendly relationship with other

---

[6] Zulu slang for "but" or "anyway".

neighbours who like her family were also African migrants from Kenya and Zambia one on the same floor as her (Felicity), and the other stayed one floor above her family. According to Felicity "we visit each other as family, they teach me how to cook their food and I also teach them how to make Congo food...I also help to drop or pick their children from school and they help me like that too". Given the nature of interactions between Felicity and her South African neighbours, we can conclude that in her case, spatial proximity did not evolve into social proximity and as such contact did not produce conviviality.

Workplace Ties
As mentioned earlier, Felicity is self-employed and owns a hair salon in the CBD of Empangeni. According to her, "the business is doing well. I also sell hair and other beauty products and I make enough to support my family". She indicates that her clients were mainly South Africans, and she has a loyal customer base who patronise her salon always. She also employs 4 South African workers including a Congolese and Ghanaian making a total of 6 employees. She has a cordial employer-employee relations with all her workers but has very friendly relations with the South African ones "because they help me get customers". However, she notes these relationships start and end at work

> I have a close relationship with my workers from here more than I have with my sister from Congo. The other worker is from Ghana and he is the one cutting men's hair. They accuse me sometimes of being too close with the Southie girls but only me know why I am close to them... They help me get lots of customers, good ones always. So I have to make them happy but our friendship ends at work. We don't visit each other at home. And it works like that for all of us. Most of them are very happy to work with me, I treat them nice too and I give them some commission from customers they bring. But there is one that is hard to please neh.... She is always frowning, always not happy and full of complains. Sometimes she is even rude to me and the others have told me she told them she wishes I was not a foreigner owning the salon so I try to accommodate her because she knows a lot of my customers. But yea, we manage and I have kept them for over 3 years now. To be honest she is getting better every day and as we get to know each other more I don't mind her at all. (Interview with Felicity, 14/09/16)

It is clear that Felicity generally has friendly relations with her work colleagues especially the South African ones who she relies on to sustain her business. According to her, they also rely on her for their employment and commissions for productivity. The relationship between them is thus one of mutual dependence that is sustained through work. Most of the hostility she experiences in her work environment is from her event ties. She identifies another unique relationship that evolved from her interaction with three South Africans that assists her financially.

Friendship Ties
On friendship ties, Felicity indicated that apart from her friendly relations with 3 of her south African employees, she does have "a special Zulu girlfriend". According to her,

> I have a lot of best friends from Africa here, and I don't have a lot of South Africans as friends because I just don't trust them. You know these women are really beautiful in this country and well-shaped, our Congolese men like them too much so I try to be careful not to get too close to them so they don't take my man (laughs). Well I know that's how we Congolese women see them and we gossip about that but I don't want to take chances. But I have this one special Zulu girlfriend. She is different. Mina, sometimes I think she is not from South Africa as in too good to be true! I think she is my best South African friend.

Clearly, Felicity's contact with South Africans did not remove her stereotypes of them, and she acknowledges that herself. These stereotypes impact negatively on her willingness to interact with and form other types of ties like friendships. Although she also indicated that her inability to understand and speak Zulu fluently impacts on her openness to relate more closely with South Africans, she has not made the effort to learn the language. In other words, her attitude to the socio-cultural differences between her and South African cultures did not enable the development of bridging social capital and allow her to develop more network ties. In essence, although she has friendship ties, language was a barrier in their interaction.

Most Important South African Tie
Felicity indicated that her most important South African tie is Ntombi Dlamini her "special Zulu girlfriend". According to her, they met in

church and Ntombi is a huge spiritual inspiration and pillar for her. For Felicity, this spiritual support from Ntombi is the bane of her friendship with Ntombi.

Ntombi Dlamini (Felicity's Tie Interviewed 21/09/16)

Ntombi is a high school teacher in Empangeni. She is from Ulundi and is in her mid-40s. According to her, she has known Felicity for over 6 years and was pleasantly surprised that Felicity choose her as her most important South Africa tie. He describes the relationship as formal and responds that

> Wow! I am really surprised she choose me as her best friend because I have never had reason to believe so on my side. Not that I don't see her as a good friend, I used to think she didn't see me the way I saw her so I always try my best to be there for her spiritually as we are in the same cell group and we meet every week in our different homes apart from church activities in church. I know our African brothers and sisters see us Zulus as not friendly and xenophobic so they don't trust us. However, as a Christian, I believe we are all one human race of brothers and sisters in Christ so I don't mind treating them same way I would treat my fellow South African. But I am very pleased that she sees me like this and I am really encouraged to even be a better friend now.

Although Ntombi had viewed her relationship with Felicity differently until she was named as her (Felicity's) most important tie, which may imply an asymmetric relationship; however, Ntombi has never seen or treated Felicity as an unimportant relationship. She was so pleasantly surprised that she even decided to be a better friend going forward. Asked if the fact that Felicity is an African immigrant impacted on their relationship Ntombi responded thus:

> Not at all. From the very first day we met I just liked her. It was clear she wasn't South African because of the way she spoke but that did not mean anything. Maybe it is because one of my relative is married to a Congolese man and they have children who are now part of our family, so I don't see them as foreigners at all. They are part of me.

Ntombi's response shows that her contact with Felicity and other Congolese has produced a "self-other merging" where she perceives the other's differences as similar to hers. In her case, intergroup contact produced conviviality and tolerance of Congolese. Furthermore, as with Jean-Pierre and Zungu, Felicity and Ntombi's relationship show the presence of mutuality and reciprocity in their dyadic tie which is also symmetric in nature. According to Ntombi, cultural differences did not impact on her relationship with Felicity because there is Congolese blood in her extended family. This made it easier for her to develop ties with Felicity in a mutually beneficial relationship.

CONCLUSION

The four life experiences presented in this chapter show the paradoxical effects of intergroup contact and how these influenced the nature of the ties that evolved. For the two Congolese migrants profiled (Jean-Pierre and Felicity), in certain spatial dimensions, contact enabled the formation of concord as contact had a more positive effect on their ties. However, within other spaces of interaction with South Africans, contact negatively impacted the nature of relations as some were characterised by hostility and exclusion. In some instances, the ties enabled integration of the migrants and in others it did not depending on the parties' responses to each other. For example, Jean-Pierre and Felicity had very good South African friends in mutually beneficial relations that enabled their integration, but they also had instances of hostile responses from South Africans in their neighbourhood (Jean-Pierre) and workplace (Felicity). Overall, the findings show that two major factors enabled South Africans to form relationships with Congolese. First, as seen in Ntombi's case, having familial ties with other Congolese made it easier for her to develop new ties with other Congolese like Felicity. Second, from Zungu's network tie with Jean-Pierre, increased contact with Congolese can enable the formation of friendship ties due to the presence of bridging capital which enables cultural exchange, cultural understanding and acceptance. This is despite the role that socio-cultural stereotypes can play in limiting the formation of ties. For instance, in Felicity's case, her stereotypical stance on the morality of South African women hindered her formation of ties with them both in her neighbourhood and workplace settings. And her very close relationship with Ntombi did not change her attitude to other South African women around her as she conveniently explains Ntombi as "different" because of her involvement in the church.

The relationship between the two Congolese migrants and two South Africans is characterised by mixed responses ranging from exclusion, to assimilation, cosmopolitanism and conviviality. This is consistent with Amin's argument that there are broader categories of relationship between strangers. These evolve with time, spanning a range of responses from hostile to friendly on both sides (Amin 2012). Therefore, alongside xenophobia, conviviality, cosmopolitanism and intercultural exchanges exist in the relationships between Congolese migrants and South Africans. In this way, the binary question of *friends or foes* misses the grey line in between and is as such too narrow to fully capture everyday realities. A network analysis of multiple relationships between African migrants and South Africans would perhaps be more revealing of the nuances that shape relations between these groups.

References

Amin, Ash. 2002. Ethnicity and the Multicultural City: Living with Diversity. *Environment and Planning* 34 (6): 959–980.

Amin, Ash. 2012. *Land of Strangers*. Cambridge: Polity Press.

Bosswick, Wolfgang, and Friedrich Heckmann. 2006. Integration of Migrants: Contribution on Local and Regional Authorities. European Foundation for the Improvement of Living and Working Conditions. http://www.eurofound.europa.eu/pubdocs/2006/22/en/1/ef0622en.pdf.

Durrheim, Kevin, Nicola Jacobs, and John Dixon. 2014. Explaining the Paradoxical Effects of Intergroup Contact: Paternalistic Relations and System Justification in Domestic Labour in South Africa. *International Journal of Intercultural Relations* 41: 150–164.

Granovetter, Mark. 1983. The Strength of Weak Ties: A Network Theory. *Sociological Theory* 1: 201–233.

Harrigan, Martin, Daniel Archambault, Padraig Cunningham, and Neil Hurley. 2012. EgoNav: Exploring Networks through Egocentric Spatializations. Paper prepared for the ACM International Working Conference on Advanced Visual Interfaces (AVI).

Hatala, John-Paul. 2006. Social Network Analysis in Human Resource Development: A New Methodology. *Human Resource Development Review* 5 (1): 45–71.

In-depth Interviews with 4 Congolese Migrants and 4 South Africans, 13–14 September 2016.

Jack, Sarah, M. Rose, and Lorraine Johnston. 2010. Tracing the Historical Foundations of Social Networks in Entrepreneurship Research. Prepared for The 32nd Annual ISBE Conference. www.isbe.org.uk/.../BP09-Sarahjack.pdf.

Jackson, Matthew. 2011. An Overview of Social Networks and Economic Applications. In *Handbook of Social Economics*, ed. J. Benhabib, A. Bisini, and M.O. Jackson, 511–585. Netherland: North Holland Press.

Kadushin, Charles. 2004. Some Basic Network Concepts and Proposition. In *Introduction to Social Network Theory*, C. Kadushin, 3–60. Boston: M.A.

Kadushin, Charles. 2012. *Understanding Social Networks: Theories, Concepts and Findings*. Oxford: Oxford University Press.

Katz, Nancy, David Lazer, Holly Arrow, and Noshir Contractor. 2004. Network Theory and Small Groups. *Small Group Research* 35 (3): 307–332.

Macy, Michael, James Kitts, Andreas Flache, and Stephen Benard. 2003. Polarization in Dynamic Networks: A Hopfield Model of Emergent Structure. In *Dynamic Social Network Modelling and Analysis: Workshop Summary and Papers*, ed. R. Breiger, K. Carley, and P. Pattison, 162–173. Washington: The National Academies Press.

Martino, F., and A. Spoto. 2006. Social Network Analysis: A Brief Theoretical Review and Further Perspectives in the Study of Information Technology. *Psychology Journal* 4 (1): 53–86.

Miguel, Veronica, and Mark Tranmer. 2009. Personal Support Networks of Immigrants to Spain: A Multilevel Analysis. CCSR Working Paper. http://www.ccsr.ac.uk/publications/working/2009-07.pdf.

Mitchell, J. Clyde. 1973. Networks, Norms, and Institutions. In *Network Analysis Studies in Human Interaction*, ed. J. Boissevain and J.C. Mitchell, 15–36. Netherland: Mouton and Co.

Monge, Peter, and Noshir Contractor. 2002. *Theories of Communication Networks*. Oxford: Oxford University Press.

de Nooy, Wouter, Andrej Mrvar, and Vladimir Batagelj. 2005. *Exploratory Social Network Analysis with Pajek*. New York: Cambridge University Press.

Pettigrew, Thomas. 1998. Intergroup Contact Theory. *Annual Review of Psychology* 49: 65–85.

Scott, Richard, and Gerald F. Davis. 2006. *Organizations and Organizing: Rational, Natural and Open Systems*. Upper Saddle River, NJ: Pearson Prentice Hall.

Tesson, Karen. 2006. Dynamic Networks: An Interdisciplinary Study of Network Organization in Biological and Human Social Systems. Ph.D. Dissertation, University of Bath.

Wasserman, Stanley, and Katherine Faust. 1994. *Social Network Analysis: Methods and Applications*. Cambridge: Cambridge University Press.

CHAPTER 10

'First Comes Love, Then Comes Marriage?': Exploring the Narratives and Experiences of South African Partners of Nigerian Male Immigrants in South Africa

Dorcas Ettang and Oluwaseun Tella

INTRODUCTION

Migration flows have occurred for decades around the world. People migrate for various reasons, some for trade and work opportunities, while others seek refuge or asylum from political turmoil and chaos in their countries of origin. As they settle into their new host communities, some immigrants enter personal and family relationships through intermarriage

D. Ettang (✉)
University of KwaZulu-Natal, Durban, South Africa
e-mail: Ettang@ukzn.ac.za

O. Tella
Institute for the Future of Knowledge, University of Johannesburg, Johannesburg, South Africa

© The Author(s), under exclusive license to Springer Nature Singapore Pte Ltd. 2022
C. Isike and E. M. Isike (eds.), *Conflict and Concord*,
https://doi.org/10.1007/978-981-19-1033-3_10

with members of the local population. They give birth to new generations within the countries they now call home.

The number of immigrants in South Africa has increased since the dawning of democracy in 1994. For this chapter, these include refugees, asylum seekers, and economic immigrants. Immigrants in South Africa come from African countries like Nigeria, Zimbabwe, the Democratic Republic of Congo (DRC), Somalia, Lesotho, and beyond, including China, India, and Pakistan. The 2011 census found about 2.2 million immigrants in the country (Statistics South Africa 2011). Immigrants generally experience different levels of integration and resistance from their host communities. For example, Phalet and Swyndegouw (2003) establish that while immigrants in Belgium desire equal rights, opportunities, and access to social services in their host society; in some cases, Belgians are reluctant to accept the increased number of foreigners in their society. Foreigners in South Africa face a similar situation, as evidenced by xenophobic sentiments, violence, and attacks on foreign nationals in different spaces.

Consequently, this chapter argues that immigration goes beyond a political and security issue and extends to socio-cultural implications of immigration. These cultural and social elements emerge from personal relationships between immigrants and key individuals in their host communities like partners, in-laws, children, extended family, and friends. As they embed themselves and build these personal relationships in host communities, similarities emerge between immigrants and hosts. Therefore, governments must consider the different groups that have a stake in the immigration process and the grave consequences their actions can have for partners, children, and the families of immigrants.

This chapter focuses on positive and negative aspects of personal relationships between Nigerian male immigrants and their South African partners. It aims to answer a key research question: What are the experiences of concord and conflict between Nigerian male immigrants and their South African partners? The chapter investigates the experiences of concord and conflict from the perspective of members of the United Nigerian Wives in South Africa (UNWISA) as women who are married or personally involved with male Nigerian immigrants. UNWISA has been selected as a case study because it is the most active organization with a large membership of South African women married to Nigerians in South Africa. They have also engaged politically and socially in a bid to promote their interests and demands. This qualitative study uses a case study approach which delves into the experiences and narratives of members of UNWISA. Focus Group Discussions and Key informant interviews were used to collect data.

Various researchers have examined the experiences of immigrants in South Africa (Vawda 2017; Mavodza 2019), while some have engaged relevant policies (Maharaj 2002), others have focused on their sexual and reproductive health (Freedman et al. 2020). Authors like Isseri et al. (2018) have studied the experiences of migrant learners in South Africa's basic education system. Tella and Ogunnubi (2014) have investigated the nexus between xenophobia and South Africa's soft power while Tella (2016) has examined xenophobia in South Africa using three levels of analysis—individual, state, and the international system. Ettang (2021) has explored the links between Xenophobia, Small Arms and Light Weapons (SALW), and crime. This chapter goes beyond this to examine a largely understudied area—the broader socio-cultural dimensions of host and immigrant relationships in South Africa. In other words, it explores personal relationships that are integral in understanding the trajectories and the various layers of host and migrant interactions.

The chapter is divided into five sections. It begins with an examination of key concepts and issues in immigration within the context of integration; it then presents the case study of UNWISA. Thirdly, it explores assimilation theory and its relevance to the subject matter and discusses key findings from the collected data. The final section reflects on some key outcomes that can be considered to enhance the integration or inclusion of immigrants who have personal and longstanding relationships in the country.

Immigration and Integration

Integration can be defined as 'protection from discrimination, social inclusion, and cultural adaptation in the public domain of the host country while allowing for (and often actively supporting) diverse ethnic cultures and identities in the private domain of family and community life' (Phalet and Swyndegouw 2003). They add that integration is incomplete without granting immigrants political rights, access to full citizenship, and the right to vote (Phalet and Swyndegouw 2003). Hamberger (2009) identifies four components of classical notions of integration, namely:

(a) Cultural integration: knowledge of the host country and some level of understanding of its society and respect for basic norms
(b) Social integration: inclusion in education and welfare systems
(c) Economic integration: access to labour markets and employment
(d) Political integration: the right to vote and to run for office, which is only possible if one obtains citizenship.

Against this backdrop, integration, for an immigrant, involves political, economic, social, and cultural inclusion into their host communities while still embracing diversities in their relationships and private spaces. In the case of UNWISA, Nigerian male migrants have integrated into South African society.

Politically, integration can be defined as a 'loose collection of policies towards immigrants and post-migration minorities' (Hamberger 2009). It, therefore, involves the 'redefinition of national socio-political spaces to incorporate new immigrants' and 'selective extension to non-nationals of legal, social, cultural, and political rights and opportunities that were once the exclusive entitlements of nationals' (Hamberger 2009). Integration, therefore, goes beyond economic integration, and a holistic approach should include political, social, and cultural aspects that are interconnected. Socio-cultural integration is evident in the relationships between male Nigerian immigrants and their partners. This chapter argues that these dimensions of integration are critical to enhancing relationships between immigrants and hosts.

Integration is not a seamless and easy process as immigrants face many challenges, limiting their access to opportunities. In the case of Belgium, for instance, ethnic inequality can be seen in residential segregation and perceptions of discrimination; significant educational inequalities with migrants at a disadvantage; and the fact that migrants are less economically active and are more likely to face unemployment (Phalet and Swyndegouw 2003). The migrant communities in this country include Italians, Turkish, and Moroccan labour migrants and their families, and refugees and asylum seekers. In addition, tensions between migrants and host communities are not new, and the causes vary. However, they are mainly centred around cultural diversity and building homogeneity in host societies. Immigration flows and related ethnic and cultural differences are significant challenges for host countries. In Belgium, public displays of ethnic cultures have been identified as a source of ethnic tension between immigrants and hosts (Phalet and Swyndegouw 2003). There is, however, strong support for immigrants among one another. Ethnic cultures have been crucial in building loyalty and solidarity while also helping groups overcome ethnic disadvantages (Phalet and Swyndegouw 2003).

Cultural integration seems to be the most advanced form of integration in many societies. In the case of Nigerian male migrants in South Africa, they speak the language of their spouse and take part in traditional practices from paying *lobola* (bride price) to different cultural rites and traditions surrounding marriage. Therefore, language is central in understanding the host nation's culture, interacting with others in society, and, most importantly, communicating with one's spouse. It is thus an important factor in ensuring successful integration in all aspects of one's life (Hamberger 2009).

Discourses on immigrants and immigrant-host relations cannot exclude spousal dimensions, which are common as many communities have become multicultural due to intermarriage. These marital dynamics are very strong in countries grappling with immigration, including the United States (US) and the United Kingdom (UK). In the United States, for example, marrying an American and having a family, job, and home are not sufficient to prevent unauthorized immigrants from being deported (Yee 2018). As of 2016, British immigration rules require that its citizens earn a certain income level before their non-European Union spouses can enter the UK, a decision upheld by the Supreme Court (Harrison 2017). In June 2018, it was reported that the South African government had stated that couples must prove that they have been in a relationship for a minimum of two years, leading to protests by immigration experts and lawyers (Thelwell 2018). These and other examples point to increasing pressure on married couples and partners to meet immigration requirements if not, face extreme measures, including deportation. This chapter investigates how Nigerian men have been integrated into South African culture and the challenges their partners and children encounter. It is hoped that the findings will assist the South African government and other key stakeholders in improving the integration of immigrant partners of South Africans.

Assimilation Theory and Host-Immigrant Relationships

Assimilation theory enables an in-depth understanding of cultural integration. Theory and research on assimilation, integration, and incorporation explain how immigrants settle and become integrated into their host societies. Originally proposed by Robert E. Park and Ernest W. Burgess, assimilation theory brings attention to the experiences and views of immigrants and reveals how they have become part of host societies. It posits that, in some instances, immigrants have changed their language and culture to fit into their host communities. A loose definition of assimilation is a decline in or eradication of ethnic and racial differences and their related culture. Assimilation theory is founded on three key ideas, namely:

> Diverse ethnic groups come to share a common culture through a natural process along which they have the same access to socio-economic opportunities as natives of the host country. Second, this process consists of the gradual disappearance of original cultural and behavioural patterns in favour of new ones. Third, once set in motion, the process moves inevitably and irreversibly toward complete assimilation. (Algan et al. 2012)

Assimilation is thus a process where immigrant groups and host communities become more similar in their values, behaviours, characteristics, and norms over time. It, therefore, introduces the notion of 'melting' into the culture of society through an 'inter-generational process of cultural, social and economic integration' (Algan et al. 2012). Assimilation theory is supported by the experiences of various European immigrants to the United States, where they underwent a process of cross-generational social mobility and intermarriage (Algan et al. 2012). As succeeding generations settle into their new host communities, they will experience further integration characterized by a shift from their original cultures. Hamberger (2009) argues that the human capital of migrants are important in their integration. This argument implies that their education and training should not be stereotyped or downplayed but should be advantageous.

In the case of South Africa, unions between South Africans and foreigners produce children who imbibe and perpetuate their parents' ideas, practices, and languages. These second-generation South Africans have greater exposure to host communities. An important premise of assimilation theory, particularly in the context of integration, is that the longer the time spent in a country and with the presence of previous immigrant generations in a host country, there will be stronger integration of immigrants and their offspring in their host communities and improved ability to navigate that environment.

While assimilation theory offers relevant ideas on how groups integrate and become part of the cultures and communities they live in, it is not without criticism. Algan et al. offer multiculturalism as an alternative theory. Multicultural societies are made up of different ethnic and racial groups, with a dominant majority group. In such a situation, immigrants actively define and shape their own identities and are far from passive in this process (Algan et al. 2012). Structuralism, on the other hand, posits that socio-economic differences determine levels of immigrant integration. Thus, unequal access to economic opportunities and social and public services like education, electricity, housing, wealth, jobs, and privilege limit immigrants from fully integrating.

Algan et al. (2012) assert that full assimilation is determined by the extent to which the dominant population accepts groups. Due to their wives' acceptance and support, Nigerian men married to South African women have somewhat assimilated to South African culture. Integration is a complex and multi-layered process that brings with it different experiences. Values, behaviours, and practices are shared between foreigners and their significant others through these experiences. In their study on migration and integration in Europe, Algan et al. (2012) note that first-generation migrants have different experiences from future generations as the former have to contend with gaps in language, citizenship, citizen participation, religion, perceptions of discrimination, and issues of trust, occupation and very importantly, income. Language and citizenship gaps seem to decrease by the second generation.

For this chapter, assimilation theory explores the social and cultural forms of integration between foreigners and South Africans. For instance, Nigerian men have increasingly embraced the culture and practices of their partners and vice versa. The complexities and challenges involved in the process of assimilation are discussed below. The theory also sheds light on immigrant group mobility and how one group's cultural ideas, characters, and behaviours reflect the other through processes like marriage and love relationships.

MIGRANTS AND RELATIONSHIPS—THE CASE OF UNWISA

The United Nigerian Wives in South Africa (UNWISA) was launched in October 2013 to support South African women married to Nigerians. It was formed because of the shared negative experiences of these women due to the nationality of their husbands. According to Respondent 1, the organization's main goal is to 'fight crime, fight stigma, stereotype and prejudices, create a healthy and safe environment for Nigerians in South Africa, and empower women.' Its social activities include hosting soccer tournaments and attending various cultural events. A Facebook page was created in 2013 to build an online community and share new developments and information. On the political front, UNWISA has participated in public protests, anti-xenophobia marches, and media interviews. It is safe to say that its members are knowledgeable on integration processes and contribute to the discourse on migrant relationships and experiences in South Africa. According to Respondent 2, UNWISA stands for every foreigner in South Africa and represents every woman married to a foreigner. Discrimination, abuse, threats of detention, and withholding government services are some of the challenges these women have had to face in their efforts to achieve their goals (Khumalo 2014).

UNWISA has spread its reach, boasting membership in Cape Town and Johannesburg, and aims to establish branches in other parts of the country. There are no statistics on how many South African women are married to Nigerians, and many are afraid to reveal this fact. The Johannesburg chapter boasted 60 members as of January 2014 (Khumalo 2014). Its members include women from various occupational backgrounds, including beauticians, nurses, teachers, traffic officers, police officers, and street hawkers (Khumalo 2014).

Several South African politicians, government departments, the media, and the police have linked Nigerians in South Africa to drug dealing. As far back as 1997, Captain Giacomo Bondesio of the South African Police Service's Aliens Investigation Unit stated that 90 per cent of Nigerian refugees were drug dealers (Morris 1998). In the absence of evidence to support this claim, it is clear that Bondesio jumped on the bandwagon of anti-Nigerian sentiments, which is rife in South Africa. While some Nigerians are involved in illicit activities in South Africa, this is only one side of the story. Many are engaged in legal activities, including professional jobs as academics, medical doctors, and engineers; legitimate small, medium, and large-scale businesses; and postgraduate studies, particularly at the masters and doctoral levels. Most Nigerians that arrived in South Africa before 1993 were in the country to either study or work, and the majority were young, single, and from middle-class backgrounds. Before the emergence of Abacha's autocratic rule in 1993, most Nigerians in South Africa were academics (Morris 1998). The factors that led to the surge in Nigerian migration to South Africa included political instability in their home country, the emergence of black majority rule in South Africa, and the possibility of being gainfully employed. Nigerians have long confronted discrimination in South Africa. Anecdotal narratives show that they are blamed for the high crime levels and the drug trade despite the lack of empirical research. It is thus important to examine both the positive and negative narratives and reports of South African partners of Nigerian male migrants. This chapter also examines their perspectives on the nature of xenophobic attacks and how this has affected relationships, including those with their fellow South Africans.

Findings and Discussions

Motivation for Marriage

The motivation for marriage sheds light on the nature of the relationship between male immigrants and their partners. Most of the respondents met their husbands through friends. It is generally believed that migrants primarily marry South Africans to regularize their stay in South Africa. According to the respondents, almost all their spouses were either asylum seekers/refugees or undocumented immigrants. Respondent 3 noted that while she was courting her spouse, he pleaded with her to marry him to apply for a permanent residence permit. He told her that she could be with another man while they were in the supposedly fake marriage:

> Yes, so he said no, he is not saying I must marry him. If I am not free with that, we can do the partnership. I say, okay, how does it work, partnership work? Then he explains to me that you can still marry another person; it's not like you going to be bound to me. Okay, so we do the partnership until erhm, 2012.

Similarly, Respondent 4 remarked:

> Like in my case, like obviously, I was in love with the guy. I was in love with him. We met in June of 1999, and we married in December. So, what

was the motivation? Of course, I agreed. And we married. I was 19, and we married without my parents there. Obviously, I was in love with the guy. I didn't want him deported.

However, it must be highlighted that these spouses are still happily married with children despite the initial motivation for their immigrant partners to regularize their stay in South Africa. While the South African spouses were involved with the Nigerian men because of love, their spouses seem to have had other motives. As Respondent 2 poignantly put it:

> It is even too sad to the point that most of the women who have even made those men to be who they are today are not there to even eat those fruits that they have put because most of these men, what happens with them, the minute they reach the level they wanted to, they now dump those women, and go and marry at home. And bring those women here.

Negative Experiences in Spousal Relationships

The respondents' general perceptions of Nigerians ranged from arrogant and stubborn individuals to involvement in child prostitution and drug trafficking in South Africa. Respondent 1 commented:

> Uh, you know, as a South African ne, not as a Nigerian wife, it's not easy to interact with Nigerians in particular because they are stubborn, number one. And they feel that they are above everybody, and they know everything [chuckles] you know? So...and they are fault finders. That's the negative side of them, and like they cannot, most of them can't see anything good from other uh person, except if it comes from their side. Ja and ja that's it [chuckles].

Respondent 2 said, 'they forever want to be the one to tell you what to do, in your own country.' She noted that her husband (a Hausa man) avoided interacting with Nigerians and preferred to socialize with Ghanaians. She also highlighted excessive use of vulgar language, particularly the 'F' word, among Nigerians, raising questions about their upbringing. It was also noted that Nigerians lack proper manners in communicating with their children and others around them.

The general disturbing consensus was that Nigerians think they can tell South Africans how to live their lives in their own country. Nigerians' perceived arrogance has been partly responsible for the high levels of anti-Nigerian sentiments. For example, while many nationalities are involved in drug trafficking in South Africa, including South Africans themselves, the general perception is that only Nigerians are involved in this menace. Respondent 2 stated:

> I am not saying Nigerians are the dirtiest people, but they happen to be the people who are exposing themselves to the dirt that is done by everybody. Reason being they don't know how to shut up. They don't know how to say, "I don't know". Everything it's I know. My husband is with Ghanaians a lot. They are doing so much corruption.

Two of the respondents noted that while some nationals, such as Ghanaians, are also involved in criminal activities, including drug trafficking, one does not often hear negative things about them because they are discreet. Many of the respondents also noted that these negative characters are mainly people of the Igbo ethnic group. Respondent 2 argued:

> I am telling you, we are having a factory there, I will be honest with you, we have never had any problem with the Yorubas. But you see, the Igbo side, we always kick them out. Many of the people who are doing tailoring job there, when they arrive in Joburg they arrive in our shop. We give them a place to stay. Most of the designers in Joburg who are from Nigeria because whenever they come, they are told go to Alhaji. And whenever they…I am telling you it's a problem to stay with Igbo people. But Yoruba, number one.

Concerns were also raised around the issue of loneliness, generating questions such as: do Nigerians have family meetings? This stems from Nigerian men's role at home. Under the guise of being busy, they are often absent, spending little time with their family. Respondent 3 shared her experience:

> Honestly, eish, with my husband, I am telling you, we were living like roommates. He will go out early in the morning to go the shop at 7 o'clock, come back at 7 o'clock or 8 o'clock. No talk. He's coming back he is hungry he is eating. Even me I will tell him it's my time to sleep. I must go to sleep. Sometimes the child, he will find the child sleeping and he will leave the child sleeping. You understand? So, it seems like we are not family, we just friends. We are housemates nje. You understand?

You tell him that okay at least one Sunday stay. Let's sit as a family. Okay, he will stay that one Sunday, but he will be sleeping the whole day. "I'm tired.

The respondents also pointed to Nigerians' involvement in drug trafficking and child pornography. Respondent 1 stated that there are Nigerian drug traffickers in every nook and cranny in Johannesburg and that Nigerian criminals kidnapped a union member's sister for child prostitution in 2014. It took the concerted efforts of the organization to rescue the girl in a house in Johannesburg.

Positive Experiences in Spousal Relationships

Despite the negative experiences between these spouses, there are positive aspects of the relationship as both parties have learned and benefited from the other. Respondents noted that the positive contributions of Nigerians include their work ethic, treating women appropriately, providing support to their families, and creating job opportunities. Most of the respondents noted that South Africans have learned a work ethic from Nigerians, who are generally perceived as hardworking. In terms of treating women properly, Respondent 2 commented:

> I would say they took some few lessons from Nigerian men, how to treat a woman. Am I lying? They learn that one, first, because hayi (no) shame bona (them) they can spoil. We can do our hair. Yoh hayi! On that part honestly, it's a positive part with them. And filling up the food in the house. I am happy for that. South African men they can buy maize meal and cabbage. Though we have South African men who do more than that. But for the positive part, also, they know how to go to your home and also help. They don't calculate that this is a child of your mother or your aunty, what. So far you are here, from home, and he has that money to help, they definitely do it.

Respondent 4 noted that this behaviour extends to the whole family:

> … and they take everybody of your family as their own family member. They not erh, erh, they don't cut. Like if you come with 100 people and say, this is my family, they will embrace that. They do embrace the family thing although we were complaining earlier about loneliness and, but they do embrace that thing. If my aunt is coming, he must make sure that, eish

I don't have money, he will go and look for 1000 [rands] that if the aunty says bye, he will say, aunty go with this one. So, ja, that is the positivity about them.

Regarding creating job opportunities, Respondent 3 said that her first job was at a Nigerian-owned cybercafé. Most of the respondents highlighted the support they received from their husbands and other Nigerians in trying times, particularly the death of family members.
Respondent 1 observed:

> In 2011, I lost my father. They were there, like, we saw something that nobody else have seen, like to the extent that the community ask us, when is one of the family dying? Because everywhere I go it was like, "hayi your father's burial, it was happening." You know, it was because of Nigerians. And the community also have adopted the style. Like you know what, you don't have to mourn like heathens.

Respondent 5 concurred:

> I experienced something that made me respect them even more. If you have death, if you are in mourning those people will never leave you on your own. They will come with whatever they can come. And they will put in whatever they can put in. And I can say from my side, when I buried my daughter, we had everything. We spent half of what we were supposed to spend. They stood by us. So, Nigerians know how to support each other.

Similarly, Respondent 2 noted:

> My grandmother passed away in 2011 as well. And it was the first time, South Africans, they saw a Nigerian man in a suit going in front there and throwing the sand there, more than anybody. And to make sure that the food, everything is set in the family. ... They can support.

The respondents also emphasized solidarity among Nigerians as a positive attribute that is worthy of emulation. Respondent 1 shared her experience with her Congolese doctor who said that most people assume that he is a Nigerian and he does not deny it because he feels that no one will mistreat him if he is perceived as a Nigerian. The doctor added that he had regularly witnessed about 10 Nigerians bringing a fellow Nigerian patient to the hospital, only to realize they did not know the patient. They simply assisted them because they are Nigerian. Respondent 1 remarked: 'They can fight as Nigerians, but they will never allow an outsider to come and fight them.'

Most of the respondents noted several ways in which they identify as Nigerian. One of the most important is courage. Many said that they have become courageous because of their relationship with their Nigerian spouse. In addition, they have learnt how to negotiate for the goods they purchase in the markets and malls. Most said that they now talk very loudly. Respondent 6 shared:

> On that point, I remember, me and my husband, and my mother. Me and my husband were talking, so not this talk, the soft talk that we are having right now. Like, [starts shouting] "why did you do that?" "erh you did that!" so my mother said, "why are you two fighting?" I was like, "no we are not fighting [laughter], this is how we communicate." So, I understand exactly what she is trying to say. That's how we communicate because if you speak softly then the person doesn't understand exactly what you are trying to say, but then if you shout that's when they understand. That "oh mummy this is what you want me to do." You see?

Through their relationships, their dress sense has improved as their husbands often emphasize the need to dress nicely in public. Respondent 1 said:

> Guys, don't forget the show-off [laughter]. No, the show-off because truly speaking, we South Africans ne, whenever we go to an occasion, you just dress up only to… for you to feel comfortable. But now I want to make sure that my gele (traditional headgear), pass all the geles that are in the house. You know my attire, my george is the latest, my everything is the latest. You know everything when I enter, the grand entrance, they must feel me, they must feel my presence.

Respondent 4 agreed:

> One other thing that is good about Nigerian men and we forgot to mention, that they can't walk with you looking anyhow. You can't go out. Even my husband will tell you, "no mama go back. I can't sit next to you. Go and change. You can't walk out with me like this." So, you must always be looking your best.

Nigerians have also contributed to the spiritual life of their South African spouses. Most of the respondents claimed that they had grown spiritually. According to Respondent 6: 'And, as you said, spiritually, right, I don't wanna lie, I learnt praying from Nigerians.' Respondent 2 presents an interesting case as she was converted by her husband from Christianity to Islam. She said that it took her seven years to understand Islam and her husband never forced her. According to her, she is now a true Muslim, and she enjoys the religion.

The respondents also expressed their admiration for Nollywood and the Nigerian pidgin English they pick up from the movies. Respondent 4's observation in this regard is noteworthy:

> Ja. This is what we were saying with my kids. You know now, even erhm, the Nigerian movies, there is 168 ROK, we don't want to see those that behave like Americans, we want that Chineeekeeee! We want those shouting. But at first we were like, why now are they trying to change the accents and take...we want those village, now we are saying, where is Mr Ibu? Why don't they put erhm...you know? You know they put all those people, these new guys now want to be like Americans. That's why they gonna lose it. We want that root one, you know? The rootness, the raw.

While Respondent 3 had visited Nigeria several times to visit her in-laws, other respondents had not travelled to Nigeria due to financial constraints. However, they attended Nigerian activities in South Africa, such as Nigeria's Independence Day celebration, the yam festival (ofala) and Anambra Day. On the other hand, Nigerians have benefitted from their interactions with South Africans, especially in public behaviour. The respondents noted that they have learned that it is wrong to spit and shout in public spaces such as malls. In addition, many Nigerian professionals, particularly in medicine and academics, have excelled in South Africa.

Challenges Encountered as a Result of Marrying a Nigerian

The respondents cited some challenges that accompany being married to a Nigerian man. These include name-calling (such as paper wives and gold diggers). According to Respondent 1, South Africans often regard women in relationships with Nigerians as prostitutes, HIV positive women, and gold diggers that run after drug dealers. South Africans do not usually get involved with a South African woman that has dated a Nigerian. On the other hand, many Nigerians do not regard South African women as suitable for marriage and often discourage Nigerian men from marrying them.

Respondent 6 noted that women who are married to Nigerians suffered discrimination at the workplace. She said they are often overlooked for promotion and must endure comments like, 'So you are married to a Nigerian, you want to bring corruption to work?' Respondent 2 noted discrimination in social welfare such as Reconstruction and Development Programme (RDP) houses. Access to funeral and medical policies is also limited. She poignantly stated that they have become aliens in their own country. When Respondent 5's father discovered that she was involved with a Nigerian, he remarked: '"Why did you choose to be with this nation? Why did you choose a Nigerian man?" and he was like, "do you know that this is the worst nation on earth?"'.

Similarly, her uncle asked: 'what were you thinking? That is the worst nation you can meet with.' Other respondents noted that several women had been disowned by their families because they are married to Nigerians. They also said that they are treated unfairly in public spaces due to their husbands' accent and children's names. During xenophobic attacks, their children cannot attend school. Respondent 2 noted that her child missed examinations during the 2008 xenophobic attacks. Children also hear bad stories about Nigeria in their schools and among their peers, with negative consequences. Respondent 1 recalled:

> On Heritage Day, my son (8-year-old) refused to put on his, erh, chief clothes. The reason being, he said South Africans are going to toyi-toyi (protest dance) against him. [chuckles] Seriously. I ask him "why are you saying that?" "No, mummy, even I don't want to be a Nigerian anymore. I want to be a Zulu now. Change my name." I am like, "no but you are a Nigerian". "Mummy, Nigerians, they are feeding children drugs, they are doing this." I am like, after he went on like warning his sister. Like, "Ngozi don't follow Nigerians. They say Nigerians are bad. They will take you, they will put you in one dark house and feed you drugs."

Many of the respondents also highlighted xenophobic tendencies among their neighbours. Respondent 4 stated:

> They have come to our house. It was said that we are drug dealers because we had a…it was a palace. So, it was always full. Like, Nigerians were holding meetings. Igbos, like the Igbos were staying in our compound.

So, it was always full. It can be full Friday, Saturday. Maybe 20 cars, 30 cars, like, because we had a huge yard. So, now the neighbours got tired and said we were manufacturing drugs. They manufactured a huge story, in such a way that it's not ordinary police that came. It was only white police. I didn't know that we still had so many white police. And they were not wearing uniform. The two people that were wearing uniform, were blacks who were watching us when we were going to the toilet, they will follow you. When you say, "I want to go and take the child", they think you are flushing the drugs. They searched and searched, white people. Searched the grounds, searched…mina, I am even thinking, my husband and his people are arrested, because I was thinking, this a frame up. What type of police who speak Afrikaans? Where did they come from, in Joburg, here? They came from the head office of police. Ja, they searched and searched and searched. Eventually, they didn't find anything, so they left. (Interview with Respondent 4, 2020)

Respondent 1 narrated her experience when the Hillbrow councillor invited her to talk about Nigeria and UNWISA's activities to a gathering of about 500 people. The moment she was introduced as a Nigerian wife, the audience started laughing and making fun of her. The Councillor then interceded: 'You know you people are hypocrites. You are dating Nigerians. You are eating their food. When you go to their restaurant, it's only you South Africans. You are watching their movies. Why are you hiding?'.

Institutional Barriers to the Integration of Nigerians in South Africa

A major barrier identified by all the interviewees is the issuance of permits to their spouses and children. They noted that they often struggle to obtain identity documents for their children because their fathers are foreigners. They are usually required to provide numerous documents to show that their children were born in South Africa. Respondent 2 noted that,'… Now, I had to go back to where my child was born, that is 16 years, because he was 16 that time. I had to go back where he was born 16 years ago, just to prove that my child, for real, that he was born here.'

While most of the respondents felt that South African immigration laws and officials are xenophobic towards foreigners, they argued that it is mainly directed at Nigerians. Respondent 2 recounted an incident she witnessed when South African police arrested a Nigerian refugee. She said that they checked his asylum permit and when they discovered that he was

Nigerian, they became furious. They then told Respondent 2: 'You know what, we are very sorry my sweetheart, but honestly the government doesn't want Nigerians again. We are even told in our offices; Nigerians are no longer accepted.' Other respondents noted that anti-Nigerian sentiment is not peculiar to South Africa but also exists in countries such as Canada and Ireland. They argued that this partly stems from Nigerians' unruly behaviour such as avoiding joining queues and taking short cuts in government departments. Respondent 5 shared her personal experience.

> Between 2007 and 2008, they refused. They asked me, no, they asked him, erh, he went with his passport and asylum document, they told him it's double identity. When he asked for the correct information, they said there was no such thing as double identity, they did not want you to get married. They took him inside a room and they started shouting at him, and telling him this, and this and this. When he came out, he said, "let's go." They told me that I should keep quiet, a child is nothing. A child doesn't mean that he loves me. A child doesn't mean that he wants to stay with me.

She added that this occurred three times before they eventually got married. Respondent 2 had a similar experience.

The respondents also narrated their ordeals with the South African police. According to Respondent 5, the police often exploit Nigerians. Traffic police often demand bribes from Nigerians irrespective of whether their vehicle and driver's licences are in order. Respondent 1 was with friends, drunk and driving at night without switching on the headlights. The police stopped them and asked for the driver's licence, but she did not have it. They argued with the police, prompting the latter to state that they prefer to deal with Nigerians and taxi drivers who are always sober and willing to bribe when they break traffic laws.

UNWISA has faced challenges concerning funding administration and various projects and activities. According to Respondent 2, funding and sponsorship have been difficult to obtain because UNWISA members are married to Nigerians. She cited one such response: 'You are having husbands who are selling drugs. You will not get such funds from me.' Funding has had to come from their donations and Nigerians outside South Africa. There have also been internal challenges. According to Respondent 1, these have included different individuals vying for leadership positions, divergent views on the role of the organization and members leaving. All of these have undermined its capacity to become an effective organization. UNWISA has also been confronted with challenges in its efforts to improve the plight of Nigerian men. According to Respondent 1, these include cultural clashes as Nigerian men are secretive and do not want others to know they are suffering; they are suspicious, and this limits their ability to open up and get assistance; there is a lack of trust between UNWISA and Nigerian men, and Nigerian men prefer to seek support through other means like the Nigerian Union of South Africa (NUSA).

Conclusion

This chapter examined the experiences of concord and conflict in the relationships between Nigerian male immigrants and their South African partners using data gathered by focus group discussions and interviews with members of UNWISA. The chapter brought out both positive and negative aspects of these relationships, the challenges both parties have encountered and the institutional barriers to their integration into South Africa. The narratives and experiences of those closest to foreigners—their partners—provide significant insight into the dynamics and challenges that both foreigners and host communities must contend with. UNWISA has taken on the role of protecting and representing the interests of foreigners by being involved in various activities, including marching against police brutality against foreigners, calling for the improvement of Home Affairs processes and activities, fighting social ills, raising awareness, and educating foreigners on their rights.

The findings suggest that integration and assimilation policies and programmes are imperative to improve relationships between foreigners and host communities. Therefore, government departments, especially Home Affairs, should play an integral role in providing the necessary documentation. Other important stakeholders include organizations representing migrants' interests, embassies, and the South African Police Service (SAPS).

Some of the recommendations gleaned from the data include:

1. Educate and inform Nigerians of their rights and the grievances South Africans have against them to create a healthy environment where Nigerians and South Africans can live together in harmony.

2. Engage Nigerian leaders, the Nigerian embassy, councillors, the police, and Home Affairs officials to guarantee a positive and healthy environment for Nigerians.
3. Organise campaigns across South African communities to inform and educate the locals about Nigerian culture and its people to forestall anti-Nigerian sentiment.
4. Conduct rigorous research through interviews to investigate the level of Nigerians involvement in criminality.
5. Educate South Africans about Nigeria's contribution to the struggle against apartheid and contemporary Nigeria-South Africa relations.

REFERENCES

Algan, Y., A. Bisin, and T. Verdier. 2012. *Cultural Integration of Immigrants in Europe*. Oxford: Oxford University Press.
Billiet, J., A. Carton and R. Huys. 1990. *Onbekend of onbemind?* Leuven : KUL Sociologisch Onderzoeksinstituut.
Boswell, C. 2003. *European Migration Policies in Flux: Changing Patterns of Inclusion and Exclusion*. Oxford: Wiley-Blackwell.
Ettang, D. 2021. South Africa: Xenophobia, Crime and Small Arms Proliferation. In *Palgrave Handbook of Small Arms and Conflicts in Africa*, ed. U.A. Tar, and P. Onwurah. Cham: Palgrave Macmillan.
Freedman, J., T.L. Crankshaw, and V.M. Mutambara. 2020. Sexual and Reproductive Health of Asylum Seeking and Refugee Women in South Africa: Understanding the Determinants of Vulnerability. *Sexual and Reproductive Health Matters* 28 (1): 324–334.
Gordon, M.M. 1964. *Assimilation in American Life: The Role of Race, Religion, and National Origins*. New York: Oxford University Press.
Hamberger, A. 2009. Immigrant Integration, Acculturation and Social Integration. *Journal of Identity and Migration Studies* 3 (2): 2–21.
Harrison, E. 2017. Couples Speak of Pain Over Spouse Visa Rules. *BBC News*, February 22. https://www.bbc.com/news/uk-35552289.
Isseri, S., N. Muthukrishna, and S.C. Philpott. 2018. Immigrant Children's Geographies of Schooling Experiences in South Africa. *Educational Research for Social Change* 7 (2): 39–56. https://doi.org/10.17159/2221-4070/2018/v7i2a3.
Khumalo, F. 2014. Fighting to Love their Nigerian Men. *Mail and Guardian*, January 24. https://mg.co.za/article/2014-01-23-fighting-to-love-their-nigerian-men/.

Maharaj, B. 2002. Economic Refugees in Post-apartheid South Africa—Assets or Liabilities? Implications for Progressive Migration Policies. *GeoJournal*, 56 (1): 47–57.
Mavodza, E. 2019. Mobile Money and the Human Economy: Towards Sustainable Livelihoods for Zimbabwean Migrants in South Africa. *Africa Development / Afrique Et Développement* 44 (3): 107–130.
Morris, A. 1998. 'Our Fellow Africans Make Our Lives Hell': The Lives of Congolese and Nigerians Living in Johannesburg. *Ethnic and Racial Studies* 21 (6): 1116–1136.
Phalet, K., and M. Swyndegouw. 2003. Measuring Immigrant Integration: The Case of Belgium. *Migration Studies* XI (152): 773–803.
Statistics South Africa. 2011. Census in Brief. http://www.statssa.gov.za/census/census_2011/census_products/Census_2011_Census_in_brief.pdf.
Tella, O. 2016. Understanding Xenophobia in South Africa: The Individual, the State and the International System. *Insight on Africa* 8 (2): 142–158.
Tella, O., and Ogunnubi, O. 2014. Hegemony or Survival: South Africa's Soft Power and the Challenge of Xenophobia. *Africa Insight* 44 (3): 145–163.
Thelwell, E. 2018. New Immigration Rules: What Rights do Foreign Spouses Have? *News24*, June 18. https://www.news24.com/News24/new-immigration-rules-what-rights-do-foreign-spouses-have-20140618.
Vawda, S. 2017. Migration and Muslim Identities: Malawians and Senegalese Muslims in Durban, South Africa. *Journal for the Study of Religion* 30 (2): 32–74.
Yee, V. 2018. A Marriage Used to Prevent Deportation: Not Anymore. *New York Times*, April 19. https://www.nytimes.com/2018/04/19/us/immigration-marriage-green-card.html.

CHAPTER 11

How Can Contact Foster Concord? An Analysis of Relations Between Mozambican Migrants and South Africans in Mpumalanga Province in South Africa

Efe Mary Isike

INTRODUCTION

Before delving into the main issues of this chapter, it is pertinent to conceptualise what xenophobia is generally and its meaning in the South African context. There exist various definitions of xenophobia in the field of migration studies. Bosch et al. (2008) define xenophobia as a tenuous fear of people who are labelled foreign and are also perceived as responsible for socio-economic problems that plague the receiving countries which invariable results in host members' penchant to stereotype them. Yakushko (2009) explains it as "a form of attitudinal, emotive, and

E. M. Isike (✉)
Department of Education Innovation, University of Pretoria, Pretoria, South Africa
e-mail: Efe.isike@up.ac.za

© The Author(s), under exclusive license to Springer Nature Singapore Pte Ltd. 2022
C. Isike and E. M. Isike (eds.), *Conflict and Concord*,
https://doi.org/10.1007/978-981-19-1033-3_11

behavioural prejudice toward immigrants and those perceived as foreign". There are various dimensions of xenophobia. This is the case because of the complexity involved in defining who is foreign. The word foreign does not always connote that the person is an immigrant. In fact, being foreign is a social classification which involves the othering of people based on various social categorisations. Brons (2015) describes othering as a process that entails

> the simultaneous construction of the self or in-group and the other or outgroup in mutual and unequal opposition through identification of some desirable characteristic that the self/in-group has, and the other/out-group lacks and/or some undesirable characteristic that the other/out-group has, and the self/in-group lacks. Othering thus sets up a superior self/in-group in contrast to an inferior other/out-group, but this superiority/inferiority is nearly always left implicit.

Flowing from this xenophobia can be described as the fear possessed by the self towards the other. Mukomel (2015) in his study identifies the various dimensions of xenophobia based on different types of hierarchical social categorisation between the in-group and the out-group. These include ethnophobia, migrantophobia, Islamophobia among others (Mukomel 2015).

Within the South African context, xenophobia takes a unique dimension. In fact, Mngxitama (2008) observes, that conceptualising it as xenophobia is myopic as it does not fully explain the historical context and nature of the othering. The othering is directed to migrants but not every type of migrant. These out-groups in the country that are targets for attacks are African migrants from within the continent. Migrants from outside Africa are referred to as tourists while those from within are labelled foreigners and stereotyped as *Amakwerekwere*, which is a derogatory name for African migrants. Neocosmos (2006) contends that xenophobia in South Africa is a product of the type of state politics which evolved after apartheid. He argues that this politics produced a kind of belonging which was based on indigeneity rather than the more inclusive type which existed during apartheid among all blacks which was built on pan Africanism (Neocosmos 2006). After the demise of apartheid, a new rainbow nation was built on the premise of South Africans for South Africans. This new nation of South Africans delineated the type of Africans to be included because it was based on a new identity that was based on the notion of exceptionalism. Thakur (2011) defines this new identity among South Africans as "positively un-African", which implies that being African is synonymous to negativity. Matthew Beetar (2015) describes this new identity as exclusionary nationalism that implies "how proud one is to be South African and if you don't buy into that then just leave the country (!). For to set up the parameters of South Africanness means to fundamentally define who does NOT belong". Flowing from this, the type of xenophobia that has evolved in South Africa was a mixture of Afrophobia and Negrophobia (Mapokgole 2014). Limiting it to Matsinhe's (2011) analogy of Afrophobia does not do justice to understanding xenophobia in South Africa. This is the case because the othering is targeted at not just blacks or the Negro race but blacks who migrated specifically from the African continent. Xenophobia in South Africa most times does not only result in hostilities towards African migrants but also violent conflicts between them Black South Africans. We, therefore, cannot exclude conflict from xenophobia in South Africa.

However, while this chapter does not debunk the existence of Afrophobia and Negrophobia, it in line with the purpose of the book, explores spaces of contact between African migrants and their South African hosts which produce conviviality and concord. The chapter thus helps foreground the argument that beyond the hostilities and intergroup conflicts, there exist spaces of interaction between African migrants and South Africans that is convivial and produces concord between them. In this, regard, this chapter focused on the relations between Mozambican migrants and South Africans in Mpumalanga, a province known to host a high number of Mozambican migrants. The study employed Contact hypothesis as a theoretical framework to answer whether contact between South Africans and Mozambicans only exacerbated conflict or also reduced discord and fostered concord between them. Contact theory argues that interaction between diverse groups in some instances reduces discord and promotes concord, thereby creating conviviality between them (Pettigrew and Tropp 2008). Contact does not always remove discord and conflict in intergroup relations. There must be certain conditions present within the spaces where contact takes place to enable the development of conviviality and concord. These conditions include the equality of status of the diverse groups; cooperation among members of diverse groups; the pursuit of shared or interdependent goals; and the presence of social norms (Hamberger and Hewstone 1997; Everett and Onu 2013). Mpumalanga province which is also described as "the place where the sun rises" is the second smallest province in South Africa. The province is a hot spot for migrants from Southern Africa because of its geographical proximity to these Southern African countries and hence the reason why this geographical site was selected for this study. The eastern part of the province borders Swaziland and Mozambique. Mozambique is known to be a labour exporting country to countries in the continent and South Africa in particular (Crush 1999). South Africa's mining and agricultural sectors have depended on labour migrants from Southern Africa for a long period of time (Maharaj 2004). Most Mozambicans are known to be migrant workers in farms and mines in South Africa. These movements date back to 1909, when the colonial government in Mozambique signed the Mozambique Convention with the government of South Africa which allowed the flow of labour migrants from Mozambique to South Africa (Azevedo 2002). The early 1990s also saw a great influx of Mozambican labour migrants into South Africa because of the economic decline in the agricultural sectors in the sending country. According to Peberdy (1998), approximately 350,000 Mozambicans migrated into South Africa between 1980 and 1990 due to civil war and drought in the sending country. These labour migrants took up jobs in the mining and farming sectors in South Africa. However, studies show that the migration flow of labour migrants from Mozambique into South Africa reduced during the twenty-first century. For instance, from 1996 to 2005, there was a decline in the number of Mozambicans employed in South African mines due to the implementation of strict immigration legislation (McDonald and Jacobs 2005; Crush et al. 2006). Irrespective of this decline, South Africa still hosts a large stock of Mozambican migrants' majority of who are resident in Mpumalanga Province. This study therefore sought to explain how these groups (the Mozambican migrants and the South Africans) have developed a space of interaction also known as a convivial dome, where the *we* and *they* divide are submerged or renegotiated through contact in ways that fostered concord among them. This is significant given the dearth of studies on how African migrants develop conviviality and concord with South Africans, which enables them to integrate into the host community.

PRESENTATION AND DISCUSSION OF FINDINGS

The study required methodological flexibility to produce a nuanced understanding of this phenomenon. As such a qualitative and network approach were combined with a view to examine the existence of positive relations between Mozambican migrants and South Africans in Mpumalanga. Network study was appropriate because it measures the views of members of diverse groups, thereby providing a nuanced understanding of intergroup relations. As it is well known, the advantaged and disadvantaged members perceive relations differently (Hopkins and Kahani-Hopkins 2004).

Using the network study approach, the central nodes (the immigrants) were asked to identify their most important South African tie, and their dyadic networks are built by the information provided by the central nodes. Simply put, Mozambican immigrants who reside across different areas in Mpumalanga were purposively sampled and each then identified their closest South African tie who also formed part of the respondents for the study. This was done to map the dyadic networks of the migrants with South Africans. This dyadic network approach to primary data generation is useful to the study as it provided a balanced perspective of both migrants and members of the host communities on the nature of relationship between the two groups.

In sum, primary data was generated through qualitative interviews which allowed for flexibility to capture the experiences of both sets of respondents as much as possible. Accordingly, two sets of semi-structured interviews were carried out: one with Mozambican immigrants and the other with their most important or closest South African ties in their various social networks. Purposive sampling was employed to identify a Mozambican migrant and then a snowballing sampling technique was used to elicit at least one close South African tie from the migrant's network.[1] Sixteen Mozambicans resident across different parts of Mpumalanga were purposively sampled and 14 of these directed the researcher to one South African tie making a total of 30 respondents; 16 Mozambicans and 14 South Africans.

---

[1] The basic approach embodied in this method of research is a combined procedure which is used to identify a targeted population and construct the social network from respondents (Rothenberg 1995).

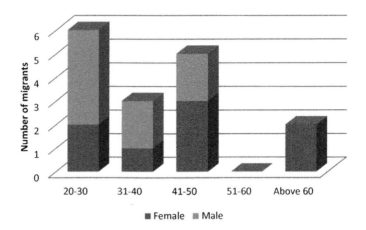

Fig. 11.1 Age and gender of the migrant sample

Demographic Profile of Mozambican Respondents

This section provides descriptive demographic information on age, employment status, and income of the Mozambican migrants to show who these migrants are. The demographics of the South Africans were also collected; however, this was not presented in the chapter because it was not the focus of this study. The demographic profile of the African migrants is presented below in line with the question sequence in the interview schedule.

Age and Gender of the Migrant Sample
Of the 16 Mozambicans sampled six were in the 20–30 years age bracket and this cohort were two females and four males. Only three migrants were between ages 31 and 40, which consisted of a female and two males. Five which consisted of three females and two males were between 41 and 50. There was not any migrant within ages 51–60 bracket. Lastly, two, which consisted of only females, were above 60 years (Fig. 11.1).

Income Qualifications
None of the migrants sampled earned above R2000. In fact, a majority of 75% earned between R0 and R1000. The rest 25% earned between R1001 and R2000. Overall, the sample consisted of working-class migrants

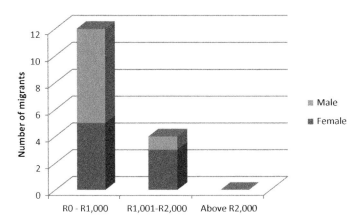

Fig. 11.2 Income of migrants

who mostly engaged in informal activities, which include farming, petty trading, and shopkeeping. Five out of the 16 which consisted of four females and a male stated that they were unemployed and had no means to generate income. This economic characteristic of the sample is intrinsic in the study of migrants' relations with host communities in South Africa. This is because studies have shown that class influences migrants' integration into the host community (Isike 2015) (Fig. 11.2).

Duration of Stay
The figure above shows that most of the migrants interviewed for this study had been in South Africa for several years. Only one had been in the country for less than three years. Three had resided in South Africa for 4–7 years, while 12 had been resident in the country for eight years and above. The duration of stay is very important to migrants' integration as the study shows later because this impacted on the formation of ties through frequent contacts across the two diverse groups. Studies have shown that this impacts on the formation and characteristics of ties between migrants and various members of the host community (Lubbers et al. 2009) (Fig. 11.3).

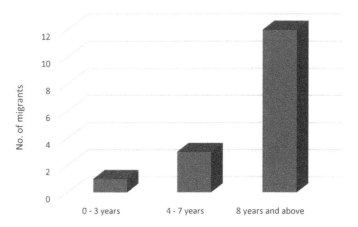

Fig. 11.3 Duration of stay

Formation of Networks

Before delving into the formation and nature of the Mozambicans' networks, it is crucial to provide some context in terms of the reasons why they migrated to South Africa. These reasons include political, economic, and social reasons. A majority of 11 stated that they emigrated from Mozambique because of economic reasons like better provision of goods and services, high poverty rate, and job opportunities. Clearly, South Africa was perceived to have better employment opportunities with better service delivery of services like shelter, education, health, and food. Three out of these stated that they were pushed out of the country due to civil war and political unrest. According to them, the political climate in the country puts their lives and security at risk. Only two migrated to South Africa for family reasons. Most of the migrants came into South Africa before the end of apartheid. They argued that apartheid was not a deterrent to their emigration from Mozambique. To them, although apartheid type of government was not practised in their home country, but the political oppression and economic challenges were worse compared to the receiving country. Only five immigrated to the South Africa during the post-apartheid era. The reasons provided why this move occurred at this latter time was their various ages; some were too young to migrate during apartheid and others were not even born. Another major factor identified by five migrants as a reason for emigration is migrants' desire to join their spouses and kin members who had migrated to South Africa. Clearly, close family networks were instrumental in the migration process of these Mozambicans. Some highlighted that without these ties, they would not have opted for South Africa. Having these networks did provide not only economic but also social support especially in allaying their fears and uncertainties. Clearly as several studies have shown, networks present in the host countries are intrinsic to migration and migrants' choice of destination (Massey and García 1987; Castles and Miller 2003). Social support through the exchange of resources such as information and financial support from personal ties with Mozambicans who had already migrated ahead of them assisted the spatial mobility of these migrants.

To provide some context for the migration trends of Mozambicans to Mpumalanga, it was also of import to explore the various accounts of the migrants on the reason why Mpumalanga Province became their chosen place of residence. The reasons provided by the respondents include the job opportunities in agricultural activities such as farming. Mpumalanga is known to be a hub for agricultural farming dating back to the apartheid era and this pulls migrants to this Province in search of employment in the agricultural market (Mather 2002). Another rationale provided is that the proximity to their country of origin to Mpumalanga makes it an ideal migration spot. This aligns with the findings of Statistics SA (2013) which states that migrants from Mozambique tend to migrate to Mpumalanga because of the geographical proximity and similar culture.

The study investigated the nature of relationships between Mozambicans and South Africans within their networks. The migrants were asked if they were treated differently by South Africans they came across within their various spaces of interaction. Most migrants which consisted of 12 Mozambicans, responded that initially when they immigrated to Mpumalanga, they were treated differently and experienced hostility from South Africans and their relationship with them was conflictual. These respondents mostly comprised those that had longer duration of stay in South Africa. For instance, Respondent F stated that being an African migrant initially impacted on her relations with South Africans.

> When I came, I felt lost because people didn't want to be close to be when I spoke (and this was) because of the difference in language... Some of them treated me like I was a nobody but after some time, we became friends because I learnt what they were about, and they understood me also...

Cultural difference in this case was a barrier to the formation of concord between her and South Africans. In Respondent F case, the initial contact with South Africans did not produce conviviality or concord. This had to do with the limited knowledge the in-group, in this case the South Africans had about the out-group. After more interactions between the diverse groups, the knowledge about the out-group increased and this diminished the prejudice from the in-group. More so, one characteristic that stood out among these migrants is that they had longer duration of stay in South Africa than their other counterparts mentioned below, and this impacted on the development and evolution of networks. Although the nature of relationship between these migrants and their host was conflictual and hostile, with time, mutual interest grew among both groups, and this led to equal perception of identity. As mentioned earlier for the right kind of contact to evolve, there must be equality of status (Pettigrew and Tropp 2008). The relationship must not be asymmetrical and hierarchical as these breed stereotypes and xenophobia. On the other hand, symmetric relationship across diverse groups is usually more "equal or stable" than asymmetric ones (Izquierdo and Hanneman 2006). In this study, Respondent F and her South African ties were able to overcome hierarchies of differences, where the Mozambican's identity is seen as the "Other" or lesser of the two and beforehand contact produced conviviality and concord between them.

There were few others which stated that their interactions with South Africans were mostly conflictual relations and contact in this case did not evolve to concord. Respondent C stated that

> They (South Africans) are not very nice to me. Even when I try to relate with them, they make me feel like an outsider... This is why I don't have a single South African friend. I only make friends with my fellow brothers from home... I also avoid them because to me their culture is very different from mine... I don't like their lifestyle; it is too wild.

Respondent C was a more recent immigrant who came into the country in 2015. However, in his case contact did not develop conviviality and concord not just because of stereotypes from host members but also because of his self-exclusion from South Africans. Berry (2005) explains that "when individuals place a value on holding on to their original culture, and at the same time wish to avoid interaction with others, then the separation alternative is defined. Here, individuals turn their back on involvement with other cultural groups and turn inward toward their heritage culture". In Respondent C's case rather than cooperation, competition existed within their interaction as it was a competition of supremacy of cultural identity. Respondent C perceived his identity as superior to that of the South Africans and rather than lose it through positive contact, he would exclude himself from them. When there is low level of cooperation in intergroup relations, it results in minimal ties and positive interactions (Isike 2015). Clearly, contact did not translate to conviviality and concord as one of the determinants for these favourable conditions was absent. Another reason identified among this group is intergroup anxiety. Swart et al. (2010) explain that this anxiety is mostly experienced by the in-group. In this case, the out-group, which include the migrants, experienced anxiety when anticipating an encounter with in-group because of cultural differences. The respondents had high levels of anxiety as their predisposition towards South Africans where they were hostile to Mozambicans. One of the respondents stated that "They (South Africans) are killers... They hate us and I am a living witness. I don't want to be killed and buried in another man's land". The high intergroup anxiety present within the out-group did not encourage the development of convivial relations or concord with South Africans. It resonates with the argument that in certain instances, contact can produce the opposite effect of reducing anxiety and producing hostility and conflict in intergroup relations (Turner et al. 2007).

The study further investigated the factors that influenced the positive nature of ties that were produced through contact. The study revealed that among most respondents, equality of status was an important factor that propagated the formation of conviviality and concord. Respondent D's dyadic tie stated that,

> We don't see ourselves as different... We are all Africans, there's no difference in this skin (pointing to her arm) ... Why will I treat her differently if she is my sister?

A Mozambican stated that identity is not an issue, he has learnt the cultures of South Africans within his networks and his South African friends have learnt his. In his words,

> ...I can speak Swathi and Tsonga, which I learnt from them...and they learnt how to eat my food.

In this situation, both groups were tolerant towards their differences when they interacted because there was no hierarchy of identity. This clearly supports Pettigrew and Tropp's (2008) argument that when there are equal power relations among group members and groups perceive themselves as equals, convivial ties develop because of contact. Equal power in this sense implies where one does not hierarchically position another identity as inferior. In this sense, equal power produces a conducive space for interaction and possibility of developing conviviality and concord among diverse groups.

However, there were few cases where inequality of status did not instigate the right kind of contact. For instance, competition of resources was an issue that produced inequality of status. Some Mozambican respondents stated that their interaction with South Africans that they work with at the informal economy was riddled with conflicts and hostility. Those migrants that did not identify any dyadic tie with South Africans were in this group. Respondent L, who is a street vendor stated that other street vendors who are members of the host community compete with him for space. He responds that

> ...I was told one time to go home that I am taking food from people's mouth... I was told one time to go back to my home, this is not my home because I was taking their customers.

This depicts a case, where inequality of status hindered positive contact. The migrant's identity was perceived as inferior irrespective of the fact that they were of the same class, engaging in similar informal business. Competition rather than cooperation was the factor that led to discord. As Dovidio et al. (2010) argue, competition fosters discord among diverse groups. This is the case because when groups compete, the "we" versus "them" attitude immediately emerges, and one group tends to see itself as entitled because of its identity that supersedes the other. Inequality of status surmounts because of this, which consequently makes intergroup conflicts and stereotypes unavoidable. This clearly shows that the relations between the two diverse groups in this case must be asymmetrical.

Another important finding was how pursuit of a common goal within the contact between Mozambicans and South Africans enabled the formation of conviviality and concord among them. Most of the respondents (63%) identified having a common interest was a very important factor which enabled the evanescence of hostility and conflict. The various common interests that acted as a bridge towards these differences, identified in the study include religious beliefs, economic activities, and geographical proximity which translated to cultural proximity. Religious communities were spaces that encouraged both parties not to abandon their social differences but relate irrespective of these differences. The common interest in this case was their belief system that emphasised conviviality and concord. For instance, Respondent F stated how that the church which propagated a belief of "oneness in the body of Christ" enabled positive relations develop between him and South Africans. As mentioned earlier, South African respondents were drawn from the most important South African tie of the Mozambicans. Similarly, Respondent F dyadic South African tie identified the church space as a platform where the dynamics of differences did not necessarily lead to hostility and conflict but the desire to pursue the Christian belief served as a mitigating factor towards the development of conviviality and concord.

A different important common interest that enabled the formation of the right kind of contact is economic interest. The study showed that when two diverse groups engaged in economic activities and cooperated in order to achieve mutual economic benefit, hostility and conflict evolved to conviviality and concord through contact. Most of the respondents that engaged in economic activities with South Africans attested that initially there existed stereotypes but these activities enabled them bridge these differences and develop convivial ties with them. Respondent K, who was under the employ of his identified dyadic tie, stated that,

> When I first got the job as a barber in his shop, he (the South African) did not trust me. He even referred to me as *amakwerekwere*... But I had to manage the shop for him. He realised I was very good at cutting and making hair and I brought him a lot of customers that made him change towards me.

When asked about their relationship, Respondent K's dyadic tie confirmed this. He stated that to ensure his business accrued profit he had to work together and develop a cooperative relationship with Respondent K. Another Mozambican migrant stated that there were cases when he had to loan monies to his dyadic tie to bail him from certain financial situations and vice versa. Clearly, mutuality or the common need to attain an objective is an important prerequisite for the right kind of contact. This as shown in the study clearly removes animosities and encourages conviviality and concord (Putnam 2000). This does not mean that it removes differences, but it creates a common ground for interaction and positive relations.

Another common interest that enabled the formation of the right kind of contact is geographical and cultural proximity. As mentioned earlier, most Mozambican migrants opt to migrate to Mpumalanga because of the geographical proximity. One of the major tribes in Mozambique is the Tsonga tribe and they are also resident in South Africa. Studies like Niehaus (2002) states that the Tsonga tribe found in South Africa and Mozambique share a common origin. This similarity in culture and language has enabled them to develop convivial relations. Personal testimonies from South Africans within the dyadic ties of the Mozambicans confirm this. One of them stated that, there is not much difference between them, they speak similar languages, eat same food, and share the same ancestry. To them, this common cultural and geographical interest acts as a bridge for the differences that exist between them. One dyadic tie even stated that there are more similarities than differences between them.

Another factor was empathy that existed between most migrants and their various dyadic ties. Most South Africans mentioned that irrespective of the differences that exist between them and the Mozambicans, they were willing to develop ties with them as there was more that connects them than divide them. As mentioned earlier, the cultural proximity between the two groups became a bridge to the diversities that exist, and this created a sense of empathy that enabled convivial intergroup relations and concord between them. Therefore, empathy produced tolerance and magnanimity among the South African dyadic ties towards the Mozambican migrants.

Moreover, the study noted that such relationships were characterised by various social exchanges and reciprocity. Again, out of the sixteen migrants sampled, only fourteen identified a South African most important tie. Among these dyadic ties, the study showed that there were exchanges of material and social resources that enabled the Mozambicans integrate into the host community and on the flip side, enabled positive attitudes and perceptions develop among South Africans. Among the migrants, these include, shelter, financial assistance, employment opportunities, and emotional support. This emotional support includes advice, affection, and care. Conversely, the South Africans accrued benefits like emotional supports, financial assistance, and cultural knowledge, among others. Hatala (2006: 50) mentions that "relational ties (linkages) between actors are channels for transfer or 'flow' of resources (either material or non-material)". These kinds of support received by South Africans enabled the integration of the Mozambican migrants in Mpumalanga.

Conclusion

In conclusion, the study noted that equality of status, cooperation, and a shared goal fostered the right kind of contact. Also, the three mediators of the contact-prejudice effect influenced the formation of convivial relations which fostered concord between African migrants and South Africans. In most cases, the knowledge about the out-group and presence of empathy led to positive relations. While vice versa was the case where intergroup anxiety was high among members of the out-group because of cultural differences. More so, these ties were avenues for support and resource exchanges between its members. In a nutshell, it can be argued that, within this study, most intergroup ties were developed through contact, and this fostered convivial intergroup relations and concord between them and the integration of migrants in the host community.

References

Azevedo, M. 2002. *Tragedy and Triumph: Mozambique Refugees in Southern Africa, 1977–2001*. Portsmouth, NH: Heinemann.
Beetar, M. 2015. South Africans are Xenophobic. *Mail & Guardian*. https://thoughtleader.co.za/mandelarhodesscholars/2015/04/16/south-africans-are-xenophobic/. April 16 2015.
Berry, J.W. 2005. Acculturation: Living Successfully in Two Cultures. *International Journal of Intercultural Relations* 29 (6): 697–712.
Bosch, N., M. Peucker, & S. Reiter. 2008. *Racism, Xenophobia and Ethnic Discrimination in Germany 2007*. (RAXEN Report / European Monitoring Centre on Racism and Xenophobia, National Focal Point Germany). Bamberg: europäisches forum für migrationsstudien (efms) Institut an der Universität Bamberg. https://www.ssoar.info/ssoar/handle/document/19246.

Brons, L. 2015. Othering, an Analysis. *Transcience* 6 (1): 69–90.
Castles, S., and J.C. Miller. 2003. *The Age of Migration*. London: Macmillan.
Crush, J. 1999. The Discourse and Dimensions of Irregularity in Post-apartheid South Africa. *International Migration* 37: 125–151.
Crush, J., S. Peberdy, and V. Williams. 2006. International Migration and Good Governance in the Southern African Region. Migration Policy Brief No. 17. Southern African Migration Programme (SAMP). file:///C:/Users/u04992726/Downloads/Migration_Policy_Brief_No._17%20(1).pdf.
Dovidio, J.F., J.D. Johnson, S.L. Gaertner, A.R. Pearson, T. Saguy, and L. Ashburn-Nardo. 2010. Empathy and Intergroup Relations. In *Prosocial Motives, Emotions, and Behavior: The Better Angels of our Nature*, ed. M. Mikulincer, and P.R. Shaver, 393–408. Washington, DC: American Psychological Association.
Everett, J.A.C. and D. Onu. 2013. Intergroup Contact Theory: Past, Present, and Future. *The Inquisitive Mind* 13 (2). http://www.in-mind.org/article/intergroup-contact-theory-past-present-and-future.
Hamberger, J., and M. Hewstone. 1997. Inter-ethnic Contact as a Predictor of Prejudice: Tests of a Model in Four West European Nations. *British Journal of Social Psychology* 2: 326–342.
Hatala, P. 2006. Social Network Analysis in Human Resource Development: A New Methodology. *Human Resource Development Review* 5 (1): 45–71.
Hopkins, N., and V. Kahani-Hopkins. 2004. Identity Construction and British Muslims' Political Activity: Beyond Rational Actor Theory. *British Journal of Social Psychology* 43 (3): 339–356.
Isike, E. 2015. Ties that Bind: A Network Analysis of Relationships Between Nigerian Migrants and South Africans in Umhlathuze. Ph.D. Dissertation, University of Kwa-Zulu Natal.
Izquierdo, L.R., and R.A. Hanneman. 2006. *Introduction to the Formal Analysis of Social Networks using Mathematica*. Riverside, CA: University of California, Riverside.
Lubbers, M., J.L. Molina, J. Lerner, U. Brandes, J. Avila, and C. McCarty. 2009. Longitudinal Analysis of Personal Networks: The Case of Argentinean Migrants in Spain. *Social Network* 32: 91–104.
Maharaj, B. 2004. *Immigration to Post-apartheid South Africa*. Geneva: GCIM Global Migration.
Mapokgole, R.B. 2014. *There iI No Black in the Rainbow (Nation): A Bikoist and Fanonian approach to Understanding 'Xenophobic' Violence in South Africa*. London and Cape Town: Trinity College.
Massey, D.S., and F. García España. 1987. The Social Process of International Migration. *Science* 237 (4816): 733–738.

Mather, C. 2002. The Changing Face of Land Reform in Post-apartheid South Africa. *Geography* 87 (4): 345–354.

Matsinhe, D.M. 2011. Africa's Fear of Itself: The Ideology of Makwerekwere in South Africa. *Third World Quarterly* 32 (2): 295–313.

Mcdonald, D.A., and S. Jacobs. 2005. *Understanding Press Coverage of Cross-border Migration in Southern Africa Since 2000*. Southern African Migration Programme (SAMP). https://samponline.org/wp-content/uploads/2016/10/Acrobat37.pdf.

Mngxitama, A. 2008. We Are Not All Like That: Race, Class and Nation After Apartheid. In *Go Home or Die Here: Violence, Xenophobia and the Reinvention of Difference in South Africa*, ed. S. Hassim, T. Kupe and E. Worby. Johannesburg: Wits University Press.

Mukomel, V. 2015. Xenophobia as a Basis of Solidarity. *Russian Social Science Review* 56 (4): 37–51. https://doi.org/10.1080/10611428.2015.1074011.

Neocosmos, M. 2006. *From Foreign Natives to Native Foreigners: Explaining Xenophobia in Contemporary South Africa*. Dakar: Codesria.

Niehaus, I. 2002. Ethnicity and the Boundaries of Belonging: Reconfiguring Shangaan Identity in the South African Lowveld. *African Affairs* 101 (405): 557–583.

Peberdy, S. 1998. Obscuring History? Contemporary Patterns of Regional Migration to South Africa. In *South Africa in Southern Africa: Reconfiguring the Region*, ed. D. Simon, 187–205. Oxford: James Currey. Perspectives No. 1.

Pettigrew, T.F., and L.R. Tropp. 2008. How Does Intergroup Contact Reduce Prejudice? Meta-analytic Tests of Three Mediators. *European Journal of Social Psychology* 38: 922–934.

Putnam, R.D. 2000. *Bowling Alone: The Collapse and Revival of American Community*. New York: Simon and Schuster.

Rothenberg, R.B. 1995. Commentary: Sampling in Social Networks'. *Connections* 18: 104–110.

Statistics SA. 2013. Provincial profile: Mpumalanga Community Survey Report 03-01-13. http://www.statssa.gov.za/publications/Report%2003-01-13/Report%2003-01-132016.pdf.

Swart, H., M. Hewstone, O. Christ, and A. Voci. 2010. The Impact of Cross-group Friendships in South Africa: Affective Mediators and Multigroup Comparisons. *Journal of Social Issues* 66: 309–333.

Thakur, V. 2011. Who is a South African? Interrogating Africanness and Afro-phobia. Paper written for Biannual SAAPS Conference, Stellenbosch, South Africa. http://www.e-ir.info/2011/07/18/who-is-a-south-african-interrogating-africanness-and-afro-phobia/.

Turner, R.N., R.J. Crisp, and E. Lambert. 2007. Imagining Intergroup Contact Can Improve Intergroup Attitudes. *Group Processes & Intergroup Relations* 10 (4): 427–441.

Yakushko, O. 2009. Xenophobia: Understanding the Roots and Consequences of Negative Attitudes Toward Immigrants. *The Counseling Psychologist* 37 (1): 36–66.

CHAPTER 12

"We Know Each Other": Analyzing Interactions Between African International and Local Students in South African Universities

Olusola Ogunnubi

INTRODUCTION

Migration refers to the movement of people from one location to another, either within or outside one's country. According to the United Nations (2004), it includes crossing the boundary of a political or administrative unit for a certain period. Over time, this process can have both negative and positive consequences (Gebre et al. 2010). Several factors influence people's need to migrate, including the desire to advance in life, evade existing conflict and violence within a country, or access better economic opportunities (Gebre et al. 2010). Studies have shown that there are more migrants in South Africa than in any other African country (Vandeyar

O. Ogunnubi (✉)
Cape Peninsula University, Cape Town, South Africa
e-mail: olusola.ogunnubi@yahoo.com

et al. 2014). The steady increase in migrants to the country was influenced by the demise of the apartheid regime, which banned the entry of black foreign nationals, particularly from other African countries.

Klotz (2000) observed that the emergence of democracy in 1994 launched South Africa on the international stage. The repeal of stringent immigration regulations enabled an influx of migrants. However, this has been accompanied by xenophobic attacks in the form of harassment and killing of foreign nationals who many South Africans accuse of taking their jobs and other opportunities (Morris 1998; Akinola 2018). Research suggests that there is little evidence to substantiate such claims (Gordon 2015). Indeed, some studies show that the migrant population in South Africa is predominantly a creator rather than a taker of jobs (Black et al. 2006; Kalitanyi and Visser 2010; Landau 2014;) and provide empirical evidence to suggest that foreigners have increased employment opportunities for South Africans.

The Advanced Dictionary of English defines xenophobia as "a strong feeling of dislike or fear of people from other countries." Given the prevalence of xenophobic attacks against foreign nationals in South Africa, this definition is too narrow as it fails to highlight the features of xenophobia in the context of physical attacks and damage to property (Harris 2001; Kollapan 1999). Studies on migration have pointed to xenophobic hostility and human rights abuses, particularly between South Africans and other African migrants.

While there can be no gainsaying that African migrants in South Africa have confronted severe challenges and successive xenophobic attacks, many have also reaped benefits while resident in the country. A sizeable number have studied and are still studying in South African universities, while many others are working in the higher education sector and supporting themselves and their families. Still others have made a name for themselves in their chosen professions.

Although there is much scholarly literature on international students globally, there is a paucity of research on the experiences of international students in South Africa (Zar 2010). It is against this background that this chapter presents a fresh perspective on social interactions between South Africans and African migrants living in the country. The study on which it is based analyzed the interactions between international African and local students in two public universities in the KwaZulu-Natal province (the University of KwaZulu-Natal [UKZN] and University of Zululand [UNIZUL]).[1] A purposive survey was employed to elicit responses from 79 African international students that were analyzed to uncover patterns of existing relationships and spaces of interaction between the groups. The responses were also used to draw inferences and evaluate African international students' contributions to South Africa's development. The findings showed that interaction between locals and foreigners in South Africa goes beyond the belabored narratives of xenophobia to include other interactions that emphasize social networks and integration (Isike 2015). They are important not only in terms of building a nuanced narrative for South Africa in the international community, but also offer a yardstick for the implementation of socio-economic transformation policies in the country.

The study posed the following critical questions: Are there spaces for positive interactions between international (African) and local (domestic) students? What level of acceptance exists within their university communities and South African society in general? What are the main forces that shape these interactions? What implications can be drawn from this for polemic discourses on migration studies?

INTERNATIONAL STUDENT MIGRATION: A LITERATURE REVIEW

This section presents a review of relevant literature in relation to international and African migration of students. It examines scholarly perspectives on the increased movement of international students in general and discusses the forces that shape rising student migration in both the source and destination countries. These factors are then considered in relation to South Africa. International students are ubiquitous around the world and form an important part of any internationally recognized

---

[1] In the South African context, Ramphele (1999, 1) attempt to resolve the dilemma of how to define international students by asserting that an international student in South Africa "...is anyone who is not a South African citizen, not a permanent resident, or does not have diplomatic exemption." In South Africa, international students are required to have a temporary residence permit as well as functional medical aid cover, which is often closely monitored by tertiary institutions before registration. For the purpose of this study, an African international student was defined as a student who is studying and living in a country other than their country of origin. It was concerned with international students who were studying in South Africa for a period of more than six months.

institution. Furthermore, internationalization of Higher Education Institutions (HEIs) has gained rapid traction in recent years (Sam, 2001). The demise of apartheid in 1994 meant that South Africa emerged from international isolation. At a broader level, globalization and internationalization have facilitated the movement of international students, mainly from developing countries to industrialized nations. While countries such as the United States, UK, Canada, Australia, and New Zealand lead the pack as preferred destinations (Aloyo 2009; Foster 2014), within Africa, South Africa has continued to be a destination of choice for many African students in search of higher education qualifications (Giles and Luxmoore 2007, 4). Ramphele (1999) noted that most international students in South Africa are from Africa, particularly from the Southern Africa Development Community (SADC). Mutula (2002, 9) observed that South Africa's re-entry into the international arena meant that neighboring states lost students to that country. For instance, Botswana lost a substantial share of its university students to South Africa. It is estimated that African students account for about two-thirds of the international student population in South Africa (Ayliff and Wang 2006). While fee remissions have been cited in some cases as one of the reasons for this inflow, there is very little evidence to suggest that this is true. At UKZN in particular, there is an undeniable presence of students from other African countries, especially at postgraduate level.

Several studies have examined external and internal factors that influence international students' decision to study overseas. In many ways, the flow of international students is a consequence of globalization (Massey et al. 1993) that has facilitated networking and communication across borders and has seen the easing of restrictions on movement between countries. The boundaries that existed decades ago have been dismantled by closer ties and activities between nations (Aloyo 2009). Massey et al. (1993) also cite differences in infrastructure between source and destination countries as impacting the mobility of international students. Thus, students choose to study in countries with better infrastructure and educational facilities. This could explain the increasing flow of international students of African origin to South Africa, which offers superior infrastructure and facilities (Aloyo 2009).

Vertovec (2002) argues that the term "movement" or "mobility" should be used rather than "migration" with respect to skilled workers.

Similarly, Castles and Miller (2003) contend that "'students' mobility is the precursor of skilled migration," while Larsen and Vincent-Lacrine (2004) compare the movement of international students with that of highly skilled immigrants. Ozden and Schiff note that the movement of skilled workers, including university students from developing countries, is concentrated in the OECD countries, which currently receive more than 85% of global international students. Arsen and Vincent-Lacrin argue that, "this increased global flow of international students have been shaped by the demand for higher education in developing (source) countries and the policy for internationalization in the developed (receiving) countries." For instance, immigration of international students to Europe has been the direct product of policy, while in the United States, it is the result of the appeal and attractiveness of its HEIs (see OECD 2004, 2). Aloyo (2009) asserts that migration connotes long-term or permanent residency while mobility has a temporary connotation, reflecting the multi-directional mobility of skilled workers.

The literature identifies several broad factors that account for the destination of international students, including increasing demand for university education in the source country, and internationalization policies in destination countries. It is, therefore, important to assess these factors in greater detail. Aloyo (2009, 20) cites a House of Commons (2007, 12) report that notes that demand for education in a source country directly impacts decisions made by an individual who is interested in the quality of their educational experience, the international comparability and value of the qualification they obtain, and the potential for better job opportunities on graduation. In other words, international students are driven to move to a country that promises to deliver on these objectives.

Social capital or networks have also been observed to contribute to increased demand and inflow of international students from developing countries (Massey et al. 1993; Massey and Espinosa 1997). Massey et al. (1993) note that "human and social capital progressively lead to cumulative causation as pioneer international students gather experience that enables them to decide whether to migrate permanently and share it with their kin or acquaintance" (see Aloyo 2009, 20). Vertovec (2002) observes that recruitment agencies have also played a role in forming institutionalized networks to facilitate the movement of professionals and students from developing to developed countries.

Zigurasa and Lawb (2006, 59) identify the low cost of education, flexible and simple immigration processes, and uncomplicated admission procedures as factors that motivate students to study abroad. Gera and Songsakul (2005) argue that international students' mobility may also be the result of internationalization policies in both the source and destination countries as well as strategies adopted by the admitting institutions. Countries in the developed world have designed carefully crafted policies on internationalization of higher education (Zigurasa and Lawb 2006). Finally, Gera and Songsakul (2005) assert that, in the new knowledge economy, countries such as the UK, Canada, and Australia continuously seek to acquire migrant skills by relaxing their immigration policies in order to facilitate the immigration of international students (see Aloyo 2009).

While it is clear that international students have become an important component of higher education, Sehoole (2008) notes that existing data on the migration of international students in Africa are inconsistent, incomplete, and are defined differently by each country. His study points to challenges such as xenophobia, bigotry, and racism that hinder African HEIs from attracting international students, particularly in South Africa. Furthermore, there is a paucity of research on the movement of international students between developing countries.

According to the ICEF Monitor 2013 Report, in 2013, there were around 74,000 international students in South Africa, accounting for almost 8% of the total student population, and constituting 15% of postgraduate and 6% of undergraduate enrollment. Sehoole (2011) noted that, in 2005, South African doctoral programs drew students from across the globe with international students totaling 2564, 27% of the 9434 candidates enrolled in such programs (see Tables 12.1 and 12.2). The 2009 data show a 2% increase in doctoral students from 9434 in 2005 to 10,529. During this period, the proportion of international students from Africa enrolled at all levels increased from 8 to 10%.

Table 12.1 Total number of international registered students in selected South African universities in 2006

	SADC	Rest of Africa	Rest of the world	Total foreign student	Total students	% of foreign students
UCT	2000	481	1842	4860	21,731	22.4
UNW	3037	126	113	3278	39,096	8.4
UKZN	1552	606	646	2804	40,761	6.9
UP	1318	648	796	2764	46,351	5.9
SU	958	307	1085	2350	22,082	10.6
WITS	1077	530	464	2086	23,241	9.0
NMMU	1301	271	476	2048	24,132	8.5
UJ	933	392	130	1455	45,503	3.2
UL	289	243	27	560	17,578	3.2

Source See Aloyo (2009, 25)

Table 12.2 International student enrolments in doctoral programs in South Africa

Region of origin	2005	%	2009	%
SADC	1156	12	1260	12
Rest of Africa	727	8	1076	10
Europe	252	3	282	3
Asia	176	2	220	2
N America	223	2	189	2
S America	17	0	23	0
Austalia Oeania	13	0	25	0
International total	2564	27	3075	29
National total	6870	73	7454	71

Source See Sehoole (2011)

METHODOLOGY

A descriptive survey was employed to sample the international student population across UKZN and UNIZUL. Convenience sampling was used at both institutions due to the researcher's access to international students (Flick 2009). Systematic random sampling was used to select the respondents. Lists of international students enrolled on all the campuses of the two universities were obtained from the international offices. With the help of research assistants, international students were randomly approached to participate in the study and to suggest colleagues who might also be willing to do so. The study areas were KwaDlangezwa, Durban, and Pietermaritzburg and the participants were from a variety of countries, including Nigeria, Democratic Republic of Congo, Mozambique, Zimbabwe, Lesotho, Congo, Swaziland, Ghana, and Botswana. This sample of international students from ten countries appears representative of the general spread of international students at the two universities. It thus yielded rich data.

A quantitative research method was employed, which enables the findings to be extended to the broader study population, and a self-administered questionnaire was used to gather data. The questionnaire was divided into two sections. The first part elicited information on the participants' demographic characteristics, while the second solicited their perceptions on their level of interaction, assimilation, and acceptance with local students in their university communities and the broader South African society. The questionnaire employed a five-point Likert scale, with Strongly Agree (SA), Agree (A), Undecided (U), Disagree (D), and Strongly Disagree (SD), and Missing System (MS) included to denote unanswered questions.

A total of 100 questionnaires were distributed to international students. Descriptive statistics were employed to analyze the data. The frequency and percentage distribution were used to summarize frequencies of observations without making further inferences. These statistics enabled observation of the occurrence of the different categories of responses.

One of the major constraints encountered was the suspension of academic activities, especially on UKZN's campuses as a result of ongoing #feesmustfall protests. However, with the help of student representatives from each participating country, 79 competed questionnaires were returned, representing a 79% response rate, a substantial proportion of the sample.

Discussion of Results

Table 12.3 reports the descriptive statistics, which mainly cover the demographic characteristics of the respondents, including gender, age, qualification, nationality, and duration of residence in South Africa. A total of 54 males and 25 females participated in the survey, with the

Table 12.3 Socio-demographic characteristics of respondents

Sex	Frequency	%
Male	54	68.4
Female	25	31.6
Total	79	100
Age		
Below 20	5	6.3
21–30	43	54.4
31 and above	31	39.2
Total	79	100
Qualification studying for		
Degree	8	10.1
Honors	8	10.1
Masters	27	34.2
Ph.D.	35	44.3
Others	1	1.3
Total	79	100
Nationality		
Nigerian	37	46.8
Zimbabwe	8	10.1
Botswana	4	5.1
Mozambique	1	1.3
Lesotho	7	8.9
Congo	4	5.1
DRC	1	1.3
Swaziland	12	15.2
Ghana	4	5.1
Others	1	1.3
Total	79	100
Duration of resident in South Africa		
1 month–2 years	36	45.6
2 years–4 years	18	22.8
4 years–6 years	15	19.0
6 years and above	9	11.4
Missing system	1	1.3
Total	79	100

Source Field Survey, 2016

former representing 68.4%. This reflects the fact that the majority of international students in South Africa are male. In terms of age, 43 respondents (54.45%) were aged between 21 and 30, with five (6.3%) below the age of 20, and 31 (39.2%) 31 years and above.

The results show that 75.5% of the respondents were postgraduate students undertaking Ph.D. and Master's studies, with 16 respondents (20.2%) enrolled for undergraduate and Honors degrees.

As noted earlier, the respondents hailed from ten African countries. The largest sample group was from Nigeria (37–46.8%), with 12 from Swaziland and eight from Zimbabwe, together accounting for 25.3% of the total sample.

Finally, the table shows that 42 respondents (54% of the sample) had lived temporarily as international students in South Africa for more than two years.

Section two of the questionnaire included 14 related questions that measured the sampled international African students' perceptions on their level of interaction, assimilation, and acceptance both with local students in their university communities and the broader South African society. In the discussion, responses that are correlated are thematically arranged in the same table in order to allow for a nuanced discussion and analysis.

The first two questions under this section generated responses on the choice of South Africa for study and preference for the South African higher education system. The study was not concerned with the factors responsible for this choice; rather, the focus was on the preference for South Africa over and above what was obtainable in the country of origin. As shown in Table 12.4, a significant number of respondents (71–89.9%) indicated that education was their primary motivation for the decision to study in South Africa. By implication, this is linked to various international rankings, which rank South African universities highly and above many of their counterparts in other parts of Africa.[2] As the responses in the second question indicate, it is clear that international students from Africa perceive that they are likely to receive a better quality education in South Africa than that on offer in their own country. They thus regard South Africa as an alternative destination for quality higher education for African students. The results show that 39 of the 79 respondents agreed with this statement, while a surprising 21 were undecided and 19 disagreed. Thus, a reasonable proportion of the sample concurred with the opinion that the South African educational system is of a higher standard than that of their country of origin. These responses were corroborated by the fact

---

[2] The Times Higher Education's University Rankings rank South African universities, the University of Cape Town, University of Witwatersrand, and Stellenbosch University 1st, 2nd, and 3rd, respectively in Africa.

Table 12.4 Responses on the preference of South African higher education system

S/N			Frequency	%
1	I migrated to South Africa primarily for educational purpose	SD	2	2.5
		D	3	3.8
		U	2	2.5
		A	16	20.3
		SA	55	69.6
		MS	1	1.3
	Total		79	100
2	South African educational system is preferred to that of my country	SD	7	8.9
		D	12	15.2
		U	21	26.6
		A	24	30.4
		SA	15	19.0
	Total		79	100
3	I am aware that the number of African international students in South African universities is on the increase	SD	1	1.3
		D	2	2.5
		U	10	12.7
		A	38	48.1
		SA	28	35.4
	Total		79	100

that 83.5% of respondents agreed that there had been an increase in the number of African international students in South African universities.

In a bid to engender more robust analysis, similar constructs and their corresponding responses were compared to observe the trend of convergence and divergence. To start with, the response to questions 1 and 2 was compared to understand if the respondents' decision to migrate to South Africa was predicated solely on educational pursuit or preference for the South African educational system. 89.9% of the respondents agreed that they only came to South Africa for educational purposes, compared to 39% that agreed that they preferred the South African educational system to that of their home country. This suggests that, to a certain extent, African international students' migration to South Africa reflects a desire to pursue higher education which precedes their preference for the

South African educational system. Similarly, on the question of integration into the South African space as an international student, distinction was drawn between whether local students are sometimes hostile toward international students (question 4).

The three questions included in Table 12.5 elicited responses on international students from Africa's perceptions on the extent of their integration with the South African community, whether within or outside the campus. The results show that although many international students (38) agreed that they sometimes experienced hostility from local students, a slightly higher proportion (39) either disagreed or strongly disagreed with this statement, and 17.7% were undecided. Thus, perceptions as regards hostility were mixed, which could be due to several factors that were beyond the purview of this study. These responses correlated positively with the question on whether the respondents were integrating easily into South African society. The majority (53–67.1%) of

Table 12.5 Responses on integration of international student

S/N			Frequency	%
1	The local students are sometimes hostile to international African students	SD	7	8.9
		D	19	24.1
		U	14	17.7
		A	23	29.1
		SA	15	19.0
		MS	1	1.3
	Total		79	100
2	I am integrating nicely into the South African society	SD	2	2.5
		D	8	10.1
		U	15	19.0
		A	43	54.4
		SA	10	12.7
		MS	1	1.3
	Total		79	100
3	I have encountered issues during the process of my integration into the South African society	SD	4	5.1
		D	13	16.5
		U	15	19.0
		A	38	48.1
		SA	9	11.4
	Total		79	100

the respondents agreed that such integration had been smooth. Only ten respondents (12.6%) disagreed with this statement, suggesting that many African international students concur that interaction between local and international students is less hostile and more interactive. However, asked whether they had confronted any issues during the process of integration into South African society, 47 respondents affirmed that they had. In other words, while there was a level of integration or acceptance of African international students into their host communities, issues may arise that challenge such integration. Taken together, the three categories of responses reveal a clear pattern of satisfaction with the integration between international students and their host communities.

Similarly, on the question of integration into the South African space as international student, distinction was attempted between whether the local students are sometimes hostile toward international students (question 4), and if international students are integrating well into South African society (question 5). The results show that 38% of the respondents agreed that local students were hostile toward international students, while only 10% disagreed that they were integrating well into South African society. This suggests that, on the whole, international students are integrating into South African society fairly easily calling into question media reports on the treatment of foreign nationals by local South Africans.

The series of related questions presented in Table 12.6 aimed to gather information on experiences of being an African international student in South Africa. The table shows that 63 respondents (79.8%) agreed that their experience had been positive. Furthermore, 61 (77.2%) agreed that they enjoyed a positive relationship with local students in their respective universities. Nevertheless, the respondents indicated that they did not enjoy equal rights with local students. This is not surprising given that scholarships and bursaries offered within these institutions may be mainly available to prospective and current local students while international students are expected to provide their own funding. Overall, the responses in the three categories of questions suggest mainly positive experiences among African international students, which correlates with previous responses on the extent of integration within host communities.

The responses on international students' rights were also compared. Only 16% of the respondents agreed that they did not enjoy equal rights with their local counterparts (question 3 of Table 12.6), while 67% concurred that they had benefited as international students while studying

Table 12.6 Responses on experiences with local students

S/N			Frequency	%
1	The experience of being an international student in a South African university is worthwhile	SD	2	2.5
		D	3	3.8
		U	11	13.9
		A	44	55.7
		SA	19	24.1
	Total		79	100
2	I have enjoyed good inter-personal relationship with local students in this university	SD	1	13
		D	5	6.3
		U	12	15.2
		A	44	55.7
		SA	17	21.5
	Total		79	100
3	I have not enjoyed equal rights with local student as an international African student since my studentship	SD	3	3.8
		D	13	16.5
		U	10	12.7
		A	36	45.6
		SA	17	21.5
	Total		79	100

in South African universities (question 1 of Table 12.7). This finding runs contrary to the popular belief that the rights of international students are not fully guaranteed in South African universities.

The questions in Table 12.7 related to assimilation. Sixty-seven respondents (84.8%) agreed that they had benefited from studying at a South African university. Furthermore, 69 (87.8%) concurred that they had been absorbed into their communities while studying in the country. Thus, the majority of the respondents responded positively in terms of the benefits and assimilation they had enjoyed as international students in South Africa. Despite this, the question on the cordiality of relations between local and international African students yielded mixed responses. While 37 respondents (46.8%) felt that this relationship was cordial and non-hostile, 20 (25.3%) pointed to a negative relationship and ten (12.7%) were undecided.

Other comparisons were made to measure the extent or nature of the relationship between international and local students. To achieve this,

Table 12.7 Responses on assimilation by international African students

S/N			Frequency	%
1	As an international African student, I have benefited from studying in one of South Africa's universities	SD	2	2.5
		D	3	3.8
		U	7	8.9
		A	37	46.8
		SA	30	38.0
	Total		79	100
2	I have gained a lot in terms of assimilation while studying in South Africa	SD	3	3.8
		D	2	2.5
		U	5	6.3
		A	50	63.3
		SA	19	24.1
	Total		79	100
3	The relationship between local students and international African student is cordial and non-hostile	SD	5	6.3
		D	15	19
		U	22	27.8
		A	28	35.4
		SA	9	11.4
	Total		79	100

the international students' perception of inter-personal relationships with local students (question 2 of Table 12.6) was compared with whether their relationships were cordial or non-hostile (question 3 of Table 12.7). 61% of the respondents agreed that they enjoyed good inter-personal relationships with local students, while 37% felt that their relationships with local students were amiable and non-hostile. This suggests that, to a large extent, African international students enjoy good inter-personal relationships with their local counterparts.

Finally, a comparison was made between the extent to which the international students had experienced assimilation in the course of their studies (question 2 of Table 12.7) and if such assimilation progressed unhindered (question 2 of Table 12.5). It was found that 69% of the respondents felt that they had been assimilated during the course of their studies in South Africa with 53% agreeing that such assimilation was, to a large extent, free from restrictions and bottlenecks.

Table 12.8 presents the results relating to the questions on perceptions of acceptance of international students in South Africa. None of the participants strongly disagreed with the statement that their good experiences surpassed the negative ones, while 14, representing 17.7%, disagreed. Conversely, 48 respondents (60.8%) agreed or strongly agreed with the statement and 51 (64.6%) agreed that the university environment was conducive for international students. This suggests that they were generally accepted within their host communities and did not feel

Table 12.8 Responses of perception of acceptance as international students in South Africa

S/N			Frequency	%
1	My good experiences as an international African student surpass the ugly ones	SD	–	–
		D	14	17.7
		U	17	21.5
		A	38	48.1
		SA	10	12.7
	Total		79	100
2	The university community is conducive for all including international African students	SD	–	–
		D	13	16.5
		U	15	19.0
		A	38	48.1
		SA	13	16.5
	Total		79	100
3	I consider South Africa more homely than a temporary abode	SD	12	15.2
		D	21	26.6
		U	17	21.5
		A	28	35.4
		SA	1	1.3
	Total		79	100
4	I am likely to live permanently in South Africa after my studies	SD	19	24.1
		D	8	10.1
		U	29	36.7
		A	13	16.5
		SA	9	11.4
		MS	1	1.3
	Total		79	100

threatened. However, 13 (16.5%) and 15 (21.5%) respondents disagreed or were undecided, respectively. Furthermore, 29 respondents agreed that South Africa was perceived as more homely than a temporary place of abode, while 33 rejected this viewpoint and 17 were undecided. Overall, it would seem that, based on positive assimilation, some African international students would consider the possibility of staying in South Africa after completing their studies to search for employment. In this regard, 27 respondents (34.2%) disagreed that there was a likelihood of their living permanently in the country, while 22 (27.9%) agreed and 29 (36.7%) were undecided.

A comparison was also made between the respondents' likelihood of considering South Africa as more like a home than a temporary abode (question 3 of Table 12.8) and the likelihood of them living permanently in the country after completing their studies (question 4 of Table 12.8). The result showed that 29% of the respondents considered South Africa as more than a temporary abode and that 22% indicated that they were likely to live permanently in South Africa after their studies. These results suggest that African international students typically consider South Africa as a study destination rather than as a future permanent place of residence.

Analysis of Findings

A number of interpretations and inferences can be made from the analysis of the survey's findings. In the first place, it is evident that many African students consider South Africa as a significant destination for higher education outside of their country. This is confirmed by available statistics on destination countries for international students. A 2013 France Report notes that South Africa is the second destination of choice for international students, with a 15% share and a continued rise in intake. The statistics show that, there are more postgraduate international students than undergraduates ones; one of the reasons for this is the relatively cheaper option that South Africa offers for postgraduate education. The results also align with statistics and the literature that show that South Africa remains the most popular destination for international students from Africa (Mudhovozi 2011). The favorable international ranking of South African universities is perhaps the chief reason. Other factors alluded to in the literature include the country's economic stability, low tuition fees, and the promise of a unique academic experience (Mudhovozi 2011; MacGregor 2011). The increasing trend of

African students embarking on post-secondary education in many South African HEIs can also be related to the shared positive experience of previous international students.

Secondly, and related to the above, the data show that despite some common challenges, African international students have great admiration for their host communities with respect to their assimilation and integration.³ Despite the challenges of relocating to a foreign land to study, local and international students at UKZN and UNIZUL find ways to build friendships and fraternize with one another. African international and local students seem to enjoy a degree of collegial relationships that transcend hostility or the xenophobia that is generally pervasive in South African society. The knowledge of one another implied by the responses to the questionnaire is indicative of more profound levels of interaction that need to be explored further in the broader South African society. The researcher is acquainted with former colleagues who were international students or local students that have married each other. Future research could further investigate the sources of conviviality among local and international students in South Africa.

Furthermore, the positive responses from the majority of the respondents on their experiences in South Africa illustrate and support the claim of acculturation (integration, acceptance, and assimilation) that accompanies the relationship between the parties (Miguel and Tranmer 2009; Kirshner 2012). Nevertheless, perceptions of unequal rights can be correlated with institutional rules that may appear to privilege local students' access to funding through bursaries, and scholarships, or even work-study opportunities. The respondents' view that integration takes place amid a positive experience of South Africa by African international students also reflects the feeling that they have been absorbed into local communities. Although relationships between local and international students may encounter problems at times, the overall feedback is one of satisfaction expressed through experiences of assimilation and integration which

---

³ Poyrazili and Grahame (2007) suggest that international students face challenges adapting to the new country, including finding accommodation, learning about the education system and academic culture of the country, developing new friendships, and forming new social support systems. Other challenges involve achieving an intercultural transition whilst remaining focused on their academic objectives (Mokhothu and Callaghan 2018; Chen 2009; Cushner and Karim 2004). Church (1982) also points to issues such as language barriers, financial problems, homesickness, and educational and social adjustment as problems international students are likely to encounter.

is perceived to be cordial and mostly devoid of hostility. The findings suggest that South African university campuses provide safe spaces for cultural assimilation and integration between local and African international students. It is also possible that, as Dominguez and Maya-Jariego's (2008) findings suggest, the length of residence of a migrant can influence the extent to which he/she is able to form social ties with a host community (see Isike 2015).

The positive experiences of African international students reported here may help to challenge negative stereotypes and perceptions of South Africa as being dangerous, and xenophobic toward foreigners. For instance, a participant in a study conducted at the University of Witwatersrand observed:

> Before you come, everyone says it's not safe, it's not safe, so you are already worried before you come, so you have be like, extra aware…when I came I knew before the sun goes down I should try to be home…but I haven't found it like dangerous or not safe, but I think it's just an act here, that people says it's not safe that makes me worried.

The respondents' perceptions of relations with their host communities corroborate the findings of an earlier study conducted in Empangeni by Isike (2015) which concluded that a variety of relationships and interactions exists across multiple social networks among migrants and South Africans in their everyday lives. Beyond xenophobic violence and other forms of abuse that have characterized South Africa in recent times, this chapter argues that foreign migrants, particularly African international students, have benefited from opportunities that build networks and acculturation with their host communities, thereby facilitating integration, assimilation and acceptance in South Africa.

Conclusion

Much of the literature on the relationship between South Africans and African migrants living in the country is awash with "misery discourses" of xenophobia and afrophobia. This is notwithstanding significant evidence which suggests that interactions between these two groups transcend the notoriety of conflictual relationships. For instance, statistics show that despite pervading xenophobic violence against African migrants in South Africa, the population of international students from Africa continues to rise significantly. This exploratory study assessed university communities' acceptance of African international students by conducting a survey among 79 African international students at two universities in KwaZulu-Natal. The analysis of their perceptions of the extent of their acceptance, assimilation, and integration into the South African environment makes a case for a more nuanced assessment of South Africa's contribution to internationalization and regional integration in Africa, not only for building a stronger global reputation for the Republic, but also in providing a recipe for Africa's socio-economic transformation in the face of challenging economic realities.

REFERENCES

Akinola, Adeoye, ed. 2018. *The Political Economy of Xenophobia in Africa: Advances in African Economic, Social and Political Development*. Switzerland: Springer.

Aloyo, N.O. 2009. *The economic impact of international students on South Africa*. MA dissertation. Johannesburg: University of Johannesburg.

Ayliff, D., and Wang, G. 2006. Experiences of Chinese international students learning English at South African tertiary institutions. *South African Journal of Higher Education* 20 (3): 25–37.

Black, R., J. Crush, S. Peberdy, S. Ammassari, L. McLean Hilker, S. Mouillesseaux, C. Pooley, and Rajkotia, R. 2006. Migration and Development in Africa: An Overview. *African Migration and Development Series* No. 1. South African Migration Project, 105. Cape Town, IDASA.

Castles, S., and M.J. Miller, 2003. *The Age of Migration*. London: The Guildford Press.

Chen, S. 2009. A Study of International Students' Life Situation—A Case Study of the International Students in University of Twente. Unpublished master's thesis, University of Twente, Enschede, The Netherlands.

Church, A.T. 1982. Sojourner adjustment. *Psychological Bulletin* 91: 540–572.

Cushner, K., and A.U. Karim. 2004. Study Abroad at the University Level. *Handbook of Intercultural Training* 3: 289–308.

Dominguez, S., and I. Maya-Jariego. 2008. Acculturation of Host Individuals: Immigrants and Personal Networks. *American Journal of Community Psychology* 42: 309–327.

Flick, U. 2009. *An Introduction to Qualitative Research*. London: Sage.

Foster M. (2014). Student destination choices in higher education: Exploring attitudes of Brazilian students to study in the United Kingdom. *Journal of Research in International Education* 3 (2): 149–162. https://doi.org/10.1177/1475240914541024.

Gebre, L.T., P. Maharaj, and K.N. Pillay. 2010. The Experiences of Immigrants in South Africa: A Case Study of Ethiopians in Durban, South Africa. *Springer Science Business Media* 22: 23–35.
Gera, S., and T. Songsakul, 2005. *How is Canada faring in the competition for internationally mobile high skilled workers?*. Paper presented to the 39th Annual Canadian Economics Association Meetings.
Giles, J., and Luxmoore, G. 2007. *Brisbane, City of Education: Economic impact of International Students*. Brisbane: Brisbane City Council.
Gordon, S. 2015. Xenophobia across the class divide: South African attitudes towards foreigners 2003–2012. *Journal of Contemporary African Studies* 33 (4): 494–509. https://doi.org/10.1080/02589001.2015.1122870.
Harris, B. 2001. A Foreign Experience: Violence, Crime, and Xenophobia During South Africa's Transition. *Violence and Transition Series* 5: 11–140.
House of Commons. 2007. The future sustainability of the higher education sector: International aspects. *Eight Report of Session* 1 (8): 4–18.
ICEF Monitor. 2013. South Africa an Important Regional Hub for International Students, ICEF Monitor.
Isike, M.E. 2015. Ties That Bind: A Network Analysis of Relationships Between Nigerian Migrants and South Africans in Umhlathuze. Unpublished PhD thesis, University of KawaZulu-Natal, Pietermaritzburg.
Kalitanyi, V., and Visser, K. 2010. African immigrants in South Africa: Job Takers or Job Creators? *South African Journal of Economic and Management Sciences* 13 (4): 376–390.
Kirshner, J.D. 2012. We Are Gauteng People: Challenging the Politics of Xenophobia in Khutsong, South Africa. *Antipode: A Radical Journal of Geography* 44 (4): 1307–1328.
Klotz, A. 2000. Migration After Apartheid: Deracialising South African Foreign Policy. *Third World Quarterly* 5 (21): 831–847.
Kollapan, J. 1999. Xenophobia in South Africa: The Challenge to Forced Migration. Unpublished seminar. Johannesburg.
Landau, L.B. 2014. Conviviality, Rights, and Conflict in Africa's Urban Estuaries. *Politics & Society* 42 (3): 359–380.
Larsen, K., and Vincent-Lacrin, S. 2004. *Internationalisation of higher education*. Organisation for Economic Co-operation and Development (OECD) Observer, Paris.
MacGregor, K. (2011). South Africa: Universities Open to Foreigners. Retrieved from http://www.universityworldnews.com/article.php?story=201 00219145415434.
Massey, D., J. Arango, G. Hugo, A. Kouaouci, A. Pellegrino, and J.E. Taylor. 1993. Theories of international migration: A review and appraisal. *Population and Development Review* 19: 431–466.

Massey, D.S., and Espinosa, K.E. 1997. What's Driving Mexico-US. Migration? A Theoretical, Empirical and Policy Analysis. *American Journal of Sociology* 102 (4): 939–999.

Miguel, V., and Tranmer, M. 2009. Personal Support Networks of Immigrants to Spain: A Multilevel Analysis. CCSR Working Paper. http://www.ccsr.ac.uk/publications/working/2009-07.pdf.

Mokhothu, T.M., and C.W. Callaghan. 2018. The Management of the International Student Experience in the South African Context: The Role of Sociocultural Adaptation and Cultural Intelligence. *Acta Commercii* 18 (1): 1–11.

Morris, A. 1998. Our Fellow African Make Our Lives Hell: The Lives of Congolese and Nigerians Living in Johannesburg. *Ethnic and Racial Studies* 21 (6): 1116–1136.

Mudhovozi, P. 2011. Adjustment Experiences of International Students at a South African University. *Journal of Psychology in Africa* 21 (2): 293–296.

Mutula, S. 2002. E-learning initiative at the University of Botswana: Challenges and opportunities. *Campus-Wide Information Systems* 19 (3): 11–99.

Poyrazili, S., and Grahame, K. M. 2007. Barriers to adjustment: Needs of international students within a semiurban campus community. *Journal of Instructional Psychology* 34 (1): 28–45.

Ramphele, M. 1999. *Immigration & education: International students at South African universities and technikons.* Migration policy series, No. 12. Cape Town: Idasa.

Sam, D.L. 2001. Satisfaction with life among international students: An exploratory study. *Social Indicators Research* 53: 313–337.

Sehoole M. 2008. South Africa and the dynamics of international student circulation. In *The dynamics of international student circulation in a global context*, eds. H. De Wit, P. Agarwal, M. Said, M. Sehoole, and M. Sirozi. Rotterdam: Sense Publishers.

Sehoole, C. 2011. Student mobility and doctoral education in South Africa. *Perspectives in Education* 29 (3): 53–63.

United Nations (UN). 2004. Economic Impacts of International Migration. *World Economic and Social Survey.* Department of Economic and Social Affairs, New York: United Nations.

Vandeyar, S., T. Vandeyar, and K. Elufisan. 2014. Impediments to the Successful Reconstruction of African Immigrants' Teachers' Professional Identities in South African Schools. *South African Journal of Education* 32 (2): 1–20.

Vertovec, S. 2002. Transnational networks and skilled labour migration. Paper presented at the Ladenburger Diskurs "Migration" Gottlieb Daimler- und Karl Benz-Stiftung Conference, Ladenburg, 14–15 February.

Zar, D. (2010). "International students from Africa: The impact that living in South Africa has on one's sense of identity." PhD dissertation (Unpublished), Johannesburg: University of the Witwatersrand.

Zigurasa, C., and S.F. Lawb, 2006. Recruiting international students as skilled migrants: The global "skills race" as viewed from Australia and Malaysia. Globalisation, *Societies and Education* 4 (1): 59–76.

CHAPTER 13

Conclusion: Contact, Concord and Social Cohesion in South Africa

Efe Mary Isike

A Synopsis

In immigration terms, democratization in South Africa in 1994 led to the abrogation of restrictive laws and policies which maintained the apartheid system. The apartheid immigration policy (Aliens Control Act) has been described as a two-gate policy which was restrictive towards Africans but open to Europeans from outside the country in order to offset the population imbalance occasioned by a black majority (Landau and Kabwe-Segatti 2009; Isike 2015, 211). The post-1994 state thus inherited the responsibility of transforming the Aliens Control Act into a more representative and inclusive legislative and policy framework. The Act was subsequently replaced by the Aliens Amendment Act (1995) which in many ways has also been exclusionary. For instance, in 1996 a number of illegal immigrants were deported from South Africa to their various home countries, and the statistics show that 98% of these deportees were from African

E. M. Isike (✉)
University of Pretoria, Pretoria, South Africa
e-mail: efe.isike@up.ac.za

countries even though there were as many illegal immigrants from outside Africa in the country then (Maharaj 2004). These kinds of developments set the tone for the racialized nature of xenophobia experienced in post-apartheid South Africa, especially between 2008 and 2019. Although there has been a few immigration legislation such as the Immigration Act No. 13 (2002), the Immigration Amendment Act of 2004 and Immigration Amendment Act of 2013 which were meant to tackle the problems of skills shortages that plagued the country's economy by encouraging the immigration of people with skills, they did not address the exclusionary nature of the previous legislation. The Immigration Regulations of 2014 were described as even more stringent and exclusive in terms of shutting out African migrant workers. According to Hamill (2014), it only served to reinforce the stereotyping of African migrants as aliens, severely limit African migration and expose African migrants in South Africa to various vulnerabilities. It is clear that, on the part of the state, the impasse on how to deal with the challenges of African immigration to South Africa remains unresolved as more migrants continue to move to South Africa in search of greener pastures given the reality of globalization and the crises of underdevelopment which plagues much of the continent.

On their part as citizens, South Africans have typically, as peoples of other nations would,[1] resisted African migration not only due to economic factors such as stiffer competition for resources and jobs, but also due to the fear of cultural differences that could fragment the perceived homogeneity of South African society. Added to this mix is the phenomenon of particular crimes that are largely associated with African migrant communities in South Africa such as drugs and women trafficking. Therefore, African migrants are viewed as the *Other* who disrupt the new rainbow nation, and xenophobia, deployed as a form of nationalism, has become a tool to prevent the diversification of a unified social fabric. That said, whilst xenophobia is not unique to South Africa, what is unique about xenophobia in South Africa is its extremely violent nature which has no comparison elsewhere in the world.

However, this is not the whole story. Even in the face of violent xenophobic actions which continue to be targeted specifically at African

---

[1] South Africans are not any more xenophobic in their attitude and behavior towards foreigners than citizens of many countries in the world where they (citizens) have and often express genuine concerns about immigration and its dual impact of reducing opportunities for them (citizens).

migrants and which this book confirms and documents in Part II, we have also shown in Part III of the book that there are spaces of positive interactions between South Africans and African immigrants that have not sufficiently come to the fore to give a more nuanced and balanced analysis of African migrant and host relations in South Africa. This was the premise on which this edited book was put together; to examine the everyday realities of migrants in ordinary places and micro public spaces where they interact with a variety of South Africans through their livelihood activities, marriages and social relationships, in their residential areas, in faith-based organizations and other elements of everyday life (Isike 2015). Its central argument is that xenophobia is only one of the varying outcomes of contact between African migrants and South Africans. Therefore, this book does not contest that there is hostility in the migrant/host relations in South Africa. Rather it argues that hostility is one end of a long spectrum with non-hostility at the other end, and many outcomes in between. Indeed, the 2015 xenophobic violence which the Minister of Home Affairs then, Mr. Malusi Gigaba aptly described as *Afrophobia*, served to reinforce popular understanding of relations between black South Africans and African immigrants as very hostile and these came to the fore again in the 2019 violence against African migrants which was even more widespread across the country. However, the activities of many other South Africans (Black and White) at various levels during both the 2015 and 2019 violence against African immigrants have shown that it would be uncritical to paint relations between South Africans and African immigrants with only a brush of hostility. For example, apart from the 15 April 2015 march by South Africans against xenophobia in Durban,[2] support for African immigrants by South Africans who were reported to have rescued, sheltered and protected immigrants during these violence serve to buttress the central argument we have tried to make in this book (Ikalafeng 2015).[3] These actions which were again in full display during the 2019 attacks against African migrants, are not simply random

---

[2] This march of more than 3000 people was led by the KwaZulu-Natal Premier and government officials at various municipal levels, with civil society representatives and ordinary citizens also in attendance. Its significance was not blighted by the opposing march of over 200 other South Africans who insisted on their anti-African foreigner stance.

[3] Ikalafeng, T. 2015. Our African Bonds Defy Borders. The Sunday Independent. 26 April SABC News, Friday 24 April 2015, and The Sowetan, 07 September 2019 There are also numerous personal accounts of African immigrants on Facebook who were assisted by South Africans during the 2015 and 2019 xenophobic violence.

acts of goodwill or kindness towards migrants but are also products of deep friendships between South Africans and migrants that have developed overtime in different spaces of contact and interaction across South Africa. Clearly then, contact between South Africans and African migrants has led to both conflict and conviviality mediated only by the absence and presence of certain predisposing conditions. These include equality of status of the diverse groups, cooperation amongst its members, the pursuit of common interdependent goals and shared social norms. Also, as different chapters show, the three mediators of the contact-prejudice effect; knowledge of the outgroup by the in-group which enables the formation of bridges across diversity, the anxiety of members within the groups and the attitude of empathy present within intergroup relations, all play out in varying degrees in the relations between South Africans and African migrants. Over 27 years after the new democracy, and in spite of increasing contact between them, South Africans still have limited knowledge of Africa and its peoples. False beliefs, stereotypes and myths about African migrants created by the media and which are reinforced by careless remarks of some political and thought leaders in the country have not been helped to bridge knowledge gap. Similarly, the closed-mindedness of some African migrants to South African culture and peoples have also not helped to bridge the knowledge gap between South Africans and their South African hosts. This hampers conviviality and concord as it exacerbates the anxiety that fuels conflict between both groups in South Africa.

Some Plausible Policy Considerations for Social Cohesion

The fact remains that Africans will continue to migrate into South Africa and South Africans will also increasingly migrate into the continent for all kinds of reasons that have traditionally fuelled migration. This is a difficult reality that South Africa needs to confront head-on. As Landau aptly puts it: "it is time to ask ourselves uncomfortable questions. At stake are the ethics of living with diversity, the nature of social membership, the value of rights and law, and the means of building unity in a country still characterized by division, inequality and fragmented institutions".[4]

Managing relations between migrant and host communities and appropriating the development potential of immigration has always been a challenge, and the case of South Africa presents a bigger challenge given its history of apartheid which disconnected black South Africans from the rest of the continent, creating a people who do not feel a sense of historical connectedness with the rest of the continent (Isike 2015, 214). Using the cases of Congolese, Kenyan, Mozambican, Nigerian and Zimbabwean migrants in different spaces of South Africa, this book has argued that there are convivial relations between African migrants and their various host communities in South Africa which developed as a result of contact with one another in the country. Although varied, the interactions and the ties that bind them together run deep beyond ethnic and national differences as we have seen in numerous cases of black South Africans choosing to protect African immigrants from xenophobic attacks, and in some instances, marching against xenophobia in show of solidarity with African migrants as we saw in 2015 and 2015. These are all products of the network ties developed through contact and interactions with one another over time in South Africa (Isike 2015), which Landau has described as communities of convenience that yet illustrate the value of solidarity in migrant-rich spaces whilst raising broader questions about the spatial scale and role of affective relationships in overcoming economic and physical precarity (Landau 2017). However, as has been argued, when we extend the focus on African migrants beyond those in the lower economic strata to those in the middle and higher economic strata who have settled, are more embedded, and in some instances, fully integrated into various South African communities, we begin to see less opportunism and precarity, and more permanence in these relations. This bodes well for concord and integration which can be appropriated for its development value for host communities in particular and South Africa in general. There is therefore a need to analyze and tell these stories of positive contacts and their nature of interactions which show conviviality and accommodation as much as we tell those that produce conflict and xenophobic responses. This is important not only for disaggregating the people who populate South Africa's towns

---

[4] Landau 2013. Xenophobia demons linger in SA. Available in https://mg.co.za/article/2013-05-17-00-xenophobic-demons-linger-in-sa/, accessed 05/08/2020.

and cities and the processes that unite and divide as Landau admonishes (Landau 2013), but also because of their implications for inclusiveness and social cohesion which are important aspirational values in South Africa's National Development Plan (NDP 2030) as a Rainbow nation. The country has already committed to social cohesion and safer communities as one of the priorities (Priority 6) of the national Medium Terms Strategic Framework (MTSF) 2019–2024. Amongst others, it aims to foster behavioural change to enable the sharing of common space and services across society recognizing that "without a high degree of social cohesion and unity of purpose, it is difficult to envisage South Africa overcoming the significant obstacles that stand in the way of prosperity and equity" (MTSF 2019–2024, 191). The Minister of Sports, Arts and Culture, Nathi Mthethwa reiterated this point when he inducted the second cohort of Social Cohesion Advocates (2020–2024) he appointed to implement the social cohesion programme of the national government in July 2020.[5] According to him, the government's efforts to achieve its goals of nation building and social cohesion in South Africa are informed by the understanding, amongst others, that:

> government works to consolidate partnerships across society to strengthen social cohesion and ensure that our nation achieves the values of a caring society, inspired by the traits of human compassion which informed our struggle against colonialism and apartheid.[6]

The minister reiterated the need for all members of the South African society, citizens and non-citizens resident in the country to stand together in unity at "a time in our history where more than ever before we need to forge our togetherness and especially our unity in diversity". He highlighted government's rollout of Social Cohesion Community Dialogues and Conversations aimed at promoting interaction on an equal basis between communities from different backgrounds in its efforts to build a

---

[5] The Social Cohesion Advocates Programme emerged as one of the resolutions of the 2012 National Social Cohesion summit in Kliptown, which involved a number of key sectors from a broad spectrum of the South African population. Its purpose is to be the engine room for realizing the idea of a non-racial, non-sexist and democratic society founded on the values of equality and human dignity in line with vision of the National Development Plan 2030.

[6] Speech by the Minister of Sport, Arts and Culture, Hon. Nathi Mthethwa, on the occasion of induction of Social Cohesion Advocates (SCAs) on 03 July 2020.

socially cohesive nation. According to him, "these dialogues were aimed at healing communities and allowing them to share common experiences bringing them closer together". They are also critical to giving life to the principles of human rights and equality, non-racialism, non-tribalism, non-sexism, unity in diversity, inclusivity and social justice, intergroup and community cooperation, and social solidarity which underlie the social cohesion programme. The government's focus in its social cohesion drive is to mobilize the broader society so that this important nation-building task becomes the responsibility of all sectors, and leaders across all sectors and fields of occupations are afforded public platforms to be champions of social cohesion. As an integral part of the South African society, African immigrants are also critical stakeholders in forging a socially cohesive nation which is pivotal for development. They should therefore be more open to seeing South Africa as home and treating South Africans as no different from their kins in their home countries by learning South African languages and cultures, and respecting the country's laws.

Flowing from these arguments, there is need for the South African state to rethink its immigration policy in relation to Africa and Africans in ways that align better with its NDP 2030. One of the arguments put forward by contact theorists is that institutional norms that favour intergroup contact enable the development of conviviality and hospitality (Pettigrew and Tropp 2008). Conviviality at the top both in policy, interpretation and action will complement it at the bottom, and the need for this parity from top to bottom has been well underscored in Chapter 3. Although this book acknowledges that contact does not always reduce prejudice, tension and conflict, the presence of the predisposing conditions and mediators of the contact-prejudice effect mentioned above do yield conviviality and concord in ways that aid integration[7] as reported from empirical findings in Chapters 8–12.

Policy suggestions in this regard include a call to government to improve on the 2014 legislation to create spaces for skilled African immigrants to come to South Africa to work, live and be integrated legally. Indeed, as was concluded in Chapter 3, there are glaring gaps in legislation including serious policy gaps (DHA 2017, III) and hiccups in implementation thereof which need to be improved on. Second, the

---

[7] Examples of these conditions in the literature which were validated by the findings of from chapters eight to twelve include economic interdependence, social bridging capital and marriage.

South African government and the media need to take the lead in changing the discourse on African immigration from "African immigrants are the problem in South Africa" to "we need migrants, both Africans and non-Africans, to grow and develop to our full potential as a developing nation". This is because understanding other peoples and societies is a way to understand ourselves as a people and society. One policy suggestion in this regard is national re-orientation of South Africans on the place of immigration in national development, focusing on the specific contributions that African immigrants make. This should also include civic responsibility orientation for all immigrants coming into the country and those applying for different levels of stay in the country to learn good citizenship practices including respecting law and order. And when they run foul of the laws of the land, law enforcement agencies must live up to their responsibility to prosecute all law breakers without fear or favour. Third, the national government can consider collaborating more with the consular offices of African foreign missions in South Africa and civil society groups to develop and implement intercultural and exchange programmes that showcase cultural diversity to enable social cohesion between African immigrants and South Africans. Inevitably, social cohesion between African migrants and South Africans is an important goal for the state to pursue given South Africa's increasing leadership role in Africa. Finally, there is a need to further study the varied spaces of interactions between South Africans and African migrants to better understand the full nature of their complex relationships. Also, based on the limitations of focusing on dyadic ties alone, there is need to conduct a more holistic analysis of social networks to examine intergroup contacts beyond micro-public spaces. A network study of multiple relationships between South Africans and African migrants would provide a more holistic and thus illuminating picture of African immigration in South Africa which may have more evidence-based policy implications for social cohesion, inclusivity, human and national development.

References

Department of Home Affairs (DHA). 2017. *White Paper on International Migration for South Africa, 2017*. Republic of South Africa: Government Printing Works.

Hamill, James. 2014. Africa: Closing the Door—South Africa's Draconian Immigration Reforms. *World Politics Review*. http://imcosa.co.za/news/458-sa-s-new-immigration.html.

Ikalafeng, Thebe. 2015. Our African Bonds Defy Borders. *The Sunday Independent*, April 26.

Isike, Efe. 2015. Ties That Bind: A Network Analysis of Relationships Between Nigerian Migrants and South Africans in Umhlathuze. PhD dissertation, University of KwaZulu-Natal.

Landau, Loren. 2013. Xenophobic Demons Linger in SA. *Mail and Guardian*, May 17. https://mg.co.za/article/2013-05-17-00-xenophobic-demons-linger-in-sa/.

Landau, Loren. 2017. Friendship Fears and Communities of Convenience in Africa's Urban Estuaries: Connection as Measure of Urban Condition, Urban Studies, Special Issue, 1–16. https://doi.org/10.1177/0042098017699563.

Landau, Loren, and A.W. Kabwe-Segatti. 2009. Human Development Impacts of Migration: South Africa Case Study. Human Development Research Paper, 173–174. https://mpra.ub.unimuenchen.de/19182/1/HDRP_2009_05.pdf.

Maharaj, Brij. 2004. *Global Migration Perspectives: Immigration to Post-Apartheid South Africa*. Global Commission on International Migration. Switzerland: Geneva. http://www.queensu.ca/samp/migrationresources/Documents/Maharaj_immigration.pdf.

Medium Terms Strategic Framework (MTSF). 2019–2024. Priority 6: Social Cohesion and Safer Communities, 191–233.

Pettigrew, Thomas, and Linda Tropp. 2008. How Does Intergroup Contact Reduce Prejudice? Meta-analytic Tests of Three Mediators. *European Journal of Social Psychology* 38: 922–934.

Index

A
Affirmative action, 120
African Academic Diaspora (AAD), 110, 111, 117, 118, 120, 124
African countries, 51, 66, 86, 110–112, 117, 120, 122, 125, 126, 180, 204, 219, 220, 222, 228, 244
African immigration, 3, 4, 6, 7, 9–11, 13, 19, 62, 63, 65, 73, 86, 87, 93, 98, 103, 105, 175, 195, 244, 245, 247, 249, 250
African international students, 13, 121, 220–225, 227–229, 231–238
African migrants, 2–4, 6–8, 10–12, 19–21, 24, 31, 32, 66, 70, 72, 85–87, 91–99, 101–105, 131, 137–141, 157–159, 173, 177, 202–204, 206, 209, 215, 220, 237, 244–247, 250
African National Congress (ANC), 53, 115, 125

Afrophobia, 11, 61, 86, 94, 117, 137, 140, 203, 237, 245
Afrophobic comments, 95
Aliens Amendment Act (1995), 243
Aliens Control Act, 243
Amakwerekwere, 97, 202, 213
  kwerekwere, 97, 100
  makwerekwere, 97, 118, 138, 172
Assimilation, 2, 8, 12, 158, 167, 168, 177, 184, 185, 197, 226, 228, 232, 233, 235–238
Assimilation theory, 181, 183–185
Asylum seekers and refugees, 45, 51, 55, 68

B
Being, 6, 11, 18, 20–22, 41, 54, 61, 64, 68, 69, 71, 72, 74, 90, 92, 96–99, 103, 109–113, 117–119, 121, 123, 124, 132, 133, 135–140, 147, 149, 152, 161, 173, 183, 187, 189, 193, 194, 197, 202, 203, 209, 231, 232, 237

non-being, ix
Belonging, 5–7, 18, 21, 40, 87, 88, 95, 99, 101, 112, 117, 125, 130, 133, 137–139, 147, 151, 153, 154, 161, 164, 167, 170, 202, 203
non-belonging, 130
Bill of Rights, 37, 39, 40
Black, 11, 12, 18, 22, 62, 66, 70, 75, 86, 88, 97, 104, 110, 113, 115, 118, 119, 123, 124, 130–132, 134, 135, 140, 146, 164, 187, 195, 202, 203, 220, 243
black African migrants, 147
Black bodies, 11, 130, 134
Black South Africans, 3, 4, 20, 31, 61, 64, 76, 78, 88, 104, 130–132, 164, 203, 245, 247

C
Cape Town, 7, 12, 67, 69, 72, 112, 114, 122, 146, 148–150, 152, 186, 228
Churches, 150, 151, 175, 176, 213
Citizenship, 40, 96, 112, 153, 181, 182, 185, 250
Co-existence, 2, 10, 12, 40, 41, 44, 56, 146, 147
Colored, 131, 134
colored bodies, 132, 134
Communities, 6, 13, 26, 39, 40, 42–44, 47, 51, 54–56, 62, 65, 70, 76, 89–91, 99, 147, 182, 183, 185, 213, 221, 226, 228, 232, 236, 238, 244, 248, 249
communities of convenience, 5, 8, 25, 247
Concord, 1–3, 6, 7, 10, 13, 17, 23, 25, 31, 111, 158, 163–165, 171, 176, 180, 197, 203, 204, 210–215, 246, 247, 249

Conflict, 1–4, 10, 11, 13, 17–19, 21, 25–27, 29–32, 51, 78, 86, 87, 96, 131, 136–141, 145, 158, 165, 180, 197, 203, 210–213, 219, 246, 247, 249
Conflictual relations, 21, 164, 210, 237
Congolese Community of Empangeni (COCOE), 162, 166, 167
Congolese migrants, 12, 146, 149, 157–159, 161–163, 176, 177
Constitution of the Republic of South Africa, 38, 40, 44, 49, 55, 116
Contact, 1, 3, 4, 6–8, 10, 12, 13, 17–19, 24–32, 66, 86, 96, 151, 158, 159, 163, 164, 166–169, 173–176, 203, 204, 207, 210–215, 245–247, 249, 250
Contact-prejudice, 13, 29–31, 215, 246, 249
Contact theory, 13, 25, 27, 30, 203, 249
Contestation for economic space, 92
Conviviality, 2–8, 12, 13, 17, 18, 21, 23–32, 41, 86, 148, 158, 162, 163, 167, 171, 173, 176, 177, 203, 204, 210–214, 236, 246, 247, 249
Convivial relations, 3, 6, 8, 10, 24, 26, 30, 169, 211, 214, 215, 247
Cosmopolitanism, 2, 8, 10, 12, 24, 158, 177
Criminalisation, 62
Cultural and geographical interests, 214
Cultural differences, 2, 10, 66, 167, 168, 171, 176, 182, 210, 211, 215, 244
Cultural integration, 182, 183
Cultural stereotyping, 66, 158, 176
Cyber social movements, 89

Cyberspace xenophobia, 11, 95, 99, 102

D
Democratic Republic of Congo (DRC), 72, 163, 171, 180, 226, 227
Department of Home Affairs (DHA), 44–50, 54, 56, 73, 74, 97, 111, 249
Descriptive statistics, 226
Development, 7, 10, 24, 28, 30, 46, 47, 78, 80, 90, 91, 94, 110, 114, 121–123, 125, 126, 159, 163, 166, 174, 186, 203, 210, 211, 213, 221, 244, 247, 249
Discriminatory treatments, 73
Diverse groups, 2, 4, 13, 22–31, 167, 203, 205, 207, 210, 212, 213, 246
Durban, 67, 69, 114, 150, 163, 164, 168, 226, 245
Dyadic relations, 8, 158, 159, 162

E
Economic immigrants, 180
Economic opportunities, 47, 64, 118, 184, 185, 219
Empangeni, 9, 12, 157–159, 162–166, 171–173, 175, 237
Entanglement and conviviality, 2, 158
Ethnographic, 12, 146
Exclusion, 1–5, 7, 8, 10–12, 18–20, 23, 24, 40, 46, 50, 87, 88, 91, 110–112, 114, 115, 117, 118, 120, 122–126, 139, 158, 163, 176, 177, 203, 210, 244

F
Facebook, 11, 86, 87, 95–98, 100, 103–105, 186, 245

Fake news, 19, 31, 92, 93, 96, 99
False belief theory, 4, 19, 31, 92–94, 102, 246
Falsehood narrative, 94
Fees must fall protests, 226
Foreign African scholars, 118, 119, 121, 124, 125
Foreign nationals, 40, 46, 52, 53, 64, 65, 68, 73, 97, 99–101, 121, 180, 220, 231
Foreign-owned business, 102
Formation of ties, 171, 176, 207
Freedom Charter, 110
Friendship, 5, 6, 13, 24, 25, 62, 80, 162, 163, 165–170, 173–176, 236, 246
Friends or foe, 8, 12, 177

G
Geographical proximity, 204, 209, 213, 214
Ghana, 110, 122, 125, 173, 188, 189, 226, 227

H
Higher education sector, 110, 112, 113, 117, 220
Host and migrant interactions, 181
Host communities, 1, 3, 4, 6, 8, 17, 30, 62, 93, 104, 153, 166, 168, 179, 180, 182, 184, 185, 197, 204, 205, 207, 212, 214, 215, 231, 234, 236, 237, 247
Hostility/hostilities, 1, 3, 7, 8, 12, 18, 19, 24–30, 42, 53, 54, 62, 64, 92, 96, 98, 135, 147, 158, 163, 166, 174, 176, 203, 209, 211–213, 220, 230, 236, 237, 245
Human rights abuses, 220
Human trafficking, 65, 71, 97, 101

Hybridity, 2, 10, 158, 169
Hybrid space, 91

I
Illegal immigrants, 86, 243, 244
Immigrants' networks, 7, 209, 247, 250
Immigration, 5, 10, 19, 25, 26, 39–42, 44–47, 51, 53–55, 64, 66, 71, 73, 74, 103, 149, 180–183, 208, 209, 220, 223, 224, 243, 244, 247, 249, 250
Immigration Act No.13 (2002), 244
Immigration Amendment Act of 2004, 244
Immigration Amendment Act of 2013, 244
Immigration amendment bill, 38, 44
Immigration experts, 183
Immigration legislation, 10, 42–44, 46, 47, 49, 204, 244
Immigration Regulation of 2014, 244
Informal economy/informal economies, 148, 212
Institutional *Naijaphobia*, 70, 73
Integration, 1–3, 5, 7, 10, 12, 13, 17, 23, 31, 44, 76, 146, 158, 166, 167, 169, 170, 176, 180–186, 195, 197, 215, 221, 230, 231, 236–238, 247, 249
Intergroup anxiety, 29, 30, 211, 215
Intergroup relations, 18, 21, 28–31, 160, 203, 205, 211, 214, 215, 246
Internationalization of Higher Education Institutions (HEIs), 222
International Organization for Migration (IOM), 43, 67
International students, 126, 220–226, 230–237
Interviews, 8, 10, 12, 75, 102, 117, 130, 133, 158, 162–165, 170–173, 175, 181, 186, 195, 197, 198, 205–207
Intimacy of contact, 171

J
Johannesburg, 5, 6, 12, 26, 52, 67, 69–74, 100, 101, 103, 130, 147, 150, 186, 190

K
Kenya, 52, 122, 126, 173
Kenyan, 41, 52, 247
Kenyan immigrants, 54
KwaZulu-Natal province, 157, 163, 170, 220

L
Language, 6, 11, 12, 18, 62, 65, 97, 114, 118, 122, 129–136, 138–141, 146, 152, 154, 167, 168, 174, 183–185, 188, 209, 214, 236
Legislative and policy framework, 55, 243
Lingua franca, 11, 135, 136
Local academics, 111
Local and international African students, 230–233, 236

M
Malawi, 100, 149
Medium Terms Strategic Framework (MTSF) 2019–2024, 248
Methodology, 7, 95, 130, 146, 159, 225
Migrant's experiences in South Africa, 11, 12, 145

Migrant integration, 45, 169, 176, 181, 207
Migration, 1, 2, 5–7, 10, 13, 17, 21, 26, 27, 31, 40–43, 45, 46, 49, 54, 66, 85–87, 96, 99, 101, 145–147, 155, 179, 185, 187, 201, 204, 209, 219–224, 229, 244, 246
Minister of Home Affairs, 44, 245
Mozambican migrants, 12, 13, 203–206, 213–215, 247
Mozambique, 52, 149, 204, 208, 209, 214, 226, 227
Mpumalanga province, 204, 209
Multiculturalism, 2, 185
Multicultural societies, 185
Mutual stereotyping, 66

N
National development, 250
National Development Plan (NDP), 248, 249
National Student Financial Aid Scheme (NSFAS), 115
Network analysis, 8, 12, 160, 177
New racism, 4, 18–20, 64
Nganda, 154, 155
Nigeria, 9, 62, 67, 68, 72, 73, 76, 78, 79, 89, 110, 119, 122, 125, 126, 180, 189, 193–195, 198, 226, 228
Nigerians, 10–12, 62–76, 78–80, 86, 97, 98, 101, 103, 137, 150, 153, 180, 182, 183, 185–198, 227, 247
Nigerian Union in South Africa (NUSA), 62, 67, 69, 70, 197
Notion of exceptionalism, 20, 203

P
Paradise gain, 11, 110

Paradise loss, 11, 111, 126
Platform for engagement, 70, 87
Politics of belonging, 130, 131, 139
Politics of language, 133, 136, 139, 140
Post-apartheid South Africa, 40, 66, 79, 92, 147, 244
Presence of reciprocity, 170

R
Racial arrogance, 134–136
Racism and xenophobia, 63, 64, 75
Relations between African migrants and South Africans, 2, 3, 11, 12, 21, 32, 85, 86, 157–159, 245–247

S
Social and structural injustices, 147
Social cohesion, 13, 246, 248–250
Social Cohesion Advocates (SCAs), 248
Social cohesion narratives, 94
Social identity, 10, 21, 22, 29
Social identity theory, 4, 18, 21, 22, 160
Social interactions, 87, 131, 220
Socialities, 5, 23, 147, 153, 154
Social media, 3, 4, 11, 21, 71, 86, 87, 89–96, 98–105
Social mobility, 109, 114, 184
Social network theory, 159, 160
Socio-economic spaces, 12, 146
South African communities, 41, 53, 137, 198, 230, 247
South African government, 4, 39, 41–43, 55, 67, 70, 74, 93, 98, 101, 102, 111, 121, 123, 126, 147, 183, 186, 204
South African partners, 153, 180, 183, 187, 197

South African Police Service (SAPS), 92, 186, 197
South African spaces, 11, 131, 137, 230, 231
South African students, 13, 120, 121, 123, 126, 220–226, 228, 230, 231, 233, 235, 236
South African universities, 11, 111, 114, 117, 120–125, 220, 225, 228, 229, 232, 235, 237
South Africa's Immigration Act of 2002, 38
South Africa spouses, 12, 76, 188, 193, 195
Southern Africa Development Community (SADC), 51, 222, 225
Space, 2, 4, 6–8, 10–13, 21, 23–28, 30–32, 61, 86–96, 98–100, 104, 112, 123, 130–136, 138, 139, 146–148, 150, 152, 154, 155, 158, 159, 162, 163, 176, 180, 182, 193, 194, 203, 204, 209, 212, 213, 221, 237, 245–250
spatial proximity, 164, 173
Spousal relationships, 188, 190
Stereotypes, 22, 27, 30, 62, 64, 66, 71–73, 80, 136–138, 141, 174, 186, 201, 202, 210, 212, 213, 237, 246
Stereotyping of African migrants, 19, 244
Supremacy of cultural identity, 211
Survival, 4, 23, 25, 97, 131, 132, 139, 148
 mechanism of survival, 31, 135, 139

T
Ties, 6, 8, 12, 13, 45, 91, 147, 157–163, 165, 166, 168, 169, 173, 174, 176, 205, 207, 209–215, 222, 237, 247, 250
Traditional media, 89, 90, 94, 99
Transformation, 11, 13, 22, 91, 109–115, 117, 118, 120–126, 221, 238
Translanguaging, 135
The Tsonga tribe, 214
Twitter, 11, 86, 87, 95–98, 100, 101, 103–105

U
Uganda, 89, 122, 125, 126
Umhlathuze municipality, 8, 157
United Nations High Commissioner for Refugees (UNHCR), 50, 64, 68
United Nigerian Wives in South Africa (UNWISA), 12, 73, 180–182, 186, 195–197
University of KwaZulu-Natal (UKZN), 221, 222, 225, 226, 236
University of Zululand (UNIZUL), 221, 225, 236

V
Violence, 4, 18, 21, 51, 53, 62, 64, 66, 68, 70, 77, 86, 90, 92–94, 102, 103, 115, 131, 147, 148, 155, 164, 180, 219, 245
Violent entrepreneurship, 65
Virtual networks, 90, 91

W
White Paper on International Migration for South Africa, 44–50

X

Xenophobia, 4, 8, 10–13, 18, 19, 24, 40, 53, 54, 61–65, 70, 73, 75, 80, 86, 92, 95, 99, 102, 103, 117, 120, 121, 124, 125, 146, 155, 164, 165, 177, 181, 186, 201, 202, 210, 220, 221, 224, 236, 237, 244, 245

xenophobia discourse, 3, 12, 13, 158

Xenophobic attacks, 7, 11, 20, 62, 65, 68, 70, 77, 92, 102, 110, 118, 131, 145–147, 152, 187, 194, 220, 247

Xenophobic sentiments, 3, 11, 18–20, 88, 93, 104, 158, 180

Xenophobic violence, 3, 27, 61, 64, 65, 92, 154, 237, 245

Xhosa, 148, 152
  IsiXhosa, 12, 146, 148, 150–153

Z

Zimbabwe, 79, 98, 119, 180, 226–228

Zimbabwean migrants, 12, 48, 247

Zulu, 9, 10, 22, 68, 112, 114, 129, 132, 133, 165, 167, 168, 170, 172, 174, 194
  isiZulu, 133, 136

Printed by Printforce, the Netherlands

Conflict and Concord